Lecture Notes in Compute

Commenced Publication in 1973
Founding and Former Series Editors:
Gerhard Goos, Juris Hartmanis, and Jan van

Ngoc Thanh Nguyen
Ryszard Kowalczyk (Eds.)

Transactions on Computational Collective Intelligence II

 Springer

Volume Editors

Ngoc Thanh Nguyen
Wroclaw University of Technology
Institute of Informatics
Str. Wyb. Wyspianskiego 27
50-370 Wroclaw, Poland
E-mail: thanh@pwr.wroc.pl

Ryszard Kowalczyk
Swinburne University of Technology
Centre for Complex Software Systems and Services
P.O. Box 218
Hawthorn, Victoria 3122, Australia
E-mail: rkowalczyk@ict.swin.edu.au

Library of Congress Control Number: Applied for

CR Subject Classification (1998): I.2, C.2.4, I.2.11, H.3-5, D.2

ISSN   0302-9743
ISBN-10   3-642-17154-0 Springer Berlin Heidelberg New York
ISBN-13   978-3-642-17154-3 Springer Berlin Heidelberg New York

springer.com

© Springer-Verlag Berlin Heidelberg 2010
Printed in Germany

Typesetting: Camera-ready by author, data conversion by Scientific Publishing Services, Chennai, India
Printed on acid-free paper   06/3180

Preface

Welcome to the second volume of *Transactions on Computational Collective Intelligence* (TCCI), a new journal devoted to research in computer-based methods of computational collective intelligence (CCI) and their applications in a wide range of fields such as the Semantic Web, social networks and multi-agent systems. TCCI strives to cover new methodological, theoretical and practical aspects of CCI understood as the form of intelligence that emerges from the collaboration and competition of many individuals (artificial and/or natural). The application of multiple computational intelligence technologies such as fuzzy systems, evolutionary computation, neural systems, consensus theory, etc., aims to support human and other collective intelligence and to create new forms of CCI in natural and/or artificial systems.

TCCI is a double-blind refereed and authoritative reference dealing with the working potential of CCI methodologies and applications, as well as emerging issues of interest to academics and practitioners. This second issue contains a collection of 10 articles selected from high-quality submissions addressing advances in the foundations and applications of computational collective intelligence. In "Integration Proposal for Description Logic and Attributive Logic – Towards Semantic Web Rules" G. Nalepa and W. Furmanska propose a transition from attributive logic to description logic in order to improve the design of Semantic Web rules. K. Thorisson et al. in "The Semantic Web: From Representation to Realization" present key ideas behind SemCard technology and its initial implementation, aiming to support management of the full lifecycle of data in the Semantic Web. "A Cross-cultural Multi-agent Model of Opportunism in Trade" by G. Hofstede et al. presents a model of deceit and trust in trade, together with a comparative multi-agent simulation of trading situations. L. Longo et al. in "Enhancing Social Search: A Computational Collective Intelligence Model of Behavioral Trait, Trust and Time" describe a social search model based on information foraging theory, effort and computational trust, showing a different way to implicitly judge Web-entities. "Group-Oriented Services: A Shift Toward Consumer-Managed Relationships in the Telecom Industry" by L. Vrdoljak et al. introduces an idea of a special type of personalized telecom services, called group-oriented services, and its application in agent-based mobile content brokerage. "Pricing the Services in Dynamic Environment: Agent Pricing Model" by D. Zagar et al. proposes an agent-based pricing architecture to enable objective and transparent assessment of the cost of the services. The next paper in this issue entitled "A Robust Approach for Nonlinear UAV Task Assignment Problem Under Uncertainty" by H.A. Le and Q.T. Nguyen includes a new robust approach to the task assignment of unmanned aerial vehicles operating in uncertain environments whose objective is maximizing the target score. In "Decision Support System Based on Computational Collective Intelligence in Campus Information Systems" Y. Saito and T. Matsuo describe a method and an application of reusing campus collective information. "Fuel Crime Conceptualization Through Specialization of Ontology for Investigation Management System" by J. Cybulka presents a conceptual model based on consensual semantics to support the teamwork of investigators of economics crimes. Finally, D. Barbucha et al. in "JABAT Middleware as a Tool for Solving Optimization Problems" present experience in developing several applications of JABAT, a middleware supporting A-Team architecture for solving optimization problems.

The research area of CCI has been growing significantly in recent years and we are very thankful to everyone within the CCI research community who has supported the *Transactions on Computational Collective Intelligence* and its affiliated events including the International Conferences on Computational Collective Intelligence: Semantic Web, Social Networks & Multiagent Systems (ICCCI). With this strong support and a large number of submissions we are very pleased that TCCI and ICCCI are being cemented as high-quality platforms for presenting and exchanging the most important and significant advances in CCI research and development. We would like to thank all the authors for their contributions to TCCI. This issue would also not have been possible without the great efforts of the editorial board and many anonymously acting reviewers. Here, we would like to express our sincere thanks to all of them. Finally, we would also like to express our gratitude to the LNCS editorial staff of Springer, in particular Alfred Hofmann, Ursula Barth and their team, who have supported the TCCI journal and the editorship of this issue in a very professional way.

September 2010   Ngoc Thanh Nguyen
                                                              Ryszard Kowalczyk

Transactions on Computational Collective Intelligence

This new journal focuses on research in applications of the computer-based methods of computational collective intelligence (CCI) and their applications in a wide range of fields such as the Semantic Web, social networks and multi-agent systems. It aims to provide a forum for the presentation of scientific research and technological achievements accomplished by the international community.

The topics addressed by this journal include all solutions of real-life problems for which it is necessary to use computational collective intelligence technologies to achieve effective results. The emphasis of the papers published is on novel and original research and technological advancements. Special features on specific topics are welcome.

Table of Contents

Integration Proposal for Description Logic and Attributive Logic – Towards Semantic Web Rules[*]

Grzegorz J. Nalepa and Weronika T. Furmańska

Institute of Automatics,
AGH University of Science and Technology,
Al. Mickiewicza 30, 30-059 Kraków, Poland
gjn@agh.edu.pl, wtf@agh.edu.pl

Abstract. The current challenge of the Semantic Web is the development of an expressive yet effective rule language. This paper presents an integration proposal for Description Logics (DL) and Attributive Logics (ALSV) is presented. These two formalisms stem from fields of Knowledge Representation and Artificial Intelligence. However, they are based on different design goals and therefore provide different description and reasoning capabilities. ALSV is the foundation of XTT2, an expressive language for rule-based systems. DL provide formulation for expressive ontology languages such as OWL2. An important research direction is the development of rule languages that can be integrated with ontologies. The contribution of the paper consists in introducing a possible transition from ALSV to DL. This opens up possibilities of using XTT2, a well-founded rule-based system modelling rule language, to improve the design of Semantic Web rules[1].

1 Introduction

The Semantic Web proposal [2], of the next generation Web with rich semantics and automated inference is based on a number of formal concepts and practical technologies. The former includes Description Logics (DL) [3] as the formalism for describing ontologies. Currently, the Semantic Web development is focused on providing a flexible rule language for the Web. It should be RIF-compatible [4] on the rule interchange level, and conceptually compatible with ontologies modelled in OWL with the use of Description Logics. Among other proposals, the SWRL language [5] aims at meeting these requirements.

The Semantic Web initiative is based on previous experiences and research of Knowledge Engineering [6] in the field of Artificial Intelligence [7]. In this field rule-based expert systems technologies are a prime example of effective reasoning systems based on the rule paradigm [8,9,10]. The formal description of these

---

[*] The paper is supported by the *BIMLOQ* Project funded from 2010–2012 resources for science as a research project.
[1] The paper extends concepts and preliminary results described in the paper [1] presented at ICCCI'09 Conference in Wrocław, Poland.

N.T. Nguyen and R. Kowalczyk (Eds.): Transactions on CCI II, LNCS 6450, pp. 1–23, 2010.

systems is based on the propositional calculus, or restricted form of predicate logic – like in the case of Prolog [11]. It is worth noting how the Semantic Web community could benefit from classic rule-based systems' tools and solutions.

A recent proposal of a new logical calculus extends the expressiveness of rule languages by introducing an attributive language for rule formulation [10,12]. This solution seems superior to the simple propositional systems, and still easier to reason with than the classical predicate logic. XTT2 is a rule language based on this approach [12,13]. It provides visual design and formal analysis methods for decision rules. These features would be beneficial for Semantic Web applications. However, the current problem with Attributive Logic with Set Values over Finite Domain (ALSV(FD)) is the lack of conceptual compatibility with DL.

The rest of this paper is organised as follows: selected DL concepts are discussed in Sect. 2, and a brief introduction to ALSV(FD) is given in Sect. 3. Sect. 4 gives a motivation for the research aiming at translation from the ALSV (FD) to DL. ALSV(FD) is oriented at forward chaining rule-based systems, while DL provides a formalized foundation for ontologies. Syntax and semantics of these two calculi are compared in Sect. 5. In Sect. 6 an integration proposal together with a description language is introduced. A simple example transition is then presented in Sect. 7. In Sect. 8 the proposal is evaluated and compared with selected existing solutions in Sect. 9. The paper ends with ideas for future work.

2   Description Logics Overview

Description Logics are a family of knowledge representation languages [3]. Historically related to semantic networks and frame languages, they describe the world of interest by means of concepts, individuals and roles. However, contrary to their predecessors such as semantic networks [6], they provide formal semantics and thus allow for automated reasoning. Basic Description Logics take advantage of their relation to predicate calculus. On one hand they adopt its semantics, which makes them more expressive than the propositional logic. On the other hand, by restricting the syntax to formulae with at most two variables, they remain decidable and more human-readable. These features have made Description Logics a popular formalism used for designing ontologies for the Semantic Web. There exists a number of DL languages that are defined and distinguished by which concept descriptions they allow, which influences the languages' expressivity.

The vocabulary in DL consists of languages are *concepts*, which denote sets of individuals, and *roles*, which denote the binary relations between individuals. Elementary descriptions in DL are *atomic concepts* and *atomic roles*. More complex descriptions can be built inductively from those using *concept constructors*. Respective DL languages are distinguished by the constructors they provide. A minimal language of practical interest is the *Attributive Language* [3] (AL).

Some of the most important definitions are presented (see [3]) below.

Definition 1. *Let A denote an atomic concept and R an atomic role. In basic $\mathcal{AL}$ concept descriptions C and D can be in one of the following forms:*

$$A \qquad \text{atomic concept} \qquad (1)$$
$$\top \qquad \text{universal concept} \qquad (2)$$
$$\bot \qquad \text{bottom concept} \qquad (3)$$
$$\neg A \qquad \text{atomic negation} \qquad (4)$$
$$C \sqcap D \qquad \text{intersection} \qquad (5)$$
$$\forall R.C \qquad \text{value restriction} \qquad (6)$$
$$\exists R.\top \qquad \text{limited existential quantification} \qquad (7)$$

In order to define a formal semantics, an *interpretation* $\mathcal{I} = (\Delta^{\mathcal{I}}, \cdot^{\mathcal{I}})$ is considered. This interpretation consists of the *domain of interpretation* which is a non-empty set and an interpretation function, which to every atomic concept A assigns a set $A^{\mathcal{I}} \subseteq \Delta^{\mathcal{I}}$ and for every atomic role R a binary relation $R^{\mathcal{I}} = R^{\mathcal{I}} \subseteq \Delta^{\mathcal{I}} \times \Delta^{\mathcal{I}}$. The interpretation function is extended over concept descriptions by Definition 2.

Definition 2.

$$\top^{\mathcal{I}} = \Delta^{\mathcal{I}} \qquad (8)$$
$$\bot^{\mathcal{I}} = \emptyset \qquad (9)$$
$$(\neg A)^{\mathcal{I}} = \Delta^{\mathcal{I}} \setminus A^{\mathcal{I}} \qquad (10)$$
$$(C \sqcap D)^{\mathcal{I}} = C^{\mathcal{I}} \cap D^{\mathcal{I}} \qquad (11)$$
$$(\forall R.C)^{\mathcal{I}} = \{a \in \Delta^{\mathcal{I}} | \forall b, (a, b) \in R^{\mathcal{I}} \rightarrow b \in C^{\mathcal{I}}\} \qquad (12)$$
$$(\exists R.\top)^{\mathcal{I}} = \{a \in \Delta^{\mathcal{I}} | \exists b, (a, b) \in R^{\mathcal{I}}\} \qquad (13)$$

The basic language can be extended by allowing other concept constructors, such as *union ($\mathcal{U}$)* , *full negation ($\mathcal{C}$)*, *full existential quantification ($\mathcal{E}$)* or *number restriction ($\mathcal{N}$)*. Resulting formalisms are called using the letters indicating the allowed constructors, e.g. $\mathcal{ALC}$, $\mathcal{ALCN}$, $\mathcal{ALUE}$ etc. The smallest propositionally closed language is $\mathcal{ALC}$ [3].

Basic DL allow only atomic roles (i.e. role names) in role descriptions. Different extensions are introduced by allowing *role constructors*. They enable introduction of various constraints and properties of roles, such as *transitive closure*, *intersection*, *composition* and *union*, or *complement* and *inverse* roles. Another kind of extension is obtained by allowing *nominals* in concept definitions and introducing primitive datatypes (see [3]). These modifications proved to be extremely valuable and important in the context of the Semantic Web and ontology engineering. However, they are sources of high computational complexity of reasoning in the resulting ontologies.

For expressive DLs, the above mentioned naming convention would be too long. Hence, for the basic $\mathcal{ALC}$ language extended with transitive roles, the symbol $\mathcal{S}$ is often used. The letter $\mathcal{H}$ is used to represent role hierarchy, $\mathcal{O}$ to indicate nominals in concept descriptions, $\mathcal{I}$ represents inverse roles, $\mathcal{N}$ number restrictions, and ($\mathbf{D}$) indicates the integration of some concrete domain/datatypes. The DL underlying OWL(1) DL language includes all of those constructs and is therefore called $\mathcal{SHOIN}(\mathbf{D})$. OWL 2 DL [14] is a very expressive language based on $\mathcal{SROIQ}(\mathbf{D})$ Description Logic.

Description Logics provide tools to build a knowledge base and to reason about it. The knowledge base consists of two parts: TBox and ABox.

TBox provides a terminology and contains a taxonomy expressed in the form of set of axioms. The axioms define concepts, specify relations between them and introduce set constraints. Therefore, TBox stores knowledge about sets of individuals in the world of interest. Formally, a terminology $\mathcal{T}$ is a finite set of terminological axioms. If C and D denote concept names, and R and S role names, then the terminological axioms may be in two forms: $C \sqsubseteq D$ ($R \sqsubseteq S$) or $C \equiv D$ ($R \equiv S$). Equalities that have an atomic concept on the left-hand side are called *definitions*. Axioms of the form $C \sqsubseteq D$ are called *specialization* statements. Equalities express necessary and sufficient conditions, whereas specialization statements specify constraints (necessary conditions) only. An interpretation (function) $\mathcal{I}$ maps each concept name to a subset of the domain. The interpretation satisfies an axiom $C \sqsubseteq D$ iff: $C^{\mathcal{I}} \subseteq D^{\mathcal{I}}$. It satisfies a concept definition $C \equiv D$ if: $C^{\mathcal{I}} = D^{\mathcal{I}}$. If the interpretation satisfies all the definitions and all axioms in $\mathcal{T}$, it satisfies the terminology $\mathcal{T}$ and is called a *model* of $\mathcal{T}$.

ABox contains explicit assertions about individuals in the conceived world. They represent extensional knowledge about the domain of interest. Statements in ABox may be: concept assertions, e.g. $C(a)$ or role assertions, $R(b,c)$. An interpretation $\mathcal{I}$ maps each individual name to an element in the domain. With regard to terminology $\mathcal{T}$, the interpretation satisfies a concept assertion $C(a)$ iff $a^{\mathcal{I}} \in C^{\mathcal{I}}$, and a role assertion $R(b,c)$ iff $\langle b^{\mathcal{I}}, c^{\mathcal{I}} \rangle \in R^{\mathcal{I}}$. If it satisfies all assertions in ABox $\mathcal{A}$, then it satisfies $\mathcal{A}$ and $\mathcal{I}$ is a model of $\mathcal{A}$.

Although the terminology and the world description share the same model-theoretic semantics, it is convenient to distinguish these two parts while designing a knowledge base or stating particular inference tasks.

- With regards to terminology $\mathcal{T}$ one can pose a question if a concept is *satisfiable*, if one concept *subsumes* another, if two concepts are *equivalent* or *disjoint*.
- A concept C is satisfiable with respect to $\mathcal{T}$ if there exists a model $\mathcal{I}$ of $\mathcal{T}$ such that $C^{\mathcal{I}}$ is not empty.
- A concept C is subsumed by a concept D w.r.t. $\mathcal{T}$ if $C^{\mathcal{I}} \subseteq D^{\mathcal{I}}$ for every model $\mathcal{I}$ of $\mathcal{T}$.
- Two concepts C and D are equivalent w.r.t. T if $C^{\mathcal{I}} = D^{\mathcal{I}}$ for every model I of T.
- Finally, two concepts C and D are disjoint w.r.t. $\mathcal{T}$ if $C^{\mathcal{I}} \cap D^{\mathcal{I}} = \emptyset$ for every model $\mathcal{I}$ of $\mathcal{T}$.

Satisfiability and *subsumption checking* are the main reasoning tasks for TBox; all others can be reduced to them, and either one can be reduced to the other.

For ABox, there are four main inference tasks: *consistency checking*, *instance checking*, *realization* and *retrieval*.

- An ABox $\mathcal{A}$ is consistent w.r.t. a TBox $\mathcal{T}$, if there is an interpretation that is a model of both $\mathcal{A}$ and $\mathcal{T}$. Furthermore, we say that an ABox is consistent, if it is consistent w.r.t. the empty TBox.
- Instance checking tests if a given assertion is entailed by the ABox.
- Realization tasks consist in finding the most specific concept for a given individual.
- Retrieval returns individuals which are instances of a given concept.

All these tasks can be reduced to *consistency checking* of ABox w.r.t. TBox.

In order to use DL in systems which describe a dynamically changing world, there is a need for a mechanism of updating the knowledge base. A short discussion of DL ABox updates with references to selected works is given in Sect. 9.4.

Let us now move to the discussion of the ALSV(FD) formalisms. It has been specifically introduced to improve the expressive power of rule languages. The introduction given below is largely based on [10,12,15,13].

3 Concepts of Attributive Logics

Knowledge representation based on the concept of *attributes* is one of the most common approaches [6]. It is one of the foundations for relational databases, attributive decision tables and trees [16], as well as rule-based systems [10].

A typical way of thinking about attributive logic for knowledge specification may be as follows. Knowledge is represented by *facts* and *rules*. A fact could be written as $A := d$ or $A(o) := d$, where A is a certain attribute (property of an object), o an object of interest and d is the attribute value. Facts are interpreted as propositional logic atomic formulae. This basic approach is sometimes extended with use of certain syntax modifications [16]. On top of these facts simple decision rules are built, corresponding to conditional statements.

In a recent book [10] the discussion of attributive logic is extended by allowing attributes to take *set values* and providing some formal framework of the *Set Attributive Logic* (SAL). The basic idea for further discussion is that attributes should be able to take not only *atomic* but *set* values as well, written as $A(o) = V$, where V is a certain set of values. In [12] the language of SAL has been extended to provide an effective knowledge representation tool for decision rules, where the state description uses finite domains. The proposed calculus *Attribute Logic with Set Values over Finite Domains* (ALSV(FD)) is proposed to simplify the decision rules formulation for classic rule-based expert system, including, business rules, using the so-called XTT2 rule language. While being a general solution, the language is oriented towards forward chaining intelligent control systems.

Here, an extended notation for ALSV(FD) is introduced, including: 1) the explicit differentiation of equality relation, denoted as $=$ used for comparison in the ALSV(FD) formulas and the fact definition operator, denoted as :=, and 2) the formalization of constants that simplifies effective formula notation.

The basic elements of the language of *Attribute Logic with Set Values over Finite Domains* (ALSV(FD)) are attribute names and attribute values. Let us consider: $\mathbf{A}$ – a finite set of attribute names, $\mathbf{D}$ – a set of possible attribute values (their *domains*), and $\mathbf{C}$ – a set of constants. Let $\mathbf{A} = \{A_1, A_2, \ldots, A_n\}$ be all the attributes such that their values define the state of the system under consideration. It is assumed that the overall domain $\mathbf{D}$ is divided into n sets (disjoint or not), $\mathbf{D} = D_1 \cup D_2 \cup \ldots \cup D_n$, where D_i is a domain related to attribute A_i, $i = 1, 2, \ldots, n$. Any domain D_i is assumed to be a finite (discrete) set. We also consider a finite set of constants $\mathbf{C} = \{C_1, C_2, \ldots, C_m\}$. Every constant C_j $j = 1, 2, \ldots, m$ is related to a single domain D_i, $i = 1, 2, \ldots, n$ such that $C_j \subseteq D_i$ There might be multiple constants related to the same domain.

Definition 3. *Attributes As we consider dynamic systems, the values of attributes can change over time (or state of the system). We consider both simple attributes of the form $A_i \colon T \to D_i$ (i.e. taking a single value at any instant of time) and generalized ones of the form $A_i \colon T \to 2^{D_i}$ (i.e. taking a set of values at a time); here T denotes the time domain of discourse.*

Let A_i be an attribute of $\mathbf{A}$ and D_i the domain related to it. Let V_i denote an arbitrary subset of D_i and let $d \in D_i$ be a single element of the domain. V_i can also be a constant related to D_i.

The legal atomic formulae of ALSV along with their semantics are presented in Def. 4 for simple, and in Def. 5 for generalized attributes.

Definition 4. *Simple attribute formulas syntax*

$$
\begin{array}{rlr}
A_i = d & \text{\textit{the value is precisely defined and equals to }} d & (14) \\
A_i \in V_i & \text{\textit{the current value of }} A_i \text{\textit{ belongs to }} V_i & (15) \\
A_i \neq d & \text{\textit{shorthand for }} A_i \in D_i \setminus \{d\} & (16) \\
A_i \notin V_i & \text{\textit{is a shorthand for }} A_i \in D_i \setminus V_i & (17)
\end{array}
$$

Definition 5. *Generalized attribute formulas syntax*

$$
\begin{array}{rlr}
A_i = V_i & \text{\textit{equals to }} V_i \text{ \textit{(and nothing more)}} & (18) \\
A_i \neq V_i & \text{\textit{is different from }} V_i \text{ \textit{(at at least one element)}} & (19) \\
A_i \subseteq V_i & \text{\textit{is a subset of }} V_i & (20) \\
A_i \supseteq V_i & \text{\textit{is a superset of }} V_i & (21) \\
A \sim V & \text{\textit{has a non-empty intersection with }} V_i & (22) \\
A_i \not\sim V_i & \text{\textit{has an empty intersection with }} V_i & (23)
\end{array}
$$

In case V_i is an empty set (the attribute takes in fact no value) we shall write $A_i = \{\}$. In case the value of A_i is unspecified we shall write $A_i = $ NULL (a database convention). If the current value of the attribute is not important we shall write $A = \_$ (a PROLOG convention). More complex formulae can be constructed with *conjunction* ($\wedge$) and *disjunction* ($\vee$); both symbols have classical meanings and interpretation.

There is no explicit use of negation. The proposed set of relations is selected for convenience and as such they are not completely independent. Various notational conventions extending the basic notation can be used. For example, in case of domains being ordered sets, relational symbols such as $>$, $>=$, $<$, $=<$ can be used with the straightforward meaning. To simplify the formula notation *constants* can also be defined as: $C := V$.

The semantics of the proposed language is presented below in an informal way. The semantics of $A = V$ is basically the same as the one of SAL [10]. If $V = \{d_1, d_2, \ldots, d_k\}$ then $A = V$ if the attribute takes all the values specified with V (and nothing more). The semantics of $A \subseteq V$, $A \supseteq V$ and $A \sim V$ are defined as follows:

- $A \subseteq V \equiv A = U$ for some U such that $U \subseteq V$, i.e. A takes *some* of the values from V (and nothing out of V),
- $A \supseteq V \equiv A = W$, for some W such that $V \subseteq W$, i.e. A takes *all* of the values from V (and perhaps some more), and
- $A \sim V \equiv A = X$, for some X such that $V \cap X \neq \emptyset$, i.e. A takes *some* of the values from V (and perhaps some more).

As can be seen, the semantics of ALSV is defined by means of relaxation of logic to a simple set algebra.

A *knowledge base* in ALSV(FD) is composed of:

1. facts defining the current state of the system, and
2. simple formulas forming rules.

The current values of all attributes are specified in the contents of the knowledge-base. From the logical point of view, the state is represented as a logical formula of the form:

$$(A_1 := S_1) \wedge (A_2 := S_2) \wedge \ldots \wedge (A_n := S_n) \tag{24}$$

where $S_i := d_i$ $(d_i \in D_i)$ for simple attributes and $S_i := V_i$, $(V_i \subseteq D_i)$ for complex ones. In order to cover realistic cases, an explicit notation for covering unspecified, unknown values is proposed; (for example to deal with the data containing the NULL values imported from a database).

Using the ALSV(FD) formalization, the so-called XTT2 [12,13] rule language is defined. Consider a set of n attributes $\mathbf{A} = \{A_1, A_2, \ldots, A_n\}$. Any XTT2 rule is assumed to be of the form:

$$(A_1 \propto_1 V_1) \wedge (A_2 \propto_2 V_2) \wedge \ldots (A_n \propto_n V_n) \longrightarrow RHS$$

where $\propto_i$ is one of the admissible relational symbols in ALSV(FD) (see legal formulas in Def. 4,5), and *RHS* is the right-hand side of the rule covering conclusion, including state transition and actions, for details see [10]. In order to fire a rule the preconditions have to be satisfied. The satisfaction of rule preconditions is verified in an algebraic mode, using the rules specified in Fig. 1. The full discussion of ALSV inference for all formulas can be found in [12].

To summarize, the main assumptions about the XTT2 representation are:

- current system *state* is explicitly represented by a set of *facts* based on attributive representation,
- facts are denoted in ALSV(FD) as: $A := V$,
- constants are facts defined as: $C := V$ to simplify compact rule notation,
- system dynamics (state transition) is modelled with *rules*,
- the conditional part of the XTT2 rule is conjunction built from simple ALSV(FD) formulas,
- rule decision contains state modification – new facts, and optionally external actions execution statements,
- to fire the rule, the condition has to be satisfied, which means that certain *inference task* in ALSV(FD) has to be solved.

$$A = d_i, d_i = d_j \models A = d_j$$
$$A = d_i, d_i \neq d_j \models A \neq d_j$$
$$A = d_i, d_i \in V_j \models A \in V_j$$
$$A = d_i, d_i \notin V_j \models A \notin V_j$$

$$A = V, V = W \models A = W$$
$$A = V, V \neq W \models A \neq W$$
$$A = V, V \subseteq W \models A \subseteq W$$
$$A = V, V \supseteq W \models A \supseteq W$$
$$A = V, V \cap W \neq \emptyset \models A \sim W$$
$$A = V, V \cap W = \emptyset \models A \not\sim W$$

Fig. 1. Inference rules

Given the basic discussion of both logical formalisms, the motivation for the research aiming at their integration is given in the following section.

4   Motivation

Rules are inevitably the next step towards the Semantic Web vision. Moreover, there is an increase in the number of applications which use rules to encode their behavior. Therefore, there is a need to define a rule representation method appropriate for the Web.

Description Logics provide an effective formal foundation for the Semantic Web application based on ontologies described with OWL. They allow for simple inference tasks, e.g. corresponding to concept classification. Currently the main challenge for DL is the rule formulation. There are several approaches to the integration of rules and ontologies. Other problems, that up until now have rarely been considered in the Semantic Web research, include effective design methodologies for large rule bases, as well as knowledge quality issues. Maintenance larger knowledge bases is not a trivial task; prone to design errors and logical misformulations. This is why scalable design methods are still being pursued.

In the classic AI field of rule-based expert systems numerous solutions for rule formulation and inference, as well as the design and analysis are have been considered for years [9,10]. A number of visual knowledge representations equivalent to decision rules are used, including decision trees and decision tables [6].

They prove to be helpful in the visual design of rules, as well as providing CASE tools for rule-based systems. The theory and practice of rule verification is a well studied field, for details see [17]. Therefore, evaluating the use of mature rule-based systems solutions is a natural choice for Semantic Web applications.

The XTT2 [12,13] rule formulation and design language based on the ALSV (FD) is an example of a rule design and analysis framework. It offers flexible knowledge representation for forward chaining decision rules, as well as visual design tools. Thanks to the formal description in ALSV(FD) a formalized rule analysis is also possible. As a rule framework XTT2 provides a subset of functionality that SWRL aims for, at least for the production systems based on decision rules. On the other hand, it has a complete design and formal rule analysis solutions.

The primary goal of this research is to allow the use of the XTT2 rule design framework for the Semantic Web rules. This would open up the possibility to use the visual design tools for XTT2 to design Semantic Web rules, as well as exploit the existing verification solutions. The following phases are considered:

1. a transition from ALSV(FD) to a subset of a selected DL language,
2. XTT2 rules formulation compatible with the above transition procedure,
3. visual design of XTT2 rules for the Semantic Web,
4. XTT2 rules translation to SWRL, with possible RIF-only extensions,
5. rule inference on top of OWL-based ontologies.

Ultimately it should be possible to design Semantic Web rules with the XTT2 visual design tools and provide a formal analysis of rules. XTT2 could be run with a dedicated XTT2 engine, or a SWRL runtime. In this paper the focus is on the first phase, with some considerations for the 2nd and the 3rd one. In order to provide a transition, a discussion of syntax and semantics of both DL and ALSV(FD) is given in the next section.

5 Comparison of DL and ALSV(FD)

Goals. Description Logics allow for complex descriptions of objects in the universe of discourse and the relations between them. The static part of a system is expressed in TBox part of a DL Knowledge Base. The actual state is represented by means of facts asserted in ABox. ABox in DL is limited in terms of its syntax and semantics. Only simple concept and role assertions are allowed, which together with knowledge expressed in TBox lay the ground for inferencing.

The main goal of ALSV(FD) is to provide an expressive notation for dynamic system state transitions in rule-based systems. The knowledge specification with ALSV(FD) is composed of: state specification with facts, and transition specification with formulas building decision rules.

Syntax and Semantics. The language of DL consists of *concepts*, *roles* and *constants* (*individuals*). The meaning of the symbols is defined by an *interpretation function*, which to each concept assigns a set of objects, to each role a binary relation, and to each individual an object in the universe of discourse.

In the ALSV(FD) language the following symbols are used: $\mathbf{A}$ – a finite set of attribute names, $\mathbf{A} = \{A_1, A_2, \ldots, A_n\}$, $\mathbf{D}$ – a set of possible attribute values (their *domains*), $\mathbf{D} = D_1 \cup D_2 \cup \ldots \cup D_n$, $\mathbf{C}$ – a set of constants. The semantics of ALSV(FD) is based on the interpretation of the symbols of the alphabet (see [18] for the detailed explanation).

Knowledge representation. Both logics describe the universe of discourse by identifying certain entities. In ALSV(FD) they are called attributes, in DL – concepts. They have their *domains*, which means sets, to which an interpretation maps the attributes' and concepts' name symbols.

Every attribute in ALSV(FD) has a domain, which constraints its values. In DL this kind of specification is done by means of TBox axioms. In order to be able to express a finite domain in DL, a *set of* constructors (denoted by $\mathcal{O}$) is needed.

Once the attributes (in ALSV(FD)) and concepts (in DL) are defined, they are used in system rules specification. Legal ALSV(FD) formulas (see Definitions 4, 5) specify the constraints that an attribute value has to match in order for a rule to be fired. The discussion on mapping the rule specification from AL to DL is conducted in Section 6.3.

Attribute values define the state of the system under consideration. A state is represented as a logical formula (24) built from a conjunction of formulas specifying the values of respective attributes. A statement in AL that an attribute A_i holds certain value v_i, corresponds to a DL statement that a certain object v_i is an instance of the concept A_i. This is valid for both simple and generalized attributes, as explained in Section 6.2.

Starting from this basic analysis, a proposal of a new language integrating DL with ALSV(FD) is introduced.

6   DAAL Rule Language

We propose a hybrid framework for integrating Attributive Logic and Description Logic. We introduce a language called *DAAL* (*Description And Attributive Logic*). It is syntactically based on Description Logics, but tries to capture ALSV(FD) semantics and thus enable expressing ALSV(FD) models in DL. The ideas of the DAAL framework can be summarized as follows:

- In the universe of discourse, we identify entities which correspond to attributes in AL and concepts in DL (from now on we also call them *concepts*).
- The domains of the entities are defined in DAAL in a form of TBox definitions.
- The formulas in rules are written in DAAL in a form of DL TBox axioms.
- The actual state is modelled in DAAL as a DL ABox.
- The actions taken as consequences of rule execution generates new states of the system, encoded in DAAL as new ABoxes.

A novel idea in the DAAL framework is the existence of a *static* TBox with definitions of the domains, *Temporary Rule TBoxes* and *Temporary ABoxes*.

Temporary Rule TBoxes express the preconditions of the system rules. During the execution of reasoning they are loaded into and unloaded from into a reasoner. Therefore, they are not a static part of an ontology. *Temporary ABoxes* correspond to system states. As the system changes its state, new ABoxes replace the previous ones.

6.1 DAAL Language Syntax

The language has syntax as definded in Definitions 6, 7, 8 and 9.

Definition 6. *DAAL vocabulary* *Vocabulary of DAAL language consists of:*

$$A, B, C, \qquad\qquad concept\ names \qquad (25)$$

$$\perp, \qquad\qquad bottom\ concept \qquad (26)$$

$$a, b, c, \qquad\qquad individuals \qquad (27)$$

$$\equiv, \neg, \sqcap, \sqsubseteq, \wedge, \rightarrow, \qquad\qquad operators \qquad (28)$$

$$(,), \{,\}, ., \qquad\qquad delimiters \qquad (29)$$

Concepts in DAAL are constructed from the vocabulary and may be in one of the following forms:

Definition 7. *DAAL concepts* *Admissible concept descriptions in DAAL:*

$$C, \qquad (30)$$

$$\neg C \qquad (31)$$

$$\{c_1, c_2, \ldots, c_n\} \qquad (32)$$

$$C \sqsubseteq D \qquad (33)$$

Formulas in DAAL are of two sorts: terminological axioms and concept assertions.

Definition 8. *DAAL syntax* *Admissible formulas in DAAL:*

$$C \equiv D, \qquad\qquad terminological\ axiom \qquad (34)$$

$$C(a), \qquad\qquad concept\ assertion \qquad (35)$$

Definition 9. *DAAL rules* *A rule in DAAL is of the following form:*

$$(C_1 \wedge \ldots \wedge C_n) \rightarrow (A_1 \wedge \ldots \wedge A_n) \qquad (36)$$

where $C_i, i = 1, \ldots n$ are terminological axioms, and $A_i, i = 1, \ldots n$ are concept assertions.

Examples:

- a terminological axiom: $Day \equiv \{sun, mon, tue, wed, thr, fri, sat\}$,
- a rule: $(Today \equiv \{workday\}) \wedge (Hour \equiv BizHours) \rightarrow Operation(bizhours)$.

The logical operator $\wedge$ denotes a *conjunction* with a classical meaning. The symbol $\rightarrow$ separates the rule preconditions and conclusion. Its interpretation follows the one from Logic Programming.

6.2 Conceptual Modelling in DAAL

In the DAAL approach, the attributes are modelled as DL concepts (corresponding to OWL classes). They are subclasses of the general Attribute class for attributes. Let the domain D_i of an attribute A_i be finite. Then, the transition shown in Table 1 holds.

Table 1. Formulas in AL and terminological axioms in DAAL – domain definitions

Attributive Logic		DAAL	
Attribute Name	Attribute domain	Concept Name	Concept constructors
A_i	D_i	A_i	$A_i \equiv D_i$
	$D = \{a_1, a_2, \ldots, a_n\}$		$D \equiv \{a_1, a_2, \ldots, a_n\}$

The actual state of a system under consideration is modelled as a set of DL assertions (individuals in OWL). To express a value of a simple attribute there appears a single assertion. For generalized attributes there appear as many assertions as many values the attribute takes. A formula $A_i := d$ denotes that the attribute A_i *takes value* d at the certain moment. In DL this can be represented as an assertion in ABox, namely: $A_i(d_i)$. In the case of generalized attributes, there is no direct counterpart in the DL for an AL formula: $A_i = V_i$, where V_i is a set. However, the same meaning can be acquired in other way. Based on the assumption that V_i is a finite set of the form: $V_i = \{v_{i_1}, v_{i_2}, \ldots, v_{i_n}\}$ one can add *all* of the following assertions to the DL ABox: $A_i(v_{i_1}).A_i(v_{i_2})....A_i(v_{i_n})..$ State specification in AL and DL is shown in Table 2.

Table 2. State specification in AL and assertions in DAAL

Attributive Logic		DAAL
Attribute Type	Formula	Assertion
simple attribute	$A_i := d_i$	$A(d)$
generalized attribute	$A_i := V_i, V_i = \{v_{i_1}, v_{i_2}, \ldots, v_{i_n}\}$	$A(v_{i_1}), A_i(v_{i_2}), \ldots, A_i(v_{i_n})$

6.3 Specification of Rules

The formulas used in rule preconditions specify the constraints of the attribute values. They constitute a schema, to which a state of a system in a certain moment of time is matched. DAAL approach to the mapping from AL to DL consists in a translation of the AL formulas into TBox-like DL axioms.

For simple attributes the transition is fairly clear. For instance, the formula: $A_i = d$ is logically equivalent to $A_i \in \{d\}$ so we express it in DAAL as: $A_i \equiv \{d\}$ (instances of concept A_i belongs to $\{d\}$). Another formula, $A_i \in V_i$ constraint the set of possible values to the set V_i. This corresponds to the DL axiom: $A_i \equiv V_i$.

For generalized attributes one cannot express all the AL formulas in DL TBox. This is due to the fact that the constraints in DL TBox apply to *individuals* and not sets of object. For example, one can say that all the instances of A_i are also instances of V_i and the DL axiom $A_i \sqsubseteq V_i$ corresponds to the AL formula $A_i \subseteq V_i$. However, it is impossible to specify that all elements of V_i appear in the ABox. Hence, the AL formula $A_i = V_i$ cannot be expressed in DL. An axiom $A_i \equiv V_i$ only restricts the values of A_i so that $\forall x A_i(x) \leftrightarrow V_i(x)$, but it cannot force the concept A_i to *take all the values* from V_i. This is a consequence of the Open World Assumption. If some values are missing in the explicit assertions, it does not mean that the assertions do not hold. Using Integrity Constraints to represent this kind of restrictions is planned to be investigated in future (see [19]).

Table 3. Simple attributes formulas in AL rules and respective axioms in DAAL

ALSV(FD)	DAAL
Formula	Axiom
$A_i = d$	$A_i \equiv \{d\}$
$A_i \in V_i$	$A_i \equiv V_i$
$A_i \neq d$	$A_i \equiv \neg\{d\}$
$A_i \notin V_i$	$A_i \equiv \neg V_i$
$A_i \in \{\}$	$A_i \equiv \bot$

Table 4. Generalized attributes formulas in AL rules and respective axioms in DAAL

ALSV(FD)	DAAL
Formula	Axiom
$A_i \subseteq V_i$	$A_i \sqsubseteq V_i$
$A_i \supseteq V_i$	$V_i \sqsubseteq A_i$
$A_i \sim V_i$	$\neg(A_i \sqcap V_i) \sqsubseteq \bot$
$A_i \not\sim V_i$	$A_i \sqcap V_i \equiv \bot$

To sum up, the ALSV(FD) formulas for simple attributes can be represented as terminological axioms in DL as shown in Table 3 and Table 4.

6.4 Inference Scenario

The axioms for rule representation introduced in the preceding section are called *temporary TBoxes*. They constitute a schema to which particular system states are matched, but they are not *always-true* knowledge of the system domain.

At a given moment of time, the state of the system is represented as a conjunction of formulae (legal formulas in ALSV(FD) or concept assertions in DAAL respectively (see Table 2). In order to check rule preconditions satisfiability, appropriate inference tasks have to be performed. The inference rules in AL are presented in Fig. 1. For DAAL the corresponding task is *consistency checking*.

For each rule a *consistency checking* of the state assertions with regards to the rule preconditions is performed. If the consistency holds, the rule can be fired.

In DAAL reasoning the rules are able to change the knowledge base of the system. Adding and removing facts is allowed. These operations generate a new ABox which represents the new state of the system.

An architecture of such a hybrid reasoning framework consists of a dedicated XTT2 tool, a control component, and a DL reasoner (see Sect. 10). Appropriate rules are loaded in a loop into the DL reasoner together with the actual state of the system. Each rule is temporarily joined with an existing TBox (in which the definitions of the concepts are stored). The state is a *temporary ABox*. The DL reasoner checks the consistency of the ontology resulting from the TBox and ABox. If the ontology is consistent, the rule can be fired. Rule axioms are then unloaded and the loop continues.

7   An Example of Translation

Let us consider a simple example of a forward chaining rule-based system. The example was originally presented in [20]. The goal of the system is to set a thermostat temperature based on the condition, namely the time specification.

Original Description in ALSV(FD). Consider a set attributes
$\mathbf{A} = \{day, month, hour, today, season, operation, therm\_setting\}$,
with corresponding domains:
$\mathbf{D} = \{D_{day}, D_{month}, D_{hour}, D_{today}, D_{season}, D_{operation}, D_{therm\_setting}\}$,
defined as: $D_{day} = \{sun, mon, tue, wed, thr, fri, sat\}$,
$D_{month} = \{jan, feb, mar, apr, may, jun, jul, aug, sep, oct, nov, dec\}$,
$D_{hour} = \{1 - 24\}$, $D_{today} = \{workday, weekend\}$,
$D_{season} = \{winter, spring, summer, autumn\}$,
$D_{operation} = \{bizhours, notbizhours\}$, $D_{therm\_setting} = \{12 - 30\}$,
Let us define two constant facts: $\mathbf{C} = \{Weekdays, Weekend\}$,
as $Weekdays := \{mon, tue, wed, thr, fri\}$, and $Weekend := \{sat, sun\}$.
In such a system we can consider simple production rules:[2]

$R1 : month \in \{dec, jan, feb\} \longrightarrow season := summer$
$R2 : day \in Weekdays \longrightarrow today := workday$
$R3 : today \in \{workday\} \land hour \in \{9 - 17\} \longrightarrow operation := bizhours$
$R4 : operation = \{bizhours\} \land season = \{summer\} \longrightarrow therm\_setting := 24$

Description in DAAL. In DAAL language the following concepts are distinguished: *Day, Month, Hour, Today, Season, Operation, Therm_setting*. The definition of the concepts is as follows:

---

[2] The author of [20] lives in Australia, so the rules concerning seasons are different than in Europe.

$$Day \equiv \{sun, mon, tue, wed, thr, fri, sat\}, \quad (37)$$

$$Month \equiv \{jan, feb, mar, apr, may, jun, jul, aug, sep, oct, nov, dec\}, \quad (38)$$

$$Hour \equiv \{1, 2, \ldots, 24\}, \quad (39)$$

$$Today \equiv \{workday, weekend\}, \quad (40)$$

$$Season \equiv \{winter, spring, summer, autumn\}, \quad (41)$$

$$Operation \equiv \{bizhours, notbizhours\}, \quad (42)$$

$$Therm\_setting \equiv \{12, 13, \ldots, 30\} \quad (43)$$

To simplify the notation one can introduce the following concepts:

$$SummerMonths \equiv \{dec, jan, feb\}, \quad (44)$$

$$Bizhours \equiv \{9, 10, \ldots, 17\}, \quad (45)$$

$$WorkingDays \equiv \{mon, tue, wed, thr, fri\}. \quad (46)$$

and using the transition specified in Tab. 3 write the rules in the following form:

$R1 : (Month \equiv SummerMonths) \rightarrow Season(summer),$

$R2 : (Day \equiv WorkingDays) \rightarrow Today(workday),$

$R3 : (Today \equiv \{workday\}) \wedge (Hour \equiv BizHours) \rightarrow Operation(bizhours),$

$R4 : (Operation \equiv \{bizhours\}) \wedge (Season \equiv \{summer\}) \rightarrow Therm\_setting(24)$

Inference process. In a given moment t_n the state is represented as a *temporary $ABox_n$*[3]. Let in moment t_0, the $ABox_0$ be:

$$Month(jan).Day(mon).Hour(11). \quad (47)$$

The inference process is as follows:

1. The state $ABox_0$ (47) and the preconditions of rule R1 are loaded into the DL reasoner.
2. The DL reasoner performs the consistency check of the state with respect to rule preconditions.
3. Because the ontology built from the state assertions and R1 precondition formulas is consistent ($Month(jan)$ is consistent w.r.t. $Month \equiv Summer$ $Months$ ($SummerMonths \equiv \{dec, jan, feb\}$)) the rule is fired.
4. The conclusion of the rule generates a new assertion in ABox. The new $ABox_1$ replaces the old one ($ABox_0$). $ABox_1$ is as follows:

$$Month(jan).Day(mon).Hour(11).Season(summer). \quad (48)$$

5. The state $ABox_1$ (48) and the preconditions of rule R2 are loaded into the DL reasoner.

---

[3] While we use terms "moments" (time points), as well as "temporary" we do not refer to or address any *temporal aspects*. In fact, these terms are used only technically, to denote a sequence of ABoxes.

6. The DL reasoner performs the consistency check of the state with respect to rule preconditions.
7. Because this time the ontology built from the state assertions and R2 precondition formulas again is consistent ($Day(mon)$ is consistent w.r.t. $Day \equiv WorkingDays$ ($WorkingDays \equiv \{mon, tue, wed, thr, fri\}$) the rule is fired.
8. The conclusion of the rule generates a new assertion in ABox. The new ABox_2 replaces the old one (ABox_1). ABox_2 is as follows:

$$Month(jan).Day(mon).Hour(11).Season(summer).Today(workday). \tag{49}$$

9. The reasoning continues with new ABox state and the next rules.

The evaluation of this approach is presented next.

8   Evaluation

In the proposed solution certain semantic discrepancies between AL and DL have became evident. In the former, on which HeKatE methodology[4] that uses ALSV(FD) and XTT2 is based [13], a Unique Name Assumption and the Closed World Assumption hold. The latter does not respect either of them. Therefore, by default, testing state specification against the rule precondition axioms does not yield the same results in Attributive Logic and Description Logics.

For instance, if an attribute A in rule precondition is defined as $A = \{d_1\}$, and in state specification there is a statement: $A(d_2)$, the ontology is still consistent. Hence, the rule precondition is satisfied and the rule could be fired. By means of the `owl:differentFrom` property one can specify the distinction between two individuals within a class. Then, if the value at a certain moment is said to be different from a value specified in the attribute definition, the consistency checking fails, which is the expected result. In order to ensure Unique Name Assumption in the whole system, one should define a property `owl:AllDifferents` with the domain in the most general class, namely the `owl:Thing`. This will result in distinguishing all of individuals of all the classes.

Another consequence is caused by the Open World Assumption in DL and Closed World Assumption in AL. Consider a rule:

$$(Month \equiv SummerMonths) \rightarrow Season(summer).$$

It should be fired if and only if the value of the attribute $Month$ is in the set denoted by $SummerMonths$. Let us consider a state, in which the value of the attribute is not specified. Then, in AL the preconditions are not true. However, in th DAAL approach, the consistency of the ontology built from the rule precondition and the state (in this case, only the: $Month \equiv SummerMonths$ axiom) is checked. This ontology is consistent, because there is no contradiction.

---

[4] For the home page of the *Hybrid Knowledge Engineering Project (HeKatE)* see `http://hekate.ia.agh.edu.pl`.

Therefore, by default the rule would be fired. The solution lays in introducing a requirement, that in every state of a system, only the rules using the attributes with defined values can fire. If the attribute *Month* was not precisely defined at a certain moment, then no rule using it should be loaded to the reasoner.

The proposal presented in this paper enables rule representation based on attributes of a system to be expressed by Description Logics. This representation is rich in a sense that in the body of rules one can test a range of values an attribute should take. This is accomplished by use of TBox axioms in rule preconditions. At the same time it is possible to use reasoning and design capabilities of the XTT2 representation.

The research results introduced in this paper are related to a number of other research efforts. Some important ones are referenced and briefly discussed next.

9   Related Research

9.1   Challenges Rules and Ontologies Integration

Rules and ontologies are complimentary approaches to knowledge representation and reasoning. In ontologies one can capture class properties and define complex classes. Rule languages are designed mainly to define how to synthesize new facts from those stored in the knowledge base. There are things that rules cannot express or infer, e.g. inferencing complex relationships among classes. Generally asserting negation (complement of classes) or disjunctive information or existential quantification is not possible either [21]. On the other hand, there are things that cannot be expressed in ontologies or only in a very complicated manner, for example complex Horn rules. Various use-cases have shown that applications often require both approaches, the ontologies and rules.

The integration of rules with the ontology layer is not trivial. There exist important differences between ontologies based on Description Logics and rule-based systems. Description Logics (DL) and Logic Programming (LP) (rule systems) are orthogonal in the sense that neither of them is a subset of the other [21]. The Unique Name Assumption (UNA) in logic programming does not hold in ontologies and DL, where the same resource may be referenced to by different names and descriptions. Databases and logic programming systems use the Closed World Assumption (CWA), whereas in the Semantic Web standards there is a tendency to use Open World Assumption (OWA).

Various proposals for rule representation for the Semantic Web have been formulated. Approaches to the integration of rules and ontologies may be generally divided into hybrid and homogeneous systems. Heterogeneous (modular) approach offers loose integration through strict semantic separation between the ontology and rule components. Resulting systems consist of an ontology component based on a DL variant, and a rule one, which usually is a variant of Datalog [22]. Homogeneous approach results in designing a single logical language. No syntactic or semantic distinctions are made between the ontology and the rule part, and both can be interpreted by the same reasoning engine. The language is typically either an expressive union of the component languages or the intersection of them. The union of the entire LP and DL fragments within First Order Logic (FOL), is undecidable in a general case.

The languages' semantics are based on various logical foundations, including subsets of FOL, and Frame Logic (F-Logic) [23]. A number of languages are based on the Datalog core. Selected solutions are briefly referenced below.

Hybrid solutions include $\mathcal{AL}$-log [24] and CARIN [25], which integrated selected DL with Datalog rules. Another approach is represented by combining DL with Answer Set Programming [26,27]. It includes some features from non-monotonic logics, and support for reasoning with constraints and preferences. The resulting semantics is incompatible with First Order semantics. Integrating closed- and open-world reasoning is an aim of the Hybrid MKNF Knowledge Bases [28]. A MKNF knowledge base consists of a description in DL and a set of MKNF rules. The approach tries to provide a framework for non-monotonic and autoepistemic extensions of DLs. Basically, it means that the system is able to revise its own beliefs. So far investigated theoretically, it is planned to be implemented in the KAON2[5] reasoner.

Homogeneous solutions include DLP, SWRL and ELP. DLP [29] are based on the intersection of a Description Logic with Horn Clause rules. The result is a decidable language, which is necessarily less expressive than either the DL or rules language from which it is formed. DLP as proposed in [29] has standard First Order semantics and thus does not support CWA. However, it is possible to treat DLP rules as having Datalog semantics based on CWA. In this case, though, they are no longer semantically compatible with OWL, nor even RDF. Such an interpretation of DLP leads to the situation presented in [30].

SWRL [5] is based on the expressive union of the function-free Horn logic and OWL-DL [31]. It includes a high-level abstract syntax, a model-theoretic semantics, and an XML syntax based on RuleML. The language enables Datalog-like rules to be combined with an OWL knowledge base. Concepts and roles are used in rules as unary and binary atoms. Subsumption and query answering with respect to knowledge bases and programs is undecidable.

In order to regain tractability subsets of SWRL has been proposed. For instance *DL-safe* as proposed [32] are applicable only to explicitly named objects. Another decidable fragment of SWRL is ELP [33], a language based on a tractable Description Logic $\mathcal{EL}^{++}$ augmented with DL Rules[6]. The authors call it a "rule-based tractable knowledge representation" allowing for reasoning in polynomial time. DL Rules must be of a certain "tree shape". ELP supports inferencing in OWL 2 EL and OWL 2 RL Profiles. The logic underpinning OWL 2 EL is $\mathcal{EL}^{++}$ DL. OWL 2 RL is based on Description Logic Programs.

9.2   Alternative Translations in HeKatE

Alternative proposals for representing ALSV(FD) attributes in DL have also been considered. One of them, originally developed by J. Szostek-Janik [34] is

---

[5] http://kaon2.semanticweb.org/

[6] http://korrekt.org/page/Description_Logic_Rules

supported by a translator framework called HaThoR[7]. The HaThoR framework has been developed by the HeKatE project and its developent continues.

In HaThoR, the system attributes are represented as *instances* of a general concept Attribute. They are described in more detail than in DAAL, by using multiple roles (see Fig. 2). These roles define if an attribute is simple or general, input or output, etc. The attributes are connected to instances of a general concept Type. These relations determine the domains of the attributes. Domains of the attributes are defined using appropriate roles (OWL datatype properties).

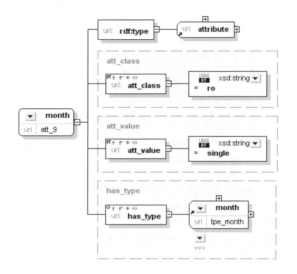

Fig. 2. Attribute representation in HaThoR

This approach has been revised for the new version of OWL. Translators to OWL2 take advantage of its support for datatype ranges, and use it in the definitions of the domains. The values of the attributes are represented with roles (datatype properties), for instance $attTakesValue(att_1, val_1)$. The rules have a form similar to SWRL rules, for instance:

$attTakesValue(att_{10}, "workday") \land attTakesValue(att_{11}, ?var\_att_11) \land swrlb :$
$greaterThan(?var\_att_{11}, 17) \rightarrow attTakesValue(att_7, "not\_business\_hours")$.

The main difference to the DAAL proposal lies in representing attributes and their values. Moreover, it is not possible to directly express set relations, such as $att_1 \in \{val_1, val_2, val_3\}$. However, if a rule has such a condition in the body, the condition can be expressed it by a set of rules, each having a single element of the set, and with the same conclusion for all the rules.

---

[7] See https://ai.ia.agh.edu.pl/wiki/hekate:hathor

9.3 Other Rule Representations

The proposal presented in this paper considers rule representation. This representation employs both TBox an ABox axioms. TBox axioms are used in rule preconditions, whereas ABox statements appear in rule conclusions.

This approach is different from SWRL [5] and its subsets. In SWRL rule preconditions may include concepts and role assertions (ABox statements). Such a representation is also possible for translation from ALSV(FD) to DL but is beyond the scope of this paper.

DL rules [33] represent rules with a certain tree structure. The approach presented here does not impose any restrictions on the rule structure. DL-safe rules [32] restrict the rules to named individuals. This is similar to our solution, where only the values of previously defined attributes are checked. Therefore, there are no variables in rules.

9.4 DL Representation of Dynamically Changing World

Describing states of a dynamic system using DL constructs implies the problem of updating the state description. Integrating action formalisms and DL may lead to more expressive representation yet with decidable reasoning [35]. The idea of updating ABox over time has been investigated [36,37] and appropriate DL languages have been defined. In our solution the updated ABoxes are treated by a separate component, so there is no direct requirement for ABox updates support. However, incorporating these ideas will be considered in future.

The idea presented here has common points with SAIL architecture for situation awareness systems [38]. Similarities lay in representing current states of a conceived world by means of DL ABox assertions and updating them over time. Moreover, a DL reasoner is a component of a system and is invoked by a control component. In [38] the idea of a *sequence of ABoxes* is introduced. The background knowledge consists of an ontology expressed in TBox and static knowledge expressed in ABox. This, together with the latest loaded ABox, is a base for inferring new facts which are stored in a new ABox.

10 Conclusions and Future Work

The research ideas presented in the paper affect integration of the selected expert system rule design method and the Semantic Web. Logical foundations of the method (developed within the HeKatE project) is Attibutive Logic ALSV(FD).

In this paper a proposal of combining Attributive Logic and Description Logic was presented. We showed how ALSV(FD) concepts can be expressed in DL and designed a language based on DL and ALSV(FD). Although conceptually similar, these two logical calculi adopt different semantics, which makes the integration challenging. A draft solution has been proposed.

For future work, we choose to investigate various solutions which facilitate bridging the identified semantic gaps. These include MKNF knowledge bases and support for integrity constraints within an ontology [19]. Integrity constraints are also considered useful when expressing restrictions on generalized attributes (taking set values at a time).

Features such as mathematical operators (e.g. $<$, $>$ etc.) in rules, as well as ordered domains of attributes, will be analyzed. Possible translation using new features of OWL 2 [39], such as support for user-defined datatypes and ranges will be investigated.

Implementation of a proof-of-concept prototype is planned. The XTT2 toolset (see `hekate.ia.agh.edu.pl`) provides a custom inference engine able to execute the XTT2 rules. The engine has an extensible architecture and is implemented in Prolog. This will allow development of an interface to an external DL reasoners and allow reasoning with XTT2 rules on top of existing OWL ontologies.

Considered tools include PrOWLog[8] and Extended DIG Description Logic Interface for Prolog.[9] The former is a hybrid system that allows access to OWL from logic programs using *any-world semantics* as explained in [40]. The system is based on KAON2, so it provides a DL reasoner. In order to use PrOWLog one needs a working SWI-Prolog installation.

The latter enables client programs to communicate with DL reasoning server via HTTP POST requests which include XML messages. The requests may be of two kinds, assert statements and queries. Using the interface, the HeaRT tool[10], a dedicated XTT2 engine, could communicate with DL reasoner like Pellet[11]. Apart from standard reasoning services (such as consistency checking), Pellet supports Datatype reasoning (user-defined datatypes allowed in OWL 2), SPARQL-Dl query answering and DL-safe rules.

Acknowledgements. The authors wish to thank Prof. Antoni Ligęza for his help in improving the preliminary version of this paper, Claudia Obermaier for her valuable remarks concerning the version of the paper presented at the ICCCI conference [1], as well as Dr. Sławomir Nowaczyk and Dr. Sebastian Ernst for their comments on the final version of the paper.

References

1. Nalepa, G.J., Furmańska, W.T.: Proposal of a New Rule-based Inference Scheme for the Semantic Web Applications. In: New Challenges in Computational Collective Intelligence. Studies in Computational Intelligence, pp. 15–26. Springer, Heidelberg (2009)
2. Berners-Lee, T., Hendler, J., Lassila, O.: The semantic web: Scientific american. Scientific American (May 2001)
3. Baader, F., Calvanese, D., McGuinness, D.L., Nardi, D., Patel-Schneider, P.F. (eds.): The Description Logic Handbook: Theory, Implementation, and Applications. Cambridge University Press, Cambridge (2003)

---

[8] http://logic.aifb.uni-karlsruhe.de/wiki/PrOWLog
[9] http://wasp.cs.vu.nl/sekt/dig
[10] https://ai.ia.agh.edu.pl/wiki/hekate:heart
[11] http://clarkparsia.com/pellet

4. Kifer, M., Boley, H.: RIF overview. W3C working draft, W3C (October 2009),
   http://www.w3.org/TR/rif-overview
5. Horrocks, I., Patel-Schneider, P.F., Boley, H., Tabet, S., Grosof, B., Dean, M.:
   SWRL: A semantic web rule language combining OWL and RuleML, w3c member
   submission 21 may 2004. Technical report, W3C (2004)
6. van Harmelen, F., Lifschitz, V., Porter, B. (eds.): Handbook of Knowledge Representation. Elsevier Science, Amsterdam (2007)
7. Russell, S., Norvig, P.: Artificial Intelligence: A Modern Approach, 2nd edn.
   Prentice-Hall, Englewood Cliffs (2003)
8. Liebowitz, J. (ed.): The Handbook of Applied Expert Systems. CRC Press, Boca
   Raton (1998)
9. Giarratano, J., Riley, G.: Expert Systems. Principles and Programming, 4th edn.
   Thomson Course Technology, Boston (2005) ISBN 0-534-38447-1
10. Ligęza, A.: Logical Foundations for Rule-Based Systems. Springer, Heidelberg
    (2006)
11. Bratko, I.: Prolog Programming for Artificial Intelligence, 3rd edn. Addison-Wesley,
    Reading (2000)
12. Nalepa, G.J., Ligęza, A.: XTT+ rule design using the ALSV(FD). In: Giurca, A.,
    Analyti, A., Wagner, G. (eds.) 18th European Conference on Artificial Intelligence:
    2nd East European Workshop on Rule-based applications RuleApps 2008 Patras,
    ECAI 2008, pp. 11–15. University of Patras, Patras (2008)
13. Nalepa, G.J., Ligęza, A.: HeKatE methodology, hybrid engineering of intelligent
    systems. International Journal of Applied Mathematics and Computer Science
    (2010) (accepted for publication)
14. Hitzler, P., Krötzsch, M., Parsia, B., Patel-Schneider, P.F., Rudolph, S.: OWL 2
    web ontology language — primer. W3C recommendation, W3C (October 2009)
15. Nalepa, G.J., Ligęza, A.: On ALSV rules formulation and inference. In: Lane,
    H.C., Guesgen, H.W. (eds.) Proceedings of the twenty-second International Florida
    Artificial Intelligence Research Society Conference, FLAIRS-22, May 19–21, pp.
    396–401. AAAI Press, Menlo Park (2009)
16. Klösgen, W., Żytkow, J.M. (eds.): Handbook of Data Mining and Knowledge Dis-
    covery. Oxford University Press, New York (2002)
17. Ligęza, A., Nalepa, G.J.: Rules verification and validation. In: Giurca, A., Dragan
    Gasevic, K.T. (eds.) Handbook of Research on Emerging Rule-Based Languages
    and Technologies: Open Solutions and Approaches, pp. 273–301. IGI Global, Her-
    shey (2009)
18. Ligęza, A.: Logical Foundations for Rule-Based Systems. Uczelniane Wydawnictwa
    Naukowo-Dydaktyczne AGH w Krakowie, Kraków (2005)
19. Motik, B., Horrocks, I., Sattler, U.: Bridging the gap between OWL and rela-
    tional databases. Web Semantics: Science, Services and Agents on the World Wide
    Web 7(2), 74–89 (2009)
20. Negnevitsky, M.: Artificial Intelligence. A Guide to Intelligent Systems. Addison-
    Wesley, Harlow (2002) ISBN 0-201-71159-1
21. Antoniou, G., van Harmelen, F.: A Semantic Web Primer. The MIT Press, Cam-
    bridge (2008)
22. Ullman, J.D.: Principles of Database and Knowledge-Base Systems, vol. I. Com-
    puter Science Press, Rockville (1988)
23. Kifer, M., Lausen, G., Wu, J.: Logical foundations of object-oriented and frame-
    based languages. J. ACM 42(4), 741–843 (1995)

24. Donini, F.M., Lenzerini, M., Nardi, D., Schaerf, A.: AL-log: integrating datalog and description logics. J. of Intelligent and Cooperative Information Systems 10, 227–252 (1998)
25. Levy, A.Y., Rousset, M.C.: Combining horn rules and description logics in CARIN. Artif. Intell. 104(1-2), 165–209 (1998)
26. Eiter, T., Ianni, G., Polleres, A., Schindlauer, R., Tompits, H.: Reasoning with rules and ontologies. In: Barahona, P., Bry, F., Franconi, E., Henze, N., Sattler, U. (eds.) Reasoning Web 2006. LNCS, vol. 4126, pp. 93–127. Springer, Heidelberg (2006)
27. Eiter, T., Ianni, G., Lukasiewicz, T., Schindlauer, R., Tompits, H.: Combining answer set programming with description logics for the semantic web. Artificial Intelligence 172, 12–13 (2008)
28. Motik, B., Horrocks, I., Rosati, R., Sattler, U.: Can OWL and logic programming live together happily ever after? In: Cruz, I., Decker, S., Allemang, D., Preist, C., Schwabe, D., Mika, P., Uschold, M., Aroyo, L.M. (eds.) ISWC 2006. LNCS, vol. 4273, pp. 501–514. Springer, Heidelberg (2006)
29. Grosof, B.N., Horrocks, I., Volz, R., Decker, S.: Description logic programs: combining logic programs with description logic. In: Proceedings of the Twelfth International World Wide Web Conference, WWW 2003, pp. 48–57 (2003)
30. Horrocks, I., Parsia, B., Patel-Schneider, P., Hendler, J.: Semantic web architecture: Stack or two towers? In: Fages, F., Soliman, S. (eds.) PPSWR 2005. LNCS, vol. 3703, pp. 37–41. Springer, Heidelberg (2005)
31. McGuinness, D.L., Welty, C., Smith, M.K.: OWL web ontology language guide. W3C recommendation, W3C (February 2004), http://www.w3.org/TR/2004/REC-owl-guide-20040210
32. Motik, B., Sattler, U., Studer, R.: Query answering for owl-dl with rules. Journal of Web Semantics, 549–563 (2004)
33. Krötzsch, M., Rudolph, S., Hitzler, P.: ELP: Tractable rules for OWL 2. In: Sheth, A.P., Staab, S., Dean, M., Paolucci, M., Maynard, D., Finin, T., Thirunarayan, K. (eds.) ISWC 2008. LNCS, vol. 5318, pp. 649–664. Springer, Heidelberg (2008)
34. Szostek-Janik, J.: Translations of knowledge representations for rule-based systems. AGH University of Science and Technology, MSc Thesis (2008)
35. Baader, F., Lutz, C., Miličic, M., Sattler, U., Wolter, F.: Integrating description logics and action formalisms: first results. In: Proceedings of the 20th National Conference on Artificial intelligence, AAAI 2005, pp. 572–577. AAAI Press, Menlo Park (2005)
36. Bong, Y.: Description logic ABox updates revisited. Master thesis, TU Dresden, Germany (2007)
37. Drescher, C., Liu, H., Baader, F., Guhlemann, S., Petersohn, U., Steinke, P., Thielscher, M.: Putting abox updates into action. In: Ghilardi, S., Sebastiani, R. (eds.) FroCoS 2009. LNCS, vol. 5749, pp. 149–164. Springer, Heidelberg (2009)
38. Baader, F., Bauer, A., Baumgartner, P., Cregan, A., Gabaldon, A., Ji, K., Lee, K., Rajaratnam, D., Schwitter, R.: A novel architecture for situation awareness systems. In: Giese, M., Waaler, A. (eds.) TABLEAUX 2009. LNCS, vol. 5607, pp. 77–92. Springer, Heidelberg (2009)
39. Hitzler, P., Krötzsch, M., Rudolph, S.: Foundations of Semantic Web Technologies. Chapman and Hall, Boca Raton (2009)
40. Matzner, T., Hitzler, P.: Any-world access to OWL from Prolog. In: Hertzberg, J., Beetz, M., Englert, R. (eds.) KI 2007. LNCS (LNAI), vol. 4667, pp. 84–98. Springer, Heidelberg (2007)

A Cross-Cultural Multi-agent Model of Opportunism in Trade

Gert Jan Hofstede[1,2], Catholijn M. Jonker[2], and Tim Verwaart[3]

[1] Wageningen University, Postbus 9109, 6700 HB Wageningen, The Netherlands
gertjan.hofstede@wur.nl
[2] Delft University of Technology, Mekelweg 4, 2628 CD Delft, The Netherlands
c.m.jonker@tudelft.nl
[3] LEI Wageningen UR, Postbus 29703, 2502 LS Den Haag, The Netherlands
tim.verwaart@wur.nl

Abstract. According to transaction cost economics, contracts are always incomplete and offer opportunities to defect. Some level of trust is a sine qua non for trade. If the seller is better informed about product quality than the buyer, the buyer has to rely on information the seller provides or has to check the information by testing the product or tracing the supply chain processes, thus incurring extra transaction cost. An opportunistic seller who assumes the buyer to trust, may deliver a lower quality product than agreed upon. In human decisions to deceive and to show trust or distrust, issues like mutual expectations, shame, self-esteem, personality, and reputation are involved. These factors depend in part on traders' cultural background. This paper proposes an agent model of deceit and trust and describes a multi-agent simulation where trading agents are differentiated according to Hofstede's dimensions of national culture. Simulations of USA and Dutch trading situations are compared.

Keywords: trust and reputation management, deceit, negotiation, trade partner selection, culture.

1 Introduction

A business transaction usually incurs cost on transaction partners, thus reducing the value of the transaction for the party bearing the cost. In transaction cost economics [1] opportunism and the incompleteness of contracts are central issues. Due to bounded rationality, contracts cannot specify solutions for all contingencies that may occur in transactions executed under the contracts. The incompleteness offers contract partners opportunities to defect. As Williamson [1] asserts, not every contract partner will take full advantage of every opportunity to defect. It is the uncertainty about a contract partner's opportunism that incurs transaction cost. *Ex ante* and *ex post* types of transaction cost can be distinguished. *Ex ante* are the cost of searching, bargaining, drafting, and safeguarding of contracts. *Ex post* are the cost of monitoring and enforcing task completion. Transaction cost economics is the basis for the process model of trading agents applied in this paper. The process model is depicted in Fig. 1.

N.T. Nguyen and R. Kowalczyk (Eds.): Transactions on CCI II, LNCS 6450, pp. 24–45, 2010.

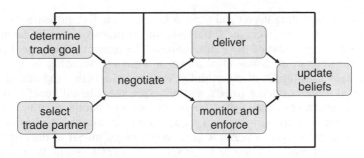

Fig. 1. Processes and internal information flows of trading agents

The outcome of successful negotiation is a contract. After that, it comes to delivery. An agent may deliver according to contract, or fail to do so intentionally (opportunism) or unintentionally (by incompetence or a flaw of its quality control system). At the same time, an agent may monitor the other party's delivery and either check if it is according to contract, or trust and accept without checking. Klein Woolthuis et al. [2] studied the relationship between trust and contracts. They concluded that trust can substitute or complement contracts: if trust is high, contracts can either be rather incomplete, because parties do not expect deceit, or more complete but not actively monitored and enforced, as a signal confirming the trusting relationship; if trust is low, a contract can either be rather complete as a safeguard against opportunism, or incomplete because of opportunistic intentions (so, contract incompleteness does not necessarily imply trust).

The trading situation of the simulation presented in this paper is based on the Trust And Tracing game [3]. In this game, players select trade partners and trade imaginary food products that have a value-adding quality attribute known by the supplier, but invisible to the customer, e.g. "organically grown". The customer can, at the cost of a fee, involve the Tracing Agency to test the actual quality. The Tracing Agency reports the test's outcome to both customer and supplier, and in case of untruthful delivery, punishes the supplier by a fine. Based on experience from negotiation and tracing results, agents update their beliefs about the market, potential partners, and the risks of opportunistic behavior. This paper focuses on the post-contract phase. The models for trust, deceit, and experience-based belief update are described in Section 2.

Human decisions to deceive and to trust are not strictly rational in the sense that is usual in neoclassical economics. Apart from financial benefits, human beings discount expectations of future deals and of social benefits that have to do with status and affiliation and can be succinctly described as 'reputation'. They do this for the simple reason that those of their ancestors who did it, or the groups and societies to which they belonged, have thrived and succeeded in reproducing [4]. The mechanisms that people use to guide their decisions to trust and deceive are largely unconscious. They include emotions [5] and intuition. Which emotions are felt in which circumstances, and which actions are taken as a result, depends on culture. As a result, the dynamics of trust and deceit depend on cultural background [6, 7]. G. Hofstede's five dimensions of national cultures [8] are widely used to identify cultural differences. G.J. Hofstede et al. described models for the influence of culture on trade processes, including deceit and trust, for each of the five dimensions separately [9, 10, 11, 12, 13]. However, the differentiation of human behavior cannot be described along a single one of these dimensions. The present paper's goal is to integrate G.J. Hofstede et al.'s individual dimension models, focusing on the decisions whether to deliver truthfully or untruthfully (*deceit*) and whether to trace the delivery or to accept it without tracing (*trust*), and on experience- based belief update about partner's trustworthiness and benevolence (i.e. its inclination to trust). Section 3 introduces Hofstede's five-dimensional model of culture and the dimensions' effects on deceit and trust. Section 4 presents the computational model of the effects of culture on deceit and trust. Section 5 describes experimental results from multi-agent simulations. Section 6 concludes the paper with a discussion of the results.

2 Modeling Deceit, Trust, and Experience-Based Belief

The simulation model represents the trade process of the Trust And Tracing game [3], where a group of 15-20 participants repeatedly trade commodities of different quality levels for an a priori unknown time. Suppliers are informed about the quality; customers are not informed. Participants are free to select a partner for each transaction,

Buyer responds	Seller offers		
	Low Q	High Q, trustworthy	High Q, deceitful
a) accepts	No-risk deal		
b1) accepts, trusts		B, S: reward	B: sucker's payoff S: temptation
b1′) accepts, trace		B: reward minus cost of tracing S: reward B,S: possibly damaged relation (distrust)	B: confirmation of distrust S: punishment
b2) requires guarantee; no trace		B, S: reward B,S: possibly damaged relation (distrust)	B: sucker's payoff S: temptation
b2′) requires guarantee; trace		B: reward minus cost of tracing S: reward B,S: possibly damaged relation (distrust)	B: confirmation of distrust, money back S: punishment, return money
b3) requires certificate		B, S: no risk; reward minus certificate cost	B: no product S: withdrawal

Fig. 2. Payoff matrix for the version of the Trust & Tracing game modeled in this paper (Q: quality; S: seller's payoff; B: buyer's payoff)

and negotiate about price, quality to be delivered, and conditions of the contract. Fig. 2 provides a graphical summary in the form of the 'Trader's Predicament' [14], a payoff matrix in the style of the Prisoner's Dilemma.

Customers may (a) avoid deceit by buying low quality or (b) buy high quality and either (b1) accept vulnerability and trust the supplier to deliver according to contract, or (b2) protect themselves by negotiating a guarantee, for instance money back in case deceit would be revealed, or (b3) have the commodity traced in advance (certification). Option (a) is free of cost and risk, and a low price may be negotiated, but the customer has to accept low quality. Options (b1) and (b2) incur risk on the customer (as they offer the seller an opportunity to defect), and additional cost only if the customer decides to monitor (trace) the delivery. The certification option (b3) excludes risk, but always incurs additional cost.

Although trust is relevant for the processes of partner selection and negotiation, the present paper focuses on the post-contract phase of transactions. It describes the decision whether to deceive or not in the delivery process, the decision whether to trust or to trace in the monitoring and enforcing process, and the update of beliefs resulting from confirmed or violated trust. The remaining part of this section discusses relevant literature from the social sciences and introduces the agents' decision models applied in the simulation.

In experiments using a repetitive ultimatum game with asymmetric information, Boles et al. [5] found that most people do not choose deceptive strategies. However, deceit occurred in their experiments, in particular when stakes were high. So, for deceit to occur, at least two conditions have to be satisfied: motive (substantial advantage for the deceiver) and opportunity (lack of information on the part of the deceived).

As Boles et al. found, the conditions of motive and opportunity are not sufficient for deceit. The decision to deceive depended on interpersonal interactions and the player's satisfaction about the behavior of the other party. They report that *"the bargainers were little like those depicted by rational economic models"* [5] and that *"responders may react emotionally and reject profitable offers in the present when they realize that they have been deceived in the past"* [5].

Role-playing research into cheating on service guarantees by consumers reported by Wirtz and Kum [15] confirms that people are not inclined to seize any opportunity to cheat. Their research also confirms that potential material gain is a condition for cheating, but they found no evidence that people who cheat let their decision depend on the expected amount of payout or the ease of the opportunity to cheat. They report cheating to be related to personality of players (morality, Machiavellianism and self-monitoring). Two factors found to decrease cheating were satisfaction about the deal and the expectation of repeated dealing with the supplier in the future. Wirtz and Kum [15] suggest that a sense of loyalty and trust may reduce cheating. They also refer to Hwang and Burgers [16] who take an economics approach and argue that the high cost of the loss of a trusted partner is an inhibitor of opportunism. Both views indicate that a high-trust relation inhibits deceit.

In the research discussed above, four factors that influence deceit are found: opportunity, expected payout, player's personal traits and values, and player's trust relationship with their counterpart. Steinel and De Dreu [17] conclude on the basis of experiments with the Information Provision Game that, due to greed and maybe to fear of exploitation, individuals are less honest when they experience their counterpart to be competitive rather than cooperative, and that this tendency is stronger for prosocial than for selfish individuals. The importance of the relationship and the behavior of the counterpart is confirmed by Olekalns and Smith [18] who contrast two models of ethical decision making: *fair trade* (my counterpart trusts me, so I will cooperate) and *opportunistic betrayal* (my counterpart trusts me, so I can easily defect). In experiments with Australian undergraduate students they found strong support for *fair trade* as the prevailing model. However, Wirtz and Kum [15] found that individuals scoring high on Machiavellianism in the personality test, were more easily tempted to seize an opportunity to cheat and actually followed what Olekalns and Smith [18] called the *opportunistic betrayal* model.

A general conclusion of the work cited so far in this section is that deceit is less likely to occur when trade partners show trust in each other, even when rational strategies to win the game would suggest cheating. As the purpose of the multi-agent simulation reported in this paper is to represent actual human behavior rather than to apply deception as a strategy to win a game, we cannot employ rational models like the ones proposed by Castelfranchi et al. [19] and Ward and Hexmoor [20].

In the simulation a supplier's decision to deceive business partner b is modeled as a Bernoulli variable with probability of deceit

$$p(\text{deceit}) = q\ (1-c)\ m_b\ (1-d_b)\ , \tag{1}$$

where:

- q represents the quality agreed in the current contract ($q=1$ for high quality; $q=0$ for low quality or no opportunity);
- $c=1$ if certification has been agreed (no opportunity); $c=0$ otherwise;
- m_b represents the supplier's motive or rationale to deceive business partner b: $m_b=1$ if the supplier expects an extra profit from deceit; $m_b=0$ otherwise, for instance if the customer negotiated a guarantee and the supplier expects the customer to trace the delivery;
- d_b represents on the interval [0, 1] seller's threshold for deceit toward business partner b, where $d_b=1$ represents perfect truthfulness; d_b is influenced by seller's personal traits and values (like risk aversion and morality), power and group relations, and seller's estimate of customer's benevolence toward the seller, i.e., seller's trust that the customer will accept deliveries without tracing; details on d_b and the influence of cultural background are discussed in Section 3.

For the purpose of the simulation, Klein Woolthuis et al.'s [2] narrow definition of trust is adopted. A customer's trust in a particular supplier is defined as the customer's estimate of the probability that the supplier will cooperate and deliver according to contract, even if the supplier has the motive and the opportunity to defect. However, this does not imply that an agent's decision to have a delivery traced can be modeled as a Bernoulli variable with $p(\text{trace})=q(1-c)(1-t_b)$ where $q(1-c)$ represent opportunity as in equation (1) and t_b represents trust in business partner b. Additional factors like power and group relationships with the supplier and the agent's cultural background also have their effect on the decision to trace. The effects of relationships and cultural background on the tracing decision are discussed in Section 3.

Trust and distrust develop during social interactions. Visual and auditory contact is relevant to develop trust and detect deceit in human interactions [21]. The multi-agent simulation does not support these effects. The only sources of information that can be taken into account are negotiation outcomes and tracing reports, which are relevant in reality as well. Every successful negotiation resulting in a transaction will strengthen partners' trust in each other. The possibility that a supplier carries out a trace is disregarded here. Customers can decide to trace a delivery and this can have its effects on mutual trust. First, if the result of tracing reveals deceit, the customer's trust in the seller will be reduced. Second, to some extent the fine and the reputational damage resulting from revealed deceit will reinforce the supplier's honesty. However, reinforced honesty will decay to its original level in the course of time. Third, the supplier delivering truthfully may be offended by tracing and the relation may be damaged. For this reason, customers may exercise restraint to trace. Tracing by a customer will always reduce the supplier's belief about customer's benevolence. So, the following dynamics have to be modeled:

- development of trust and benevolence belief by successful negotiations;
- for customers: reduction of trust in case of revealed deceit;
- for suppliers: reinforcement of honesty in case of revealed deceit;
- for suppliers: decay of reinforced honesty to a base level;
- for suppliers: reduction of benevolence belief in case of tracing.

Formal models for representing the development of trust were analyzed by Jonker and Treur [22]. They distinguish six types of trust dynamics: blindly positive, blindly negative, slow positive – fast negative, balanced slow, balanced fast, and slow negative – fast positive. The most realistic type of dynamics for trust in trading situations is slow positive – fast negative: it takes a series of positive experiences to develop trust, but trust can be destroyed by a single betrayal (e.g., Boles et al. [5] report that deceit leads to emotional reactions and consequences beyond what is in their own interest; Steinel and De Dreu [17] refer to *"punitive sentiment"* towards deceivers).

The trust dynamics are modeled as follows. After the n'th experience a consumer's trust in business partner b is updated according to belief update factors u_+ and u_-:

$$
\begin{aligned}
t_{b,n} &= t_{b,n-1} + u_+(1- t_{b,n-1}) &&\text{if } n^{\text{th}} \text{ experience is positive },\\
t_{b,n} &= (1-u_-)\, t_{b,n-1} &&\text{if } n^{\text{th}} \text{ experience is negative },\\
t_{b,n} &= t_{b,n-1} &&\text{if } n^{\text{th}} \text{ experience is neither positive nor negative },
\end{aligned}
\tag{2}
$$

with $0 < u_+ < u_- < 1$, where $t_{b,n} = 1$ represents complete trust and $t_{b,n} = 0$ represents complete distrust in b; a successful negotiation counts as a positive experience; a tracing report revealing deceit counts as negative; all other experiences are considered neither negative nor positive with respect to trust.

A supplier's belief $v_{b',n}$ about a partner's benevolence is updated similarly:

$$v_{b',n} = v_{b',n-1} + u_+ (1 - v_{b',n-1}) \quad \text{if } n^{th} \text{ experience is positive ,}$$
$$v_{b',n} = (1 - u_-) \, v_{b',n-1} \qquad\quad \text{if } n^{th} \text{ experience is negative ,} \qquad\qquad (3)$$
$$v_{b',n} = v_{b',n-1} \qquad\qquad\qquad\; \text{if } n^{th} \text{ experience is neither positive nor negative ,}$$

For the supplier a successful negotiation counts as a positive experience. However, tracing always counts as a negative experience for a supplier, whether it reveals deceit or not, because it is interpreted as distrust.

An effect of revealed deceit on the supplier's part is that supplier's current honesty h_k (a personal trait, representing the inclination to deliver truthfully) is reinforced to 1, representing maximal honesty in the supplier's cultural background. h_k will subsequently decay to a base value h' on each interaction, whether it is successful or not, with a decay factor f.

$$h_k = h' + f(h_{k-1} - h'), \text{ with } 0 < h' < 1 \text{ and } 0 < f < 1 . \qquad\qquad (4)$$

with $0 < h' < 1$ and $0 < f < 1$.

3 Deceit and Trust across Cultures

The preceding section introduced models for deceit, trust and belief update in a process of trade. The roles of deceit and trust are known to be different across cultures [6, 7]. Therefore, a multi-agent simulation of international trade that models the effects of deceit and trust should include the effects of culture. This section proposes an approach to model the effects of culture on the parameters and variables introduced in the previous section (deceit threshold, inclination to trace, and positive and negative trust update factors), based on G. Hofstede's dimensions of culture [8]. First culture and Hofstede's dimensions and their effects on deceit and tracing are discussed.

Hofstede describes culture as *"the collective programming of the mind that distinguishes the members of one group or category of people from another"* [8], p. 9. This implies that culture is not an attribute of individual people, unlike personality characteristics. It is an attribute of a group that manifests itself through the behaviors of its members. For a trading situation, culture of the trader will manifest itself in four ways. First, culture filters observation. It determines the salience of clues about the acceptability of trade partners and their proposals. Second, culture sets norms for what constitutes an appropriate partner or offer. Third, it sets expectations for the context of the transactions, e.g., the enforceability of regulations and the possible sanctions in case of breach of the rules. Fourth, it sets norms for the kind of action that is appropriate given the other three and, in particular, the difference between the actual situation and the desired situation.

G. Hofstede [8] identified five dimensions to compare national cultures (Table 1). For the dimensions, indices are available for many countries in the world. The indices

Table 1. Hofstede's dimensions of culture [8]

Dimension	Definition
Power Distance	*"The extent to which the less powerful members of institutions and organizations within a country expect and accept that power is distributed unequally"* [8], p. 98
Uncertainty Avoidance	*"The extent to which the members of a culture feel threatened by uncertain or unknown situations"* [8], p. 161
Individualism and Collectivism	*"Individualism stands for a society in which the ties between individuals are loose: Everyone is expected to look after him/herself and her/his immediate family only. Collectivism stands for a society in which people from birth onward are integrated into strong, cohesive in-groups, which throughout people's lifetime continue to protect them in exchange for unquestioning loyalty"* [8], p. 255
Masculinity and Femininity	*"Masculinity stands for a society in which social gender roles are clearly distinct: Men are assumed to be assertive, tough, and focused on material success; women are supposed to be more modest, tender and concerned with the quality of life. Femininity stands for a society in which gender roles overlap: Both men and women are supposed to be modest, tender and concerned with the quality of life."* [8], p. 297
Long- Versus Short-Term Orientation	*"Long Term Orientation stands for the fostering of virtues oriented towards future rewards, in particular, perseverance and thrift. Its opposite pole, Short Term Orientation, stands for the fostering of virtues related to the past and the present, in particular, respect for tradition, preservation of 'face' and fulfilling social obligations"* [8], p. 359

are usually named PDI, UAI, IDV, MAS, and LTO. For the multi-agent model, we scale the indices to the interval [0, 1] and refer to the scaled indices as PDI^*, UAI^*, IDV^*, MAS^*, and LTO^*. E.g., IDV^* refers to the degree of individualism and $1-IDV^*$ to the degree of collectivism, both in the range [0, 1].

G.J. Hofstede et al. [9, 10, 11, 12, 13] modeled the influence on trade processes of each of the five dimensions separately. However, single dimensions do not fully represent the differentiation of human behavior. A realistic simulation must take the simultaneous effect of all dimensions into account. The purpose of the present paper is to develop a first version of integrated models for deceit, trust and belief update. The remaining part of this section summarizes the effects of individual dimensions as described in [9, 10, 11, 12, 13].

Power Distance. [9] On the dimension of power distance, egalitarian societies are on the one extreme (small power distance), hierarchical societies on the other (large power distance). In hierarchical societies, status and position in the societal hierarchy are the main issue in relations. Trust is only relevant among partners that have equal status. The lower ranked have no choice but to show trust in the higher ranked, whatever belief about their trustworthiness they may have. The higher ranked have no reason to distrust the lower ranked, because they assume that deceit of a higher ranked would not even be considered. With respect to deceit, the higher ranked do not have to fear for repercussions when trading with lower ranked, so the decision, whether to defect or not, merely depends on their morality. The lower ranked on the other hand will not easily consider to defect. They will usually cooperate when trading with higher ranked and will only defect if in need.

For egalitarian traders, decisions to deceive and to trust are not influenced by status difference. Trust is equally important in every relation, regardless of partner's status. However, showing distrust may be harmful to relations, so there may be other incentives for benevolent behavior.

Uncertainty Avoidance. [10] Uncertainty avoidance must not be confused with risk avoidance. People in uncertainty avoiding societies accept risks they are familiar with, but they fear the unknown. They are willing to take risks in order to reduce uncertainty about things they are not familiar with, or to eliminate them.

Uncertainty avoiding traders fear and distrust strangers. They follow the rules when dealing with familiar relations, but easily deceive strangers. A foreign partner will be distrusted until sufficient evidence for the contrary has been found. Once, in the course of repeated transactions, sufficient evidence for trustworthiness has been found through tracing of deliveries, and partners have become familiar, the uncertainty avoiding may finally come to trust their partners and expect them to follow the rules like they do themselves. After they have come to trust, any unexpected revelation of deceit provokes furious reactions from uncertainty avoiding traders. They will not easily deal again with a partner that abused their trust.

In this simulation it has been hypothesized that the tracing agency is always trusted. This is a deliberate simplification. In uncertainty avoiding societies, institutions in general and government in particular tend to be distrusted.

Individualism and Collectivism. [11] In individualistic societies, people have a personal identity and are responsible for their personal actions and view a business partner as an individual. In collectivistic societies, a person's identity is primarily given by group memberships (such as extended family, village, and clubs) and relations. People from collectivistic societies feel responsible for their in-group and prefer to trade with their in-group. Serious negotiations with out-group business partners must be preceded by some form of familiarization. In collectivistic societies harmony must be preserved, so the threshold for showing distrust by tracing is high. Tracing is also less likely because the idea of calling in outsiders to perform the tracing runs counter to a collectivistic way of thinking.

In collectivistic societies trust and deceit are based on group memberships and norms. People from collectivistic societies primarily trust in-group members and distrust out-group members. After a long-lasting relation, outsiders may be trusted as in-group members. Deceiving an out-group partner is acceptable if it serves in-group interests. In individualistic societies opportunistic behavior and trust are based on personal interests, personal values, and interpersonal relations.

Masculinity and Femininity. [12] On the masculine extreme of the dimension are competitive, performance-oriented societies; on the other are cooperation-oriented societies. A stereotypical trader with a feminine, cooperation-oriented cultural background is interested in the relationship. Building trust is important. In principle, the cooperation-oriented trader does not trace, since in his mind this would constitute ostentation of distrust. If conned, then the cooperation-oriented trader will avoid the conman if possible, or give him one more chance.

Trust is irrelevant in extremely performance-oriented, masculine societies. A performance-oriented trader sticks to the contract of the deal, and deceives the trade partner to the limits of the contract without any compunction. As a consequence, the performance- oriented trader sees no problems in dealing again with a trader that conned him in the past: "It's all in the game". The performance-oriented trader always traces the goods after buying, since he expects the possibility of deception. The trader learns from mistakes to make sure that new contracts will not lead to new and uncomfortable surprises on his side.

Long- Versus Short-Term Orientation. [13] Traders from long-term oriented societies value their relations. They value a deal not only by the financial pay off, but also by the relational gains. They are inclined to invest in relations by behaving truthfully and by trusting their partners. They value their business relations by the prospect of future business. They have no respect for others that put their relations at stake for some short-term profit. If they turn out to be deceived by a business partner they will not easily forgive the deceiver.

People from short-term oriented cultures find it hard to understand the sacrifice of the long-term oriented. The short-term oriented tend to grab a chance for an easy profit and are willing to put their relations at stake for it, especially if they are in need to fulfil other social obligations, like showing off for family members. They calculate the bottom line of the transaction. Their threshold to deceive or to distrust depends on the value they attach to the relation in their social life. They can understand that a business partner may be tempted to defect if a profitable opportunity occurs, and they have trouble understanding that people from long-term oriented cultures cannot.

4 Integrated Computational Model

Hofstede et al. [9, 10, 11, 12, 13] proposed formal models of the effects of each of the dimensions of culture on trade processes, including effects on deceit threshold, inclination to trace, and positive and negative trust update factors. The models are based on expert knowledge, gained with a classical knowledge acquisition approach. This section presents an approach to integrate the knowledge about individual dimensions into a model of the joint effect of the dimensions on deceit and trust.

The expert knowledge is formulated as "cultural factors" having an increasing or decreasing effect on the strength or occurrence of behaviors along one of the dimensions of culture. Apart from the dimensions of culture, the behaviors can be influenced by attributes of the relation with the business partner. Examples of such relational attributes are status differences and in group relations. This kind of relational attributes have different relevance in different cultures.

The expert knowledge about the effects of cultural factors is expressed as effects on parameters or variables of the agents' decision models. The dimensions of culture provide a linear ordering of cultures with respect to the strength or frequency of phenomena associated with the dimensions. Therefore, we model the effect of a cultural factor as either no effect at all or as strictly monotonic, i.e. increasing or decreasing. As long as no further evidence is available, we assume the most simple monotonic relation: a linear relation between a cultural factor and the effective value of a parameter or variable. Table 2 summarizes the effects of cultural factors that were identified as relevant for the present simulation. The effects are grouped by dimension. In some cases the effects of the cultural dimensions stand alone; in other cases the effects depend on attributes of the relation with the business partner.

The types of cultural factors in Table 2 are:

- a normalized index I^* of one of the dimensions, as a characterization of a culture;
- $(1-I^*)$, as the characterization of the opposite culture on that dimensions;
- an index I^* or $(1-I^*)$ multiplied with a relational characteristic, such as agent a's group distance D_{ab} with business partner b or status difference s_a-s_b.

D_{ab} and s_a and s_b are reals on the interval $[0, 1]$, as are the normalized dimension indices; so, the value of every cultural factor is a real on the interval $[0, 1]$.

Table 2. Effects of Hofstede's dimensions of culture and relational characteristics on deceit and trust parameters (+ indicates increasing effect; - indicates decreasing effect)

Dimension index	Culture and relational characteristics	Cultural factor to be taken into account	deceit thresh-old	inclination to trace	negative update factor	positive update factor
PDI	Large power distance	PDI^*				
	- with higher ranked partn.	$\max\{0,PDI^*(s_b-s_a)\}$	+	−		
	- with lower ranked partn.	$\max\{0,PDI^*(s_a-s_b)\}$		−		
	Small power distance	$1-PDI^*$				
UAI	Uncertainty avoiding	UAI^*			+	−
	- with stranger	$UAI^*\cdot D_{ab}$	−	+		
	Uncertainty tolerant	$1-UAI^*$				
IDV	Individualistic	IDV^*				
	Collectivistic	$(1-IDV^*)$			+	
	- with in-group partner	$(1-IDV^*)(1-D_{ab})$		−		
	- with out-group partner	$(1-IDV^*)D_{ab}$	−			
MAS	Masculine (competitive)	MAS^*	−	+		−
	Feminine (cooperative)	$1-MAS^*$		−		
LTO	Long-term oriented	LTO^*	+	−		+
	Short-term oriented	$(1-LTO^*)$				
	- with well-respected part.	$(1-LTO^*)s_b$	+	−		
	- with other partners	$(1-LTO^*)(1-s_b)$	−			

4.1 The Decision to Deceive on Delivery

In the preceding sections a model is developed of factors that influence the agents' decision to cooperate or to defect. In the agent model the decision whether to deceive or to deliver truthfully is modeled as a Bernoulli variable, taking the probability according to equation (1) into account.

$$p(\text{truthful delivery}) = 1 - p(\text{deceit}) . \qquad (5)$$

This decision is taken in the delivery phase of the transaction, after a contract has been negotiated.

The opportunity to deceive depends on contract attributes q (quality) and c (certification required). If $q=0$ or $c=1$, there is no opportunity to deceive and the agent delivers truthfully: $p(\text{deceit})=0$ and $p(\text{truthful delivery})=1$ if $q=0$ or $c=1$. Otherwise, the motive and the deceit threshold are relevant.

The motive to deceive is present if the value difference between high quality and low quality exceeds the cost of the estimated risk of deceit. The motive depends on:

- Δy , value difference between high and low quality,
- v_b , the agent's belief about the partner b's benevolence (interpreted as the subjective probability that b will not put the delivery to the test),
- r, the amount of the fine in case deceit would be revealed;
- $g \cdot y$, where $g=1$ if the contract entails a guarantee, $g=0$ if not, and y, the value to be restituted in case of a guarantee).

The motive to deceive b is computed as:

$$m_b = 1 \text{ if } \Delta y > (1 - v_b)(r + gy) \text{ ;}$$
$$m_b = 0 \text{ otherwise .} \qquad (6)$$

It follows from (1) that $p(\text{deceit})=0$ and $p(\text{truthful delivery})=1$ if $m_b=0$. If motive and opportunity are present, the decision is affected by the agent's current honesty h_k and its belief about the quality relation with the customer b. We assume that the deceit threshold toward agent b has $\max(h_k, v_b)$ as a basis:

$$d_b' = \max(h_k, v_b) \qquad (7)$$

The actual deceit threshold equals basic value d_b' modified by increasing cultural effect $e^{d+}{}_b$ in the direction of 1; by decreasing effect $e^{d-}{}_b$ in the direction of 0:

$$d_b = d_b' + (1 - d_b') e^{d+}{}_b - d_b' e^{d-}{}_b , \qquad (8)$$

The joint increasing effect $e^{d+}{}_b$ is modeled as a weak disjunction of all increasing factors from Table 2; The joint decreasing effect $e^{d-}{}_b$ is modeled as a weak disjunction of all decreasing factors from Table 2:

$$e^{d+}{}_b = \max \{\text{PDI}^*(s_b - s_a), \text{LTO}^*, (1 - \text{LTO}^*)s_b\} \text{ ;} \qquad (9a)$$

$$e^{d-}{}_b = \max \{\text{UAI}^* D_{ab}, (1 - \text{IDV}^*)D_{ab}, \text{MAS}^*, (1 - \text{LTO}^*)(1 - s_b)\} . \qquad (9b)$$

In the present model, if opportunity and motive for deceit are present, the probability that an agent acts truthfully equals the culturally adapted deceit threshold d_b according to equations (8) and (9); the probability that an agent defects under these conditions equals $1 - d_b$. If motive or opportunity are absent, the agents will always deliver truthfully.

4.2 The Decision to Trust or Trace Deliveries

According to Castelfranchi and Falcone [23] *"Trust is the mental counter-part of delegation"*. The mental aspect of trust in the present agent model is the experience-based belief about a business partner b's trustworthiness t_b. The delegation aspect of trust is in the act of trusting: to delegate the responsibility to deliver high quality to b, without safeguard that b will actually do so.

Across cultures different norms exist for the showing of trust or distrust. The probability that an agent will show trust is not necessarily equal to its subjective, experience-based belief t_b about the probability that b will act truthfully. In the present model, believed trustworthiness is the basis for the act of trusting, but the actual act of trusting does not necessarily correspond with it.

The decision to trust a delivery from business partner b or to trace is based on the estimated trustworthiness t_b. An agent's belief t_b about b's trustworthiness can be interpreted as a subjective probability that b will not deceive. $(1 - t_b)$ is the agent's distrust in b, or the subjective probability that b will defect. So, the basis for the inclination w_b' to trace b's delivery is:

$$w_b' = (1 - t_b) , \tag{10}$$

which is adapted by culture, similar to equation (8):

$$w_b = w_b' + (1 - w_b') \, e^{w+}{}_b - w_b' \, e^{w-}{}_b , \tag{11}$$

where

$$e^{w+}{}_b = \max \{UAI^* D_{ab}, MAS^*\} ; \tag{12a}$$

$$e^{w-}{}_b = \max \{PDI^* |s_a - s_b|, (1 - IDV^*)(1 - D_{ab}), 1 - MAS^*, LTO^*, (1 - LTO^*) s_b\} . \tag{12b}$$

The culture-dependent probabilities that agent a will trace or trust b's delivery are:

$$p(\text{trace}) = q \, (1 - c) \, w_b ; \tag{13a}$$

$$p(\text{trust}) = 1 - w_b . \tag{13b}$$

4.3 Belief Update Factors

The values of the belief update factors to be applied in equations (2) and (3) for positive and negative experience, u_+ and u_-, respectively, are agent parameters that do not depend on the partner. They may be modeled as global parameters u_+' and u_-', respectively. In the latter case, the global values are culturally adapted as follows, in analogy with the preceding subsections.

u_+' is influenced by only a single factor according to Table 2. The value is reduced in societies with high uncertainty avoidance:

$$u_+ = u_+' - u_+' \, UAI^* . \tag{14}$$

u_-' is influenced by more factors, under the constraint that $u_- > u_+$:

$$u_- = u_-' + (1 - u_-') \, e^{u-+} - (u_-' - u_+') \, e^{u--} , \tag{15}$$

where

$$e^{u \rightarrow} = \max \{ UAI^*, 1\text{-}IDV^*, LTO^* \} ; \tag{16a}$$

$$e^{u--} = MAS^* . \tag{16b}$$

5 Testing the Implementation

The model described in the preceding sections is implemented in a multi-agent model in Cormas[1]. The decision functions and plans are implemented as methods in the software agents. The agents can communicate through the Cormas synchronized message system. They can exchange messages to communicate or to transfer the ownership of commodities. Each commodity has slots for

- real quality, not visible for the trading agents;
- stated quality, visible and modifiable by the agents; a commodity is initialized with stated equal to real quality, but may be modified during the simulation;
- traced quality, visible for the trading agents, but only modifiable by the tracing agent; it is initially empty.

In the simulation there is a tracing agent to which the trading agents may, at the cost of a fee, send a commodity for inspection (the stated quality slot may deceitfully be modified by a supplier). Upon request, the tracing agent sets traced equal to real quality, returns the commodity, informs the suppliers that their product has been traced, and, in case of deceit, traces deceivers to punish them with a fine. A product that has the traced value set, can be seen as certified. A supplier can have a product certified before selling it, to increase the value. The amount of the tracing fee increases with each transaction in the history of a commodity, so certification in advance is cheaper than tracing by the customer.

The agents have access to a central directory with references to all agents and the tracing agent. The agents have labels for status and group membership. Labels are visible for all other agents. In some cultures group distance and status difference with trade partners are very relevant. The agents use the label information to estimate these parameters. Experience gained while trading, using the update mechanism described by equations (2) and (3), results in beliefs about trustworthiness and benevolence for each partner. Agents propose to negotiate to potential partners and they may accept or ignore negotiation proposals.

Partner selection is based on the model of Weisbuch et al. [24]. This model is based on a nonlinear probability of selecting a particular partner according to experience of profitability of previous deals – which we call fairness belief – and an agent-specific loyalty parameter. The loyalty parameter determines the relevance of the fairness belief for partner selection. The fairness belief is updated through a mechanism like the ones describes by equations (2) and (3). The cultural adaptation of Weisbuch et al.'s model for the application in the simulation is described in [25].

In the process of negotiation, the agents exchange proposals with the following attributes:

- identifying attributes: sender; receiver; time; is it a first bid, reply to a previous bid or acceptance of a bid;

---

[1] http://cormas.cirad.fr/

- price;
- quality;
- an indicator if is the commodity is to be certified in advance by the supplier;
- an indicator of a money-back guarantee in case deceit be revealed in future tracing.

The negotiation process is based on work by Jonker and Treur [26]. Their negotiation architecture is based on a multi-attribute utility function. In the present implementation the utility function is a linear combination of an economic value term, a quality preference term and a risk attitude term. The relative weights of quality preference and risk avoidance determine the agent's trade strategy and are culture-dependent. The other parameters modeled to depend on culture are the agents' willingness to make concessions, the step size of concessions, impatience, and the remaining utility gap that is acceptable between own and partners proposal. The agents' culturally adapted negotiation model is described in detail in [27].

A negotiation may end with a contract, or it may fail, because one of the agents quits. In the latter case the agents select a partner, to try and start new negotiations with. In case of a contract, the processes of trust and deceit modeled in the present paper come into effect.

To test the implementation of the model, simulations were run in the environment described above. Eight supplier agents and eight customer agents could trade repeatedly, approximately 30-40 times per run, resulting in approximately 240-320 deals per run. The negotiation process was limited to result in $q=1$, $c=0$, and $g=0$, so the agents were forced to decide on trust and deceit. They could only negotiate about price, and let negotiations fail in case of distrust.

A series of runs were made, with "synthetic" cultures: the culture dimensions were set to 0.5, except one dimension, which was set to 0.1 or 0.9 in order to represent a cultural extreme. For instance, in the first run, $PDI^*=0.9$, $UAI^*=0.5$, $IDV^*=0.5$, $MAS^*=0.5$, and $LTO^*=0.5$; in the second run, $PDI^*=0.1$, $UAI^*=0.5$, $IDV^*=0.5$, $MAS^*=0.5$, and $LTO^*=0.5$. In all runs, the agents were divided into two groups of four suppliers and four customers with equal labels, having group distance $D_{ab}=0$ in the ingroup and group distance $D_{ab'}=1$ with members of the other group. Status was mixed: four agents had status 0.1, four agents 0.4, four agents 0.6, and four agents status 0.9, divided equally over ingroups of suppliers and customers. A summary of the results is presented in Fig. 3.

The first variable displayed in Fig. 3 displays the percentage of transactions that were traced and turned out to be truthful. Together with the second variable (traces that revealed deceit) it is a measure for the level of distrust that is shown. High values occur in the uncertainty avoiding and masculine societies. In the masculine society this results directly from the increased inclination to trace, equation (12), which reduces the relevance of the mental aspect of trust. In the uncertainty avoiding society, the high tracing ration results mainly from low trust: trust cannot develop because of the adapted positive belief update, equation (14). In addition, equation (12) has its effect on tracing frequency on deals with strangers.

The second variable in Fig. 3 indicates deceit revealed in traces, i.e. the confirmed distrust. There no obvious relation with the tracing frequency. In the societies where a

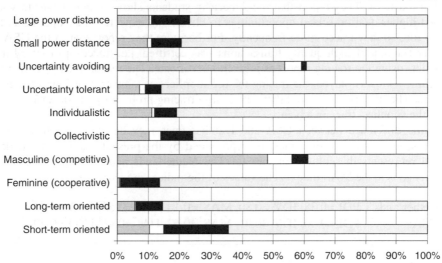

Fig. 3. Results of simulations in societies with synthetic cultures; in the synthetic cultures all scaled cultural dimensions have index 0.5, except one, which has either 0.1 or 0.9

considerable amount of the transactions is traced and distrust is frequently confirmed (the collectivistic and short-term oriented societies), this does not lead to even more tracing by the influence of equation (8), while the tracing ratio in the uncertainty avoiding society remains high, even if distrust is less frequently confirmed.

The third variable displays the frequency of unrevealed deceit. The high deceit frequency in the short-term oriented societies stems from the combination of the opportunity offered to higher ranked through equation (12b) - a low inclination to trace higher ranked – and the reduced deceit threshold toward lower ranked through equation (9b) – the opportunity is gratefully seized. This dimension is the only one where such a mutually reinforcing effect on deceit occurs in the equations. On the other dimensions, deceit frequency is lower and there is no obvious relation with the frequency of tracing (first column) across cultures. This is realistic.

In the masculine society the deceit frequency remains high while most of the deceit is revealed. This suggests that the competitive orientation is correctly implemented. In the feminine society, deceit is rarely revealed, but it does not occur more frequently than in the masculine society. This suggests that the cooperative orientation is also correctly implemented. In the short-term oriented society, the wrong partners are traced: the percentage revealed is lower than the actual percentage of deceit, in spite of the rather high tracing frequency.

The results presented in Fig. 3 give confidence that the model can differentiate trade behavior across the Hofstede's dimensions of culture in a way that is qualitatively realistic.

The remaining part of this section discusses an example on the basis of experiments with the Trust And Tracing game, the human gaming simulation that the present model represents. Meijer et al. [28] report, among others, gaming simulations with the Trust And Tracing game with business school students in The Netherlands and in the USA. They report that the American students showed more eager to win, traded higher quality, seized opportunities to cheat, and expected their opponents to do so too, so they traced more frequently. Furthermore they report that in the USA a greater fraction of high quality transactions was certified, i.e. traced up-front by the supplier, using the tracing report as a quality certificate. The reason for this is that in the game as it was played, the tracing fee for suppliers was lower than it was for customers. The players discovered that with a high tracing probability, it was efficient to have the suppliers trace in advance.

If the difference between USA and Dutch games may be attributed to culture, which seems plausible, they must be reproduced by the present multi-agent model. Fig. 4 represents the cultural indices for The Netherlands and the USA. The main difference is in the MAS index. The values of the indices are [8]:

– Netherlands: $PDI^*=0.38$, $IDV^*=0.80$, $MAS^*=0.14$, $UAI^*=0.53$, $LTO^*=0.44$;
– USA: $PDI^*=0.40$, $IDV^*=0.91$, $MAS^*=0.62$, $UAI^*=0.46$, $LTO^*=0.29$.

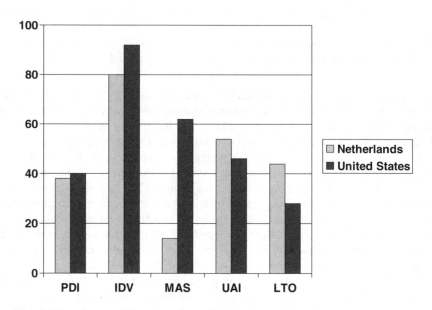

Fig. 4. The cultures of The Netherlands and the USA compared (data source: [8])

From the work of Meijer et al. [28] the following hypotheses can be formulated to be tested against simulation results:

1. The quality ratio (top quality transactions/all transactions) is higher in USA than in the Netherlands
2. The certification ratio (certified transactions/top quality transactions) is higher in USA than in the Netherlands

3. The defection ratio (untruthful deliveries/uncertified top quality transactions) is higher in USA than in the Netherlands
4. The tracing ratio (traces/uncertified top quality transactions) is higher in USA than in the Netherlands

For this purpose, simulations were run. As parameter values are unknown the following procedure was followed. For 1000 simulation runs, parameter sets were drawn at random from the joint space of parameters defined in the present paper (update factors u_+' and u_-', minimal honesty h_k, and honesty decay factor f, group distance D_{ab}, and status s_a and s_b) and parameters defined in the partner selection and negotiation models [25, 27]. All parameters were drawn independently from a uniform distribution on [0, 1], with some exceptions: u_+' was drawn from [0, u_-'], β (loyalty parameter in partner selection) from [0.5, 1.5], and the utility weight factors for quality and risk in the negotiation process were both drawn from [0, 0.2]. With these parameters agents were homogeneously configured, for a run where all agents had USA parameter settings and a run where all agents had Dutch parameter settings. So, in a single run, all agents had equal parameter settings, and for each setting, results for the USA and The Netherlands can be compared in pairs.

For each of the 1000 parameter sets, a simulation was run for each country. Each run had a length of 100 time steps, which practically limits the average number of transactions to a maximum about 20 per agent. To allow for partner selection, runs were configured for 8 suppliers and 8 customers, homogeneously parameterized. Negotiation was restricted to $g=0$ (no guarantees), with free choice between basic quality and top quality, and free choice of certification. Agents had the choice to deliver truthfully or untruthfully (equation 5) and to trust or to trace (equations 13).

Because of the wide range of parameters, many runs ended with zero or very few transactions. From the 1000 pairs of runs, the runs were selected that had a joint sum of at least 40 transactions per pair. Beneath this limit, many runs occur with zero transaction for one or both of the countries. The selection resulted in 317 run pairs.

Analysis of the results confirmed hypotheses 1, 3, and 4, but did not confirm hypothesis 2. The certification ratio as defined in hypothesis 2 was approximately equal for the USA and The Netherlands. According to the negotiation model reported in [27], customers do not take a differentiation of certification cost between themselves and suppliers into account. This difference was an important factor in the human gaming simulations in the USA. Therefore, the negotiation model from [27] was modified to take tracing fee difference and probability to trace into account. The original equation for customers' risk evaluation according to [27] was

$$r_c = (1 - c)(1 - t_b)q . \tag{17}$$

The modified equation is

$$r_c = (1 - c)(1 - t_b)q + p(\text{trace})\phi_c , \tag{18}$$

with $p(\text{trace})$ according to equation (13a) and ϕ_c representing customers' tracing fee.

This model adaptation is an example of the cyclic research approach proposed by Tykhonov et al. [3]. Their proposed approach entails stepwise refinement of models by alternating human gaming and multi-agent simulation.

Table 3. Test data for 310 run pairs for USA and NL with randomly generated parameter sets

Average of 310 runs	USA	NL	Test stat. [a]	Sample [a]	Probability [a]
Number of transactions	72	61	219	302	< 0.001
Quality ratio	0.37	0.15	277	285	< 0.001
Certification ratio	0.48	0.41	191	281	< 0.001
Defection ratio	0.25	0.13	128	154	< 0.001
Tracing ratio	0.40	0.07	169	177	< 0.001

[a] Test statistic, effective sample size, and two-sided probability level for Sign test.

The simulation was repeated after replacing equation (17) with equation (18) and setting the tracing fee equal to 0.2 for suppliers and 0.3 for customers. This resulted in 310 run pairs with a sum per pair of at least 40 transactions. Table 3 summarizes the results. Differences are significant for all variables, with $p < 0.001$ according to the Sign test. Histograms of differences are included in the Appendix.

The simulation results confirm the hypotheses 1 through 4. However, some care must be taken. The hypotheses are formulated as stylized facts. The results reproduce these stylized facts, but cannot be interpreted to represent actual values for Dutch or American behaviors, as the model has not been tuned to actual data. Nevertheless, the tests give confidence that the model has been implemented correctly and can show cultural differentiation of deceit and trust in trade.

6 Conclusion

Culture is known to have its effects on honesty in trade, and on trust as a mechanism to compensate for the inevitable incompleteness of contracts. Occurrence of deceit, and mechanisms and institutions to reduce it, vary considerably across the world. For research into these mechanisms, multi-agent simulations can be a useful tool.

In intelligent agent research, much attention has been paid to trust. Little research has been published about the simulation of deceit. Publications such as [19] and [20] modeled deceit as a rational strategy to gain advantage in competitive situations. A strictly rational approach of deceit neglects the emotional impact that deceit has, not only on the deceived, but also on the deceivers. Feelings of guilt and shame result from deceiving [6]. The extent to which these feelings prevail is different across cultures [6]. People have emotional thresholds for deceit, that cannot be explained from rational evaluation of cost and benefit, but that are based on morality and cooperative attitudes [5, 15, 17]. Once deceived, people react to an extent that goes beyond rationality [5], especially when they are prosocial rather than selfish [17]. In human decision making a model based on *fair trade* prevails over a model of *opportunistic betrayal* [18]. In addition to psychological factors, evolutionary reasons [4] or rational economic motives [16] can be given for the human inclination to cooperative behavior.

This paper contributes by introducing an agent model of deceit and placing it in a cultural context. It takes human deceptive behavior as a point of departure. Building on the work of [9, 10, 11, 12, 13] that modeled single dimensions of culture, this paper proposes an integrated model of culture's effects on deceit and trust. Example results have been generated that verify the implementation and illustrate that cultural effects can be generated. However, for realistic experiments, the model has to be tuned to and calibrated by observations and results of experiments, for instance to simulate effects like the ones reported by Triandis et al. [6] from human experiments on deceit across cultures. Before such experiments can be performed, the integration of this model with culturally adapted models for partner selection and negotiation, based on [25] and [27], has to be tested and tuned in more detail. The integration task and experiments remain for future research.

References

1. Williamson, O.E.: Transaction cost economics: how it works; where it is headed. De Economist 146(1), 23–58 (1998)
2. Klein Woolthuis, R., Hillebrand, B., Nooteboom, B.: Trust, Contract and Relationship Development. Organization Studies 26(6), 813–840 (2005)
3. Tykhonov, D., Jonker, C., Meijer, S., Verwaart, T.: Agent-Based Simulation of the Trust and Tracing Game for Supply Chains and Networks. Journal of Artificial Societies and Social Simulation 11(3), 1 (2008),
   http://jasss.soc.surrey.ac.uk/11/3/1.html
4. Wilson, D.S.: Evolution for Everyone. Bantam Dell, NewYork (2007)
5. Boles, T.L., Croson, R.T.A., Murnighan, J.K.: Deception and Retribution in Repeated Ultimatum Bargaining. Organizational Behavior and Human Decision Processes 83(2), 235–259 (2000)
6. Triandis, H.C., et al.: Culture and Deception in Business Negotiations: A Multilevel Analysis. International Journal of Cross Cultural Management 1, 73–90 (2001)
7. Zaheer, S., Zaheer, A.: Trust across borders. Journal of International Business Studies 37, 21–29 (2006) T.A. Judge
8. Hofstede, G.: Culture's Consequences, 2nd edn. Sage Publications, Thousand Oaks (2001)
9. Hofstede, G.J., Jonker, C.M., Verwaart, T.: Modeling Power Distance in Trade. In: David, N., Sichman, J.S. (eds.) MABS 2008. LNCS, vol. 5269, pp. 1–16. Springer, Heidelberg (2009)
10. Hofstede, G.J., Jonker, C.M., Verwaart, T.: Modeling Culture in Trade: Uncertainty Avoidance. In: 2008 Agent-Directed Simulation Symposium (ADSS 2008), Spring Simulation Multiconference, pp. 143–150. SCS, San Diego (2008)
11. Hofstede, G.J., Jonker, C.M., Verwaart, T.: Individualism and Collectivism in Trade Agents. In: Nguyen, N.T., Borzemski, L., Grzech, A., Ali, M. (eds.) IEA/AIE 2008. LNCS (LNAI), vol. 5027, pp. 492–501. Springer, Heidelberg (2008)
12. Hofstede, G.J., Jonker, C.M., Meijer, S., Verwaart, T.: Modeling Trade and Trust across Cultures. In: Stølen, K., Winsborough, W.H., Martinelli, F., Massacci, F. (eds.) iTrust 2006. LNCS, vol. 3986, pp. 120–134. Springer, Heidelberg (2006)
13. Hofstede, G.J., Jonker, C.M., Verwaart, T.: Long-term Orientation in Trade. In: Schredelseker, K., Hauser, F. (eds.) Complexity and Artificial Markets. LNEMS, vol. 614, pp. 107–118. Springer, Heidelberg (2008)

14. Meijer, S., Hofstede, G.J.: The Trust and Tracing game. In: Riis, J.O., Smeds, R., Nicholson, A. (eds.) Proceedings of the 7th International Workshop on Experiential Learning, IFIP WG 5.7, Aalborg, Denmark, pp. 101–116. University of Aalborg - Centre for Industrial Production, Aalborg (2003)
15. Wirtz, J., Kum, D.: Consumer Cheating on Service Guarantees. Journal of the Academy of Marketing Science 32(2), 159–175 (2004)
16. Hwang, P., Burgers, W.P.: Apprehension and Temptation: The Forces against Cooperation. Journal of Conflict Resolution 43(1), 117–130 (1999)
17. Steinel, W., De Dreu, K.W.: Social Motives and Strategic Misrepresentation in Social Decision Making. Journal of Personality and Social Psychology 86, 419–434 (2004)
18. Olekalns, M., Smith, P.L.: Mutually Dependent: Trust, Affect and the Use of Deception in Negotiation. Journal of Business Ethics 85, 347–365 (2009)
19. Castelfranchi, C., Falcone, R., De Rosis, F.: Deceiving in GOLEM: how to strategically pilfer help. In: Castelfranchi, C., Tan, Y.H. (eds.) Trust and Deception in Virtual Societies, pp. 91–110. Kluwer, Dordrecht (2001)
20. Ward, D., Hexmoor, H.: Towards deception in agents. In: Proceedings of AAMAS 2003, pp. 1154–1155. ACM, New York (2003)
21. Burgoon, J.K., Stoner, G.M., Bonito, J.A., Dunbar, N.E.: Trust and Deception in Mediated Communication. In: Proceedings of HICSS 2003 - Track1, p. 44. IEEE, Los Alamitos (2003)
22. Jonker, C.M., Treur, J.: Formal analysis of models for the dynamics of trust based on experiences. In: Garijo, F.J., Boman, M. (eds.) MAAMAW 1999. LNCS, vol. 1647, pp. 120–134. Springer, Heidelberg (1999)
23. Castelfranchi, C., Falcone, R.: Principles of trust for MAS: cognitive anatomy, social importance, and quantification. In: Proceedings of the 3rd International Conference on Multi Agent Systems, pp. 72–79. IEEE Computer Society, Washington (1998)
24. Weisbuch, G., Kirman, A., Herreiner, D.: Market Organisation and Trading Relationships. Economic Journal 110, 411–436 (2000)
25. Hofstede, G.J., Jonker, C.M., Verwaart, T.: Simulation of Effects of Culture on Trade Partner Selection. In: Hernández, C., et al. (eds.) Artificial Economics: The Generative Method in Economics, pp. 257–268. Springer, Heidelberg (2009)
26. Jonker, C.M., Treur, J.: An agent architecture for multi–attribute negotiation. In: Nebel, B. (ed.) Proceedings of the seventeenth International Joint Conference on AI, IJCAI 2001, pp. 1195–1201. Morgan Kaufman, San Francisco (2001)
27. Hofstede, G.J., Jonker, C.M., Verwaart, T.: Cultural Differentiation of Negotiating Agents. Group Decis Negot, doi: 10.1007/s10726-010-9190-x (2010)
28. Meijer, S., Hofstede, G.J., Beers, G., Omta, S.W.F.: Trust and Tracing game: learning about transactions and embeddedness in a trade network. Production Planning and Control 17, 569–583 (2006)

Appendix

Fig. 5 presents histograms of the (non-zero) differences reported in Table 3 between results of paired runs for simulated cultures of the USA and The Netherlands: in the top row the difference of the total number of successful transactions per run and the difference of the quality ratio; in the second row the certification ratio and the defection ratio; in the bottom row the tracing ratio.

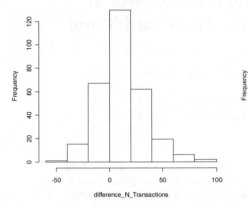
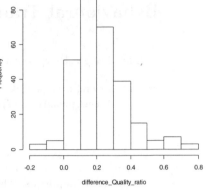

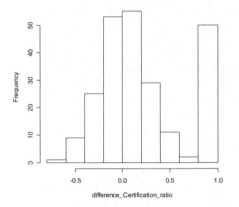
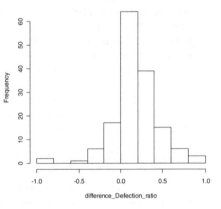

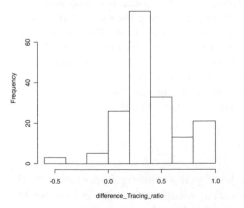

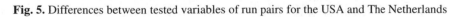

Fig. 5. Differences between tested variables of run pairs for the USA and The Netherlands

Enhancing Social Search: A Computational Collective Intelligence Model of Behavioural Traits, Trust and Time

Luca Longo, Pierpaolo Dondio, and Stephen Barrett

Department of Computer Science and Statistics, Trinity College, Dublin
{llongo,pdondio,stephen.barrett}@cs.tcd.ie

Abstract. The Web has been growing in size and with the proliferation of large-scale collaborative computing environments, Social Search has become increasingly important. This recent field focuses on assigning relevance to Web-pages by considering the reader's perspective rather than Web-masters' point of view. Current searching technologies of this form tend to rely on explicit human recommendations. In part because it is hard to obtain user feedback, these methods are hard to scale. The challenge is in producing implicit rankings, by reasoning over users' Web-search activity, without recourse to explicit human intervention. This paper focuses on a novel Social Search model based on Information Foraging Theory, Effort and Computational Trust, showing a different way to implicitly judge Web-entities. The formalism has been divided in two sub-models. The first considers the effort expended by users, in viewing Web-sites, to assess their relevance to a given searching problem. The second enhances the first sub-model by considering only the most trustworthy users' opinions, identified by Computational Trust techniques.

100 university students explicitly evaluated the usefulness of 12 thematic Web-sites and their browsing activity were gathered. Correlation indexes suggests the existence of a considerable relationship between explicit feedback and implicit computed judgements that were further compared to the ones, provided by the Google search engine. The proposed nature-inspired approach suggests that, by considering the same searching query, Social Search to be more effective than the Google Page-Rank Algorithm. The consideration of the only identified trustworthy students' implicit feedback provides a way to increase the accuracy of the effort-based approach. This evidence supports the presentation of a schema for a Social Search engine that generates implicit rankings by considering the collective intelligence emerged from users on the Web.

1 Introduction

Recently, the concept of *Social Search* has been acquiring importance in the World Wide Web as large-scale collaborative computations have become feasible. The main advantage of such systems is that the value of Web-pages is determined by considering the reader's perspective, rather than merely the perspective of page authors. This approach takes many forms, from the simplest

N.T. Nguyen and R. Kowalczyk (Eds.): Transactions on CCI II, LNCS 6450, pp. 46–69, 2010.

based on sharing bookmarks [9], to more sophisticated approaches that combine human intelligence with computational paradigms [6]. The *Social Search* approach contrasts with that of the leading searching engines, such as Google, whose Page-Rank algorithm [24] relies on the link structure of the Web to find the most authoritative pages. However, a key open challenge in designing *Social Search* systems is to identify human values in the Web automatically.

A particular practical problem for any potential solution, one key to our motivation, is that users tend to be resistant to explicit and invasive techniques for information gathering and so it is not easy to generate strong recommendations. In contrast, implicit feedback techniques gather data indirectly to produce Web-rankings automatically deduced by reasoning on the activity performed by users over Web-pages during a search. Reading time, bookmarking, scrolling, cut-paste, form filling, saving pictures are all considered relevant implicit sources of user preferences [12].

In this paper we propose a novel approach to collaborative *Social Search* that takes into account users' behaviour during Internet browsing sessions, capturing browsing activity indicators such as, for instance, scrolling, clicking, cut & paste. Such activity embodies implicit 'human judgement' where each Web-page has been viewed and endorsed by one or more people concluding that it is relevant and worthy of being shared among the community. Appropriate computational analysis allows the achievement of useful page ranking. In particular, in this study, a novel computational *Social Search* model, based on *Information Foraging theory and effort* is presented. This new approach shows how it is possible to evaluate the relevance of a Web-page by taking into account the effort performed by users, upon it. The key benefit of systems supporting this kind of collective intelligence is that the *Social Search* engine operates concurrently over continuously updated user activity and so it is well positioned to display stronger results synchronised with even rapidly changing of Web-content. A further benefit of the approach is a reduction of the impact of link spam since the link structure of Web-pages is less important. The accuracy of our formal model for *Social Search* is then enhanced by applying *Computational Trust* paradigms whose aim is to identify the most trustworthy users in the Web-community so acting to filter the user set that determines page ranking. The consideration of their implicit judgements show a refined approximation of the community's opinion along with a reduction of complexity, in term of computations, and an enhancement, in term of quality.

The specific contributions of this study are organised as follows. In section 2 we present the background of *Social Search*, *Information Foraging Theory*, *Collective Intelligence* and *Computational Trust*; in section 3 we underline the hypothesis behind this work; we describe the software tool used for gathering behavioural traits of Web-users, in section 4; in 5 we present our heuristic formal models; in 6 we describe the experiment design and the evaluation method. Section 7 presents a discussion on the results. We conclude in section 8, presenting future work and open issues related to this research.

2   Related Works

2.1   Social Search

Social Search is a type of Web-search technique that infers the relevance of Web-search results by considering the opinions of end-users as to the value of Web-content. Several computational methods have been conceived combining human intelligence with computer paradigms [1] [2] and implicit feedback techniques appear to be useful candidates to automatically evaluate Web-content that users show interest in. Feedback need not to be explicit.

When users surf the Internet they interact with a browser and generate a data set regarding actions such as clicking, scrolling, submitting forms, cutting and pasting text and so on. This data-set presents an indicative pattern of behaviour for the evaluation of Web-pages.

In [12] three sources of implicit feedback are taken into account (reading time per document, scrolling and interaction) focused on the hypothesis that users will spend more time, scroll more often and interact more with those documents they find relevant.

In [3] the authors focused on tasks such as classifying the user with regard to computer usage proficiency or making a detailed assessment of how long it took users to fill in fields of a form. For this, an HTTP logger was developed, that collects data about mouse movements, keyboard input and more. Similarly, in the work of Velayathan and Yamada [29], a framework has been proposed to gather logs of users' behaviour. These logs are then analysed in order to extract effective rules to evaluate Web-pages using machine-learning techniques.

2.2   Collaboration and Collective Intelligence

Social Search implies a degree of *implicit collaboration* [16] that is a process where people interact with each other toward a common goal, by sharing their knowledge, learning and building consensus. This concept does not require a leadership figure and it can deliver good results if applied in decentralised systems. The Internet is the most popular scenario where entities are widely distributed, without any kind of authority and Wikipedia is a good example of where it is possible to achieve a good degree of collaboration. The fact that this online encyclopaedia is written by an open community of users around the world and the majority of its articles can be edited by anyone with access to the Internet, underlines the intrinsic degree of collaboration and several studies suggest that its content can be as accurate as other encyclopaedias [30].

Web 2.0 provide a context in which users can contribute independently to build up a new collaborative architecture so creating worldwide network effects. The contribution is intended as a process where an entity, usually an individual, provides a judgement about another entity, either digital or human, by using specific graded relevance system such as numbers, letters, descriptions. As suggested in [16] there are mainly two ways to provide judgements:

- explicitly: users can provide feedback using a specific metric. The most important example are eBay[1] and Amazon[2] where buyers and sellers can rate transactions using a given graded system;
- implicitly: implicit judgements are automatically inferred by analysing user behaviour while performing a specific task.

Collaboration applied to Web 2.0 supports a new kind of shared intelligence, named *Collective Intelligence*, where users are able to generate their own content building up an infrastructure where contributions are not merely quantitative but also qualitative [31].

Several definition of *Collective Intelligence* have been proposed so far. However, a shared agreement suggests that *Collective Intelligence* is a group/shared intelligence that emerges from the collaboration and competition of many entities, either human or digital. The study of *Collective Intelligence* may be considered a subfield of sociology, computer science and of mass behaviour. *Social Search* may be considered a sub-field of *Collective Intelligence* or an application of it, due to the fact that multiple entities' behaviour is taken into account. The resulting information structures can be seen as reflecting the collective knowledge of a community of users and can be used for different purposes. For instance, as in collaborative tagging systems such as Del.icio.us[3], where users assign tags to resources and Web-entities shared with other users, the emerged community's knowledge, due to users interaction, can be used to construct folksonomy graphs, which can be efficiently partitioned to obtain a form of community or shared vocabulary [27]. However, this example is a form of *explicit collaboration*, as Web-users must explicitly provide judgements. In this paper, the opposite approach is studied: Web-users' behaviour is implicitly gathered in order to form a base of knowledge useful for studying tendencies, trends and therefore to predict the most useful Web-resources.

2.3   Effort and Information Foraging Theory

The theories of *Information Foraging* [25] are based on the ecological theories of foraging behaviour. The *Optimal Foraging theory* [28] explains the foraging behaviour of organisms in response to the environment in which they live. Foraging theory considers the foraging behaviour of animals by taking into account the payoff that animal obtains from different foraging options. *Information Foraging Theory* seeks to explain and predict how people will best adapt themselves for their information environments and how information environments can thus be best adapted to people. The human propensity to gather and use information to adapt to everyday problems in the world is a core concept in *human psychology* that has been largely ignored in cognitive studies. Humans have not only personal memory, but also external technology, as the Word Wide Web, for storing information. This extended information store thus enables us to perform

---

[1] http://www.ebay.com
[2] http://www.amazon.com
[3] http://www.delicious.com

knowledge based activity, but it is dependent on efficient information retrieval. Information foraging strategies can be adapted to identify the right knowledge, at the right time in order to take useful action or to make appropriate decisions.

The effort spent by users to take an action represents the central aspect of our study. The *Information Foraging Theory* assumes that people prefer information-seeking strategies that yield more useful information per unit cost of interaction. Users tend to arrange their environments to optimise this rate of gain, hence they prefer technology designs that improve returns on information foraging. One of the goal of the study presented here is to determine the mechanism for the generation of implicit feedback correlated with explicit human judgements as to Web-page quality and value. To test this we monitor users' behaviour while surfing the Internet and with appropriate reasoning technique and analysis of the cost, over time, of each user activity such as scrolling, bookmarking, printing, filling form, cut and paste, we aim to predict users' interest and to build up a useful and trustworthy rank among Web-pages. Our approach differs from the strategy proposed by Pirolli et. al. [26] in their SNIF-ACT model where various backtracking mechanisms are adopted to study how users make navigation choices when browsing over many Web-pages until they either give up or find what they were seeking. Similarly, our *effort-based model* differs from two other recent models of Web navigation: MESA [21] and COLIDES [14] that simulate the flow of users through the tree structures of linked Web-pages.

2.4   Computational Trust

The relevance of Trust and Reputation in human societies is indisputably recognised. Several studies have been carried out in different perspectives: psychology [11], economy [5], philosophy [10] and sociology [4]. These concepts have been acquiring a great relevance in the last decade in the area of Distributed Artificial Intelligence as multi-agent systems become feasible. These systems are used by intelligent software agents bots as an incentive in decision-making. A trust-based decision is a multi-stage process on a specific domain. This process starts identifying and selecting pieces of trust evidence, therefore the proper input data, generally domain-specific, conducting an analysis over the application involved. Subsequently, trust values are produced performing a trust computation over the pieces of evidences that means, the estimation of the trustworthiness of entities in the domain considered. Both the steps, evidence-extraction and trust computation, are informed by a notion of trust in the Trust model and the final trust decision is taken by considering the computed values along with exogenous factors such as disposition or risk assessments.

Trust has emerged as a core element of decision-support tools helping agents in the selection of good collaborative partners, selection of reliable pieces of information or as part of soft-security access control mechanisms. Trust, as intended by the Computational Trust community, is a prediction (subjective probability) that the trustee entity will fulfil trustier's expectations in the context of a specific task [8]. The proliferation of collaborative environments, for example the ones based on Wiki[4], represent good examples in which Computational Trust paradigms are applied in order to evaluate the trustworthiness of virtual identities. Dondio et al.[7] performed a set of experiments by mapping onto a model of Wikipedia expertise derived from studies in *collaborative editing* and *content quality*. Longo et al. [17] conceived a set of trust evidences based on time and applied to encyclopaedia, demonstrating how plausible trust decisions can be reached using exclusively temporal factors. Another area of application of these concepts, in agent technology, is teamwork and co-operation [22] where the game theory is the predominant paradigm considered to design Computational Trust model.

Since the first model of trust was identified by S. Marsh [20] in 1994, one of the main rationales for the investigation of trust was its ability to decrease complexity. According to Luhmann [19], trust is adopted by humans to decrease the complexity of the society we are living using delegation. By considering only the trustworthy set of entities/information, a decision making process is clearly quicker, since less information has to be analysed, and better, since the set of information contains less noise and more quality. In the *Social Search* paradigm pages are ranked according to how users of the community are consuming and judging those pages in relation to some searching needs, either implicitly or explicitly. Many *Social Search* engines employ implicit solutions that rank Webpages according to an automatic algorithm by elaborating users' search activity, while explicit social engines rely on humans ratings. We propose to enhance implicit Social Search engines with a Trust module able to filter data and make an engine's predictions more accurate. In this context, a level of trust, for each user, is assessed by considering his/her expertise in gathering information within the Web, and his/her ability to fulfil a search problem. In other words, trustworthy users are the ones able to find the most relevant information when they need it.

3   Hypothesis

This work is firstly focused on a comparison between explicit human judgements and implicit derived feedback considering an Internet Web-page. We hypothesise that in the context of Web-page media, by applying our formal model based on *Information Foraging theory*, explicit human judgements will be correlated positively with the corresponding implicit derived feedback. If the correlation between them is considerable this then suggests that it is possible to build up a collaborative environment that achieves good predictions in an implicit and non-invasive way. We seek a method of reasoning over users' behaviour inspired by the *Information Foraging Theory* to generate a set of ranked results of the most valuable content, as determined by users, which is by implication valuable to other similar users. We refer to this kind of collaborative determiner of value as *Implicit Collaboration* to distinguish from the classic, *Explicit Collaboration*, where users expressly provide judgements and feedback. The second issue we wish to investigate is the comparison between the rank proposed by Google [24]

---

[4] http://www.wikipedia.org

(Google Vector), the rank obtained by our effort-based formal model (Implicit vector) and the rank with the average of explicit judgements (Explicit vector). If the Euclidean distance between the Google and the Explicit vector is equal or greater than the distance between the Implicit and the Explicit vector, our approach will succeed as our algorithm will show an accuracy proximal to the Google PageRank. This evidence would support our formal model demonstrating how a useful rank can be achieved by using an automatic approach based on reasoning on human behaviour and no more on the link structure of the Web. Finally, by adopting *Computational Trust* techniques, trustworthy users may be spotted within the Web-community. The last hypothesis is that, by considering the implicit feedback of just a portion of the spotted trustworthy users, the previous Euclidean distance between the implicit judgements (Implicit vector) and the explicit judgements (Explicit vector) will decrease. This will support a refinement of the effort-based formal model and consequently a more accurate ranking of Web-documents may be achieved.

The 3 main hypothesis are summarised as follows:

1. *if the comparison between explicit users' judgements and related implicit feedback, derived by the effort-based formal model, is significant in term of correlation, we can avoid to explicitly ask users to rate Web-documents;*
2. *if the Euclidean vector distance between the implicit and the explicit judgements is less or equal than the vector distance between the explicit and the Google judgements, we can validate the effectiveness and the accuracy of the effort-based formal model (Google rank is used as benchmarking);*
3. *if the distance between the explicit judgements and the related implicit judgements, after the individuation of the set of the trustworthy Web-user, is lower or at least as good as the one obtained by considering all the users, we can enhance or maintain the overall accuracy of the effort-based formalism with a lower computational cost.*

4   Gathering Web-Users' Behaviour

To evaluate a Web-page automatically, we have developed a client-side logging tool that unobtrusively gathers logs of users' behaviour through the user's natural interaction while surfing the Internet. Our software solution has been built by using javascript and it runs transparently without affecting the user's browsing experience[5].

4.1   The User-Behaviour Pattern

The events (E_i) logged by our client-side piece of software, are presented in the following list:

---

[5] Collecting implicit judgements raises privacy/anonymity concerns and ethical questions. Considering these issues we designed our piece of software in such a way that users have to explicitly confirm the usage by installing it.

- E_1: bookmark;
- E_2: print;
- E_3: save as (page);
- E_4: download;
- E_5: submit (text form filling);
- E_6: save as (picture);
- E_7: Im not alive (inactivity period);
- E_8: cut & paste (clipboard using);
- E_9: scroll;
- E_{10}: find in page,
- E_{11}: focused time (focus on a certain client-window).

These events form a *'user-behaviour pattern'* containing the occurrences generated by a user while surfing a particular domain. We refer to this as $BP_n^d[E_i]$, this being a vector containing all the occurrences of each event E_i generated by a user n on a Web-site d.

5   Heuristic Formalisms

5.1   A Model Based on Information Foraging Theory and Effort

We have defined a computational model, inspired by the Foraging Theory and Effort described in 2.3, that considers the occurrences of the events in the *'user-behaviour pattern'* and computes a real value to assess a Web-sites' degree of relevance to a specific searching problem. This model is based on the hypothesis that, Web-sites on which users spend greatest effort over time, may be considered more interesting and worthy viewing. The relevance of Web-sites is particularly connected to searching activity by end users that starts with a search query, usually in browsers.

Justification of Effort. Since 'scrolling' events are more frequent than 'save as' events or 'cut & paste' events should require more effort than 'click' events, a hierarchy is needed to discriminate their importance. The importance or strength of each event E_i is the complement of the probability P^d of that event to occur in the Web-site d, and we refer to it as *justification of effort* (GE^d):

$$\forall x \neq (7 \mid 11) , P^d(E_i) = \sum_{n=1}^{z} BP_n^d[E_i] \cdot \left(\sum_{n=1}^{z} \sum_{x=1}^{y} BP_n^d[E_x] \right)^{-1} , \; x \neq (7 \mid 11)$$
$$GE^d(E_i) = 1 - P^d(E_i)$$

where the left side of the first formula represents the total probability of the event of type i to occur in the Web-site d, while the right side indicates the sum of the occurrences of all the events y (in this work $y = 11$) generated by all the z users who have previously visited the domain d, excluding the event 7 and 11, that are respectively the 'inactivity time' and the 'focused time'.

Time Properties. In order to monitor a time period of inactivity, we conceived the *'Im Not Alive'* event, based on a reasonable threshold (Th) of 10 seconds. In other words, if a user does not generate any event for more than 10 seconds, the logger generates an *'Im Not Alive'* event. By considering the focused time $(BP^d[11])$ spent on a domain d by a user and subtracting the occurrences of the *'Im Not Alive'* event $(BP^d[7])$, multiplying by the threshold (Th), it is possible to monitor the activity period. For example, if the focused time is 55 seconds for a Web-site d, and there are 2 *'Im Not Alive'* events related to it, the activity period spent on the Web-site d is $55 - (2 \times 10) = 35$ seconds. By considering the above interpretations, the time-activity function (Act) is formalised as:

$$Act_n^d(BP_n^d[E_{11}], \ BP_n^d[E_7]) = BP_n^d[E_{11}] - (BP_n^d[E_7] \ \cdot \ Th)$$

where $BP_n^d[11]$ is the focus time, $BP_n^d[E_7]$ is the number of occurrences of the *'Im not Alive'* event as gathered by the monitor in seconds, generated by the user n on the domain d and Th is the time threshold defined before (10 seconds). Our threshold value is subjective: unsupervised techniques may help identify the right value for this threshold in any particular context.

Effort. Now we are able to compute the effort expended by a user n on a domain d: the effort is the total activity per time unit (E_n^d). In particular, the total effort performed by a user n on a domain d is the sum of all the occurrences, for all the events, generated by him/her while surfing the Web-site d, multiplied by the related *justification of effort*, over the *activity time*. y refers to all the possible events (excluding 7 and 11) in the *'user-behaviour pattern'*. Formally:

$$E_n^d = \left(Act_n^d(BP_n^d[E_{11}], BP_n^d[E_7])\right)^{-1} \cdot \sum_{i=1}^{y} BP_n^d[E_i] \cdot GE(E_i) \ , \ i \neq (7 \mid 11)$$

At this stage we are able to compute the average effort (AE^d) of all the users z who previously have surfed the domain d. Formally:

$$AE^d = \frac{1}{z} \sum_{n=1}^{z} (E_n^d)$$

Ranking. Finally, we can compute the ranking of Web-sites by taking into account the average effort on each domain. We adopt a sigmoid function to assign almost null importance to those Web-sites that have not been endorsed/viewed by several Web-users. The more a Web-site d is visited, the more the average effort spent on it is emphasised, so its reliability and usefulness increase underlying the real common users' behaviour on it. Formally, the ranked value of a domain d, for a given query, is modelled as:

$$RV^d = AE^d \cdot \frac{1 - e^{-kz^d}}{1 + e^{-kz^d}}$$

where the first part represents the average effort spent on the domain d and the second part is the sigmoid function that assigns 0 to an input of 0 and grows in the number of users z^d who visited the domain d. The constant k is a value in [0..1] that supports the threshold of minimum users to start to be confident of the emerged common behaviour. The more this constant tends to 0, the higher the threshold of minimum user is. A value of 1 indicates that with 6 users or more, the sigmoid function returns value in the range [0.99..1] so it grows very slowly. The constant may be learned with unsupervised techniques but in this experimentation is set to $k = 1$. The ranking algorithm of our Computational model based on *Information Foraging Theory* and *effort* is summarised as in the follow:

```
For each Web-sites d {
    For each event i :
        GE^d(E_i)               Justification of effort of event i
    For each user n :
        E_n^d                    Effort by user n on domain d
    AE^d                         Average efforts on domain d
    RV^d                         Ranking Value of domain d
}
Order Web-sites by RV^d in descending way
```

5.2 A Model Based on Computational Trust

We have designed a further model based on *Computational Trust* whose aims is to enhance and improve the accuracy of the previous approach presented in 5.1. The model takes into account the skill of users based on the hypothesis that skilled users may be considered more trustworthy than novice users as they have more experience in surfing the Web, and they are likely therefore to have acquired greater ability in gathering information appropriate to their needs.

Justification of Skill. We propose to model the degree of users' skill by reasoning on the type and the occurrences of events generated by users over Web-pages. In particular, we call *justification of skill (GS)* the intrinsic degree of skill that an event i supports. We define this as the complement of the probability P of an event i to occur in general, in all the Web-sites considered in a certain context. This differs from the previous definition of *justification of effort (GE^d)* which was the complement of an event to occur just at the selected Web-site d. Formally:

$$P(E_i) = \sum_{d=1}^{w} \sum_{n=1}^{z} BP_n^d[E_i] \cdot \left(\sum_{d=1}^{w} \sum_{n=1}^{z} \sum_{x=1}^{y} BP_n^d[E_x] \right)^{-1}, \forall x \neq (7 \mid 11)$$

$$GS(E_i) = 1 - P(E_i)$$

where w is the total number of Web-sites, z are the users who visited the Web-site d and y is the number of events $(y = 11)$ excluding the event 7 and 11, that are respectively the 'inactivity time' and the 'focused time'.

User's Skill. The degree of intrinsic skill associated with each event type, as captured by our *justification of skill*, is useful to compute the users' degree of ability in gathering information in the Web. Our assumption is that implicit judgements, generated by skilled users, should be considered more robust and accurate than ones generated by novice users. Formally we define the degree of expertise (S):

$$S(n) = \sum_{d=1}^{w} \sum_{x=1}^{y} \left(BP_n^d[E_x] \cdot GS(x) \right), \quad \forall x \neq (7 \mid 11)$$

In other words, we take into consideration all the occurrences, for each event, generated by a user n on each Web-site, weighted by the associated *justification of skill*. For instance, as the "find in page" event implies a greater users ability and skill to generate it, as it requires a particular combinations of more keyboard keys such as "ctrl + f", and therefore unlikely to be generated, users who generate a considerable volume of this event, may be considered more expert and therefore more trustworthy.

5.3   Enhancing Implicit Judgements

The *Computational Trust* model proposed here aims to increase the robustness of the algorithm designed in 5.1, based on effort. Once trustworthy Web-users have been identified, by considering their expertise and ability in gathering information within the Web, it is possible to modify the previous effort values, one for each Web-site, by taking into account only those users ranked as trustworthy. Therefore, at this stage, we may compute the *skill weighted average effort* ($SWAE^d$) for the domain d, just by considering a subset of all the users z who previously have surfed it. This subset may have the same cardinality of the z set or may be a subset of users, considered more trustworthy.

$$SWAE_{sz}^d = \frac{1}{|sz|} \sum_{n \in sz} (E_n^d \cdot S(n)), \quad sz \subseteq z$$

Formally, we consider a subset sz of the z users who visited the Web-site d, and for each user n we take the skill influencing strength $S(n)$ multiplying it by the related effort E_n^d showed on the Web-site d. Finally, the average of the weighted efforts is computed ($\frac{1}{|sz|}$).

Skill Ranked Value. Finally, as in 5.1, we can compute the ranking of Web-sites by taking into account the skill weighted average effort $SWAE_{sz}^d$ for each domain d, and a subset sz of the most trustworthy users. The adoption of the same sigmoid function, proposed in section 5.1, is useful to assign almost null importance to those Web-sites that have not been endorsed/viewed by several Web-users. Formally:

$$SRV_{sz}^d = SWAE_{sz}^d \cdot \frac{1 - e^{-k \cdot |sz|^d}}{1 + e^{-k \cdot |sz|^d}}$$

where the first part represents the skill weighted average effort spent on the domain d, and the second part is the sigmoid function that assigns 0 to an input of 0 and grows in the number of trustworthy users, belonging to the sz^d set, who have visited the domain d.

The ranking algorithm of our *Computational Trust* model based on Web-users' trustworthiness is summarised as in the follow:

```
For each event d (excluding event 7 and 11){
```
$\quad\quad GS(E_i)$ $\quad\quad$ Justification of skill of event i
```
}
For each user n{
```
$\quad\quad S(n)$ $\quad\quad\quad$ Skill of user n
```
}
define sz          Define the sz set of users (trustworthy)
For each Web-sites d {
```
$\quad\quad SWAE_{sz}^d$ $\quad\quad$ Skill weighted average effort for d
$\quad\quad SRV_{sz}^d$ $\quad\quad$ Skill ranked value
```
}
```
Order Web-sites by SRV_{sz}^d in descending way

6   Evaluation and Experiments

We have conducted experiments in order to investigate the viability of our approach. 100 university students with different social background were recruited to participate in this study. Their ages was between 19 and 35 years, and students have been selected from different schools such as Computer Science, Psychology, Arts, Languages, Medicine. 30% of them usually spend more than six hours per day surfing the Internet. 40% use the World Wide Web just two hours per day and the rest spend just a couple of hours per week browsing Web-pages.

6.1   The Searching Problem: A Proposed Web-Task

We asked each student to organise a trip to Morocco, a couple of weeks long, providing them with a context-dependent pre-defined list of Web-sites, listed in the table 1, from which it is possible to collect information. The list was created by selecting 12 URLs from the Google ranking list obtained typing in the Google search box the keyword 'morocco' in the second week of October 2008. The thematic URLs were selected from a set of Google pages. Furthermore, the selection process considered the content and the structure of each Web-page in order to discriminate useful and non-useful Web-documents. In particular, the authors aimed to test whether, for instance, URLs H, J and K, which we show being useful for gathering appropriated information related to the task, would be automatically considered not relevant by the heuristic formalisms proposed in this paper.

During the experiment, the participants had to naturally interact with the browser, collecting useful data in order to recover it in the future. At the end of

Table 1. List of URLs, for participants, and their position in the Google's Rank

U.ID.	Http link	Google Pos.	Description
A	en.wikipedia.org/wiki/Morocco	01	General info
B	www.morocco.com/	02	A lot of travelling info
C	www.visitmorocco.com	05	Cities info
D	www.geographia.com/morocco/	11	History & geographic info
E	www.morocco-travel.com/	13	Several travelling info
F	wikitravel.org/en/Morocco	14	General info
G	www.magicmorocco.com/	19	Cities info
H	rabat.usembassy.gov/	26	Rabat USA embassy
I	www.lonelyplanet.com /maps/africa/morocco/	29	Specialised travelling site
J	allafrica.com/morocco/	39	Bad structure & useless
K	www.worldstatesmen.org/ Morocco.htm	57	Plenty of statistics
L	www.naturallymorocco.co.uk/	67	Some info

the task, we asked each of them to explicitly provide a judgement of the usefulness, related to our goal ('morocco' - organising a trip), of each Web-site listed, using a common scale from 1 to 10 (1 means not useful & 10 means very useful). In this experiment we have assumed that users do not act maliciously, such that the data contained in the log files is the proper representation of the real actions performed by them while surfing the Internet. In other words, if participants did not change their usual behaviour while surfing the Web, generated logs data are assumed to be not altered.

6.2   The Process toward Useful Assessments

At the end of the experiment, a set of noisy information had been obtained from each user, containing his/her activity while surfing Web-sites. Since volunteers can jump from one Web-document to another of the list (table 1), gathered logs needed to be filtered and pre-processed in order to produce a well defined set of data useful for an accurate set of *'user-behaviour patterns'*. For these reasons, a 'Pre-processing filter', filtered all the URLs not in the list and eliminated empty pages and other sources of noise, such as pop-ups or automatic opened pages. This process of monitoring behaviour, producing logs and filtering out noise, is called "Monitor level". This process produces a *user behaviour set*s, which is a set of *user's behaviour pattern*, one for each Url visited by each user. The set of behavioural patterns represents the input for the *reasoning model level*. At this stage, the behavioural patterns are aggregated, grouped per domain, and as result, a set of 12 aggregated *user's behaviour pattern*s, one for each Web-domain in the table 1, forms the data-set used by our reasoning techniques. Each aggregated behaviour pattern contains the occurrences of all the events generated on the main domain and its sub-domains. Finally, by applying our heuristic formalism based on *Information Foraging Theory and Effort*, we can generate a unique value representing an assessment of the usefulness of a given Web-site. The overall process toward this assessment is depicted in the figure 1 and summarised as in the follow:

1) MONITOR LEVEL
   a) the client-side logging tool
      unobtrusively gathers Web-users' behaviour
   b) a set of logs is produced
   c) the logs are pre-processed and noise is filtered out

2) USER'S BEHAVIOUR SET
   a) for each Web-site (included sub-domains)
         for each user
            a user's behaviour pattern is produces
   b) the set of total patterns, produced in 2a,
      represents the 'user's behaviour set'

3) REASONING MODEL
   a) the patterns in the 'user's behaviour set',
      produced in 2b, are aggregated
   b) a set of aggregated user's behaviour pattern
      is produced, one for each Web-domain
   c) for each aggregated user's behaviour pattern in 3b
         the heuristic formalism based on Information
         Foraging Theory assesses a usefulness/relevance value

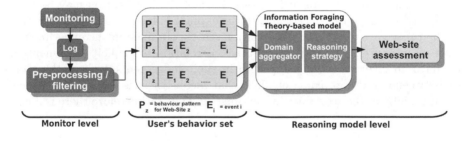

Fig. 1. Summary of the process toward the assessment of Web-site's usefulness

7   Results and Discussion

In this section we discuss results obtained in our experiments. We focus individually on each hypothesis stated in section 3, presenting the steps involved in the tests along with the statistical tools adopted.

7.1   Test Hypothesis 1

The 12 values produced by our formalism based on *Information Foraging Theory and Effort*, and the 12 explicit judgements provided by each participant are statistically correlated to test the hypothesis number 1. We have adopted the *Pearson's correlation coefficient* that measures the strength of the linear dependence between two variables. One interesting aspect of using the Pearson score is that it corrects for *grade inflation*: if one participant is inclined to give explicit higher scores than another, there can still be perfect correlation if the difference between their scores is consistent. If the correlation value obtained by considering the implicit values and the explicit judgements, for a given Web-site and a given volunteer, tends to 1, a linear equation describes the relationship positively with the implicit values increasing with the explicit values. A score of −1 shows the inverted relationship between the two values and a score tending to 0 shows the absence of a linear dependence.

In order to test the hypothesis 1 behind this research, the experiment has to produce high correlation scores. If the majority of these scores tend to 1, our hyphotesis is confirmed and we can sustain there exists a considerable relationship between implicit feedback and explicit human judgements as captured by our effort-based model. On the other hand, if our solution produces low correlation scores, that means scores tending to 0 or −1, we are not able to fully support the hypothesis so further studies and different methods have to be considered. Participants with a coefficient close to 1 are the ones who support our hypothesis and their explicit judgements can be nearly perfectly approximated by our heuristic presented in section 5.1. On the contrary, coefficients close to 0 underline the fact that our model did not succeed in automatically approximate explicit judgements in implicit feedback. Part of the justification may be found in the intrinsic degree of uncertainty in the explicit judgements provided by user.

The ranked set of Pearson's correlation scores, obtained in the experiment, is depicted in figure 2. There is no negative correlation so explicit judgements do not have an inverted relationship with implicit judgements. 22% of the scores are between 0 and approximately 0.25, that means there is a weak positive correlations. 59% of the scores are in the range [0.25..0.75] therefore there is a good

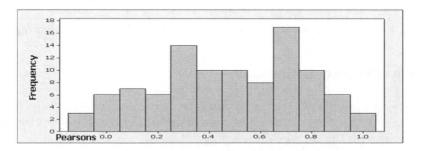

Fig. 2. Pearson's Correlation scores between each user's explicit judgement and the related computed implicit feedback

degree of relationship between explicit and implicit feedback. Finally, 19% of the participants' scores lies in the range [0.75..1]: these people have the highest approximation of their explicit judgements by the derived implicit ones. The results are encouraging: due to the existence of a relevant approximation of explicit judgements by implicit computed feedback, hypothesis 1 may be accepted. This evidence is a promising step toward the analysis of Web-users' behaviour in a non-invasive, non explicit way.

7.2 Test Hypothesis 2

For hypothesis 2, as stated in section 3, we examine how, with implicit feedback, an implicit degree of collaboration can be reached automatically. In particular, by focusing on users' behaviour and by applying the schema proposed in section 5.1, it is possible to create a ranked list of Web-sites, and thus to try to predict users' interests and tendencies. At the top of this list there will be those Web-sites with the higher average of usefulness/relevance scores, and at the bottom those ones in which users' behaviour had not significant influence for a given searching problem, and therefore, by implication, such activity was not useful. The application of our effort-based model, inspired by the *Information Foraging Theory*, has produced the ranked list summarised in table 2, ordered by the average effort values: B, D, C, L, E, F, A, I, G, H, J, K.

Table 2. List of experiment's URLs emerged from the application of the formalism, based on the *Information Foraging Theory and Effort*, ranked by the average effort showed by Web-users

U.ID.	Http Url	AVG. Effort
B	www.morocco.com/	0.054
D	www.geographia.com/morocco/	0.049
C	www.visitmorocco.com	0.038
L	www.naturallymorocco.co.uk/	0.032
E	www.morocco-travel.com/	0.031
F	wikitravel.org/en/Morocco	0.030
A	en.wikipedia.org/wiki/Morocco	0.029
I	www.lonelyplanet.com/maps/africa/morocco/	0.025
G	www.magicmorocco.com/	0.023
H	rabat.usembassy.gov/	0.012
J	allafrica.com/morocco/	0.010
K	www.worldstatesmen.org/Morocco.htm	0.006

The application of our solution over the collected data indicated that Web-sites B, D contain relevant and useful information in organising a trip to Morocco according to our analysis. URLs C, L, E, F, A, I, G are not that helpful in providing good information about Morocco compared to the previous ones: this judgement is reflected by the moderate users' average effort computed by our formal model. Web-sites H, I, J are not appropriate for the context at all, as users spent very little energy in resolving the searching problem. For instance, H relates to the Morocco USA's Embassy Web-site: despite the fact it contains key-words related to Morocco, it is totally unrelated and useless to extract relevant travel information. Finally, the url K belongs to a Web-agency that offers trip packages already assembled and therefore not relevant.

The achieved results are encouraging as they reflect what the authors expected: the URLs H, J, K in the last positions of the computed ranking, as they do not give any advantage in finding information related to the task proposed in section 6.1. One interesting point in adopting such an approach is that, by enclosing the ranking value to the URLs, more accurate justifications of their position can be achieved. For instance, it is clear that URLs H, J, K, other than being at the bottom of the ranking, are far away from those URLs relevant to the searching problem. Furthermore, Web-pages with a very low chance to be visited, such as the url L in position 67 of the Google-Rank, may carry useful information as computed by our model. By taking into account the list of URLs proposed in the table 1, ordered by the position of each Web-site selected in the Google' s List (table 4 - Google V.), and by considering the ordered list (table 4 - Implicit V.) obtained by applying our effort-model, it is possible to study their distance to the explicit participants' judgements ordered list (table 4 - Explicit V.).

The scatterplots, depicted in figure 3, show both the comparisons: explicit judgements are more correlated to the implicit computed feedback (left), in fact, points rely close to the straight line than the scatterplot in which the Google-list and the Explicit-list are compared (right).

We have adopted the *Kendall tau rank correlation coefficient* [13] which is a non-parametic statistics used to measure the strength of correspondence between two rankings, that means the degree of association of the cross tabulations. The Kendall tau coefficient τ is formally defined as:

$$\tau = \frac{2 \cdot S}{\frac{1}{2}n(n-1)} - 1$$

where n is the number of items and S is the sum, over all the items, of items ranked after the given item by both rankings. S may be interpreted as the number of concordant pairs while the denominator may be interpreted as the total number of pairs of items. The higher is S, the most pairs are concordant, indicating that the two rankings are highly correspondent. The coefficient has the following properties:

- if the two rankings are the same, that means they totally agree, the coefficient has value 1;
- if one ranking is the reverse of the other one, that means they totally disagree, the coefficient has value -1;
- for the other values lying in the range $[-1..1]$, if they tend to 0, their rankings are proportionally independent, while if they tend to the border of the range, their agreement increase either positively or negatively.

In this experiment, the number of items n is 12, that corresponds to the number of Web-sites considered. The Explicit Vector is ordered from the lower position,

Table 3. Kendall tau correlation coefficient for both Explicit list vs. Implicit list, and Explicit list vs. Google list

Explicit Vector	1	2	3	4	5	6	7	8	9	10	11	12	S	τ
Implicit Vector	5	6	4	1	7	3	8	9	2	12	10	11	(7+6+6+8+5+5+4+3+3+0+1+0)=48	0.454
Google Vector	5	6	12	2	1	3	9	7	4	11	8	10	(7+6+0+7+7+6+2+3+3+0+1+0)=42	0.272

Table 4. Position of each URLs (U.No.) in each evaluation method: our model (Implicit Vector), the Explicit feedback provided by users (Explicit Vector) and the Google Page-Rank (Google Vector)

U.No.	Effort Avg	Implicit V.	Explicit V.	Google V.
E	0.031	5	1	5
F	0.030	6	2	6
L	0.032	4	3	12
B	0.054	1	4	2
A	0.029	7	5	1
C	0.038	3	6	3
I	0.025	8	7	9
G	0.023	9	8	7
D	0.049	2	9	4
K	0.006	12	10	11
H	0.012	10	11	8
J	0.010	11	12	10

that means the Web-site with high ranking, to the higher position, the Web-site less relevant. Accordingly, the Implicit Vector and the Google Vector are ordered as well. The values for S are computed as in the table 3.

The results are encouraging as the Kendall tau coefficient of $\tau = 0.272$, emerged by considering the Explicit Vector and the Google Vector, is less than the coefficient computed by taking into account the Explicit Vector and the Implicit Vector, which is $\tau = 0.454$. The interpretation is that the Google ranked list is relatively independent from the Explicit ranked list which seems to be better approximated by the Implicit vector. Further analysis of the lists have been done by computing the Euclidean distance of both the Google vector and the Implicit vector compared to the Explicit vector. These distances are respectively 13.64 and 10.58. As depicted in the figure 3, in Web-sites C, E, G, K and L cases, the implicit computed feedback are closer to the straight line, that represents the judgements provided explicitly by users: in these cases our strategy succeeded. Url A, B, F and H have the same distance both in the Google and Implicit vectors: in these cases our model performs as well as Google. Eventually, in cases D, I and J, our approach does less well than Google. Nevertheless, our heuristic based on effort produces better results for the higher ranked half of the URLs. The distance of both the lists to the straight line (Explicit vector) are respectively 11.92 (Google Vector) and 7.42 (Implicit Vector) for the first half, 6.63 (Google Vector) and 7.55 (Implicit Vector) for the second half. This

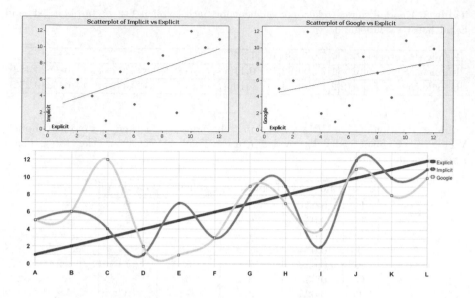

Fig. 3. Scatterplots between the Implicit and the Explicit lists, and between the Google and the Explicit lists (Top). Comparison graph among the three ordered lists (Bottom).

suggests our formalism is promising in approximating explicit Web-users' opinions about Web-sites, thus supporting the hypothesis 2.

7.3   Test Hypothesis 3

The *Computational Trust Model*, designed in section 5.2, aims to enhance the overall accuracy of the effort-based model, designed in section 5.1, in approximating explicit judgements. This Trust-based heuristic assigns to each user, involved in the experiment, a degree of skill that corresponds to the ability of gathering information and surfing, in general, the Web. Users are then ranked by considering their computed skill strength and their opinion is proportionally taken into account. In particular, a Web-user's effort, expended in viewing a given Web-site, is weighted multiplying it by the user's degree of skill. This operation is looped for each user and each Web-site, obtaining a new ranked implicit judgements list. This process is then repeated taking into consideration just the "implicit opinions", that means the average of implicit computed effort-based feedback, of just a portion of users, considered to be trustworthy due to their high degree of skill. The results, considering portions of trustworthy users, are presented in table 5.

The table 5 shows the ranked list of Web-sites computed by using the formalism presented in section 5.2 and the relative portion of trustworthy users taken into account. For instance, T-100 means we have considered the full set of users in computing the implicit vector, T-87.5 means we have taken into account the top 87.5% skilled/trustworthy users to assess each Web-site's usefulness degree,

Table 5. Implicit list ranked by considering implicit opinions of just a percentage of the overall set of users with the related Euclidean distance and the Kendal Tau coefficient

U.ID.	Explicit	T-100%	T-87.5%	T-75%	T-62.5%	T-50%	T-37.5%	T-25%	T-12.5%
E	1	4	4	4	4	3	5	3	3
F	2	5	5	5	5	5	2	6	6
L	3	6	6	7	6	6	6	12	12
B	4	1	1	1	1	1	1	1	1
A	5	7	7	6	7	9	9	7	7
C	6	3	3	3	3	4	3	2	2
I	7	8	8	9	9	8	7	4	4
G	8	9	9	8	8	7	8	8	8
D	9	2	2	2	2	2	4	5	5
J	10	11	11	11	11	11	11	9	9
H	11	10	10	10	10	10	10	10	10
K	12	12	12	12	12	12	12	11	11
Euclidean	distance	10.3	10.3	10.58	10.39	10.39	9.49	12.88	25.5
Kendall	Coeff.	0.52	0.52	0.45	0.48	0.45	0.52	0.33	0.33

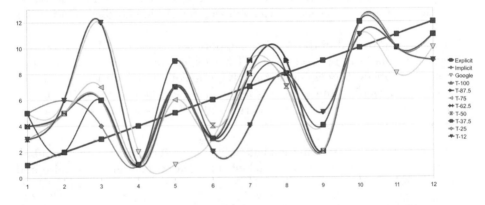

Fig. 4. Comparisons graph among implicit rankings, produced by the effort-based model enhanced by our *Computational Trust* reasoning technique, and the Explicit vector

and so forth. The same results are depicted in figure 4 where all the curved lines try to be close to the straight line which represents the explicit feedback vector.

The last 2 lines of the table 5 show the Euclidean distance among all the vectors and the Explicit rank along with the Kendall Tau correlation coefficient. The Euclidean distance of the vectors to the Explicit vector is close if we consider all the users (100%), or portion of the most trustworthy/skilled users up to 37.5% (87.5%, 75%, 62.5%, 50%, 37.5%). These results are positive as they are smaller than the Euclidean distance of 10.58 obtained while testing the hypothesis 2. In particular, by considering the portion of just 37.5% of the top trustworthy users, the enhancement, in term of accuracy in approximating the explicit judgements, is encouraging, with a percentage of improvement of:

$$Enhancement_{Euclidean} : \frac{10.58 - 9.49}{10.58} = 10.3\%$$

After this point, the consideration of a smaller portion of trustworthy users deteriorates the results as the Euclidean distance increases at a faster rate, meaning that the approximation of the explicit judgements is loosing accuracy.

Similarly, the Kendall Tau correlation coefficients behaves nearly in the same way: up to 37% as a portion of trustworthy users, the results are greater or equal the Kendall Tau coefficient of $\tau = 0.454$ obtained while testing the hypothesis 2. Yet, this fact may be interpreted positively as the related T-ranked list are closer to the ranked explicit list than the implicit one obtained while testing the hypothesis 2. With a Kendall tau value of 0.52, the enhancement, in term of accuracy in approximating the explicit judgements is:

$$Enhancement_{Kendall} : \frac{0.52}{0.45} = 15.5\%$$

After this point, the consideration of a smaller portion of skilled users decreases the accuracy of the results as the Kendall tau correlation coefficient decreases at a faster rate.

The results, provided in this section, support the hypothesis 3 of the section 3, suggesting that the opinion coming from expert individuals may be more valuable for a *Social Search* engine than the one collected from the crowd. For a *Social Search* engine, information is more valuable when it supports a better and more accurate ranking. By considering only the trustworthy set of users, a decision-making process is:

– clearly faster as less information has to be analysed and therefore computed;
– better due to the fact that the set of information contains less noise and more quality.

As a consequence, *Computational Trust* techniques are useful to increase the accuracy of *Social Search* engines either in terms of quality or scalability.

8   Open Issues and Future Work

In this study we have performed a comparison between explicit context-dependent human judgements and implicit feedback, as computed over data capturing user browsing activity. The experiment included 12 thematic URLs explicitly evaluated by 100 students with different social background and age, providing a degree of usefulness and relevance for a searching problem. During browsing sessions we have automatically monitored their activity to study their behaviour. A '*user behaviour-pattern*', containing the occurrences of browser's events, has been extracted, for each user and Web-site, and then evaluated by using a computational effort-based model inspired by the *Information Foraging Theory*. Even if a small and simple set of information has been considered, in the *users' behaviour pattern*, the Pearson's coefficient has helped us to show the existence of an encouraging correlation between explicit and computed implicit judgements.

Furthermore, we made a comparison between the explicit judgements provided by users, respectively with the ones provided by the Google' s Page-Rank algorithm and our heuristic based on user's effort. The Kendall tau coefficient and the Euclidean distance among the vectors have proved that our strategy is, in our experiment, more effective than the Google' s Page-Rank to predict user tendencies and interests. This result is promising but supplementary experiments are needed in different contexts with different constraints. Further data has to be collected about more Web-users and more Web-pages to try to generalise the ability of our strategy.

A final experiment has been carried on testing the hypothesis that, by relying only on the opinion of trustworthy users, as identified by our *Computational Trust* model, the ability of a *Social Search* engine, in identifying piece of information relevant to a search need, will be enhanced or at least maintained with less computational cost. The advantages of using our approach are promising. Firstly, a *Social Search* engine will generate a rank based on a smaller set of data, requiring less computations therefore improving scalability. Secondly, the sub-set of trustworthy information will produce a less noisy and more accurate data-set. However, further investigations on this last direction are needed as the results obtained represent a sufficient presumption but not a strong evidence.

The authors believe their approach represents a starting point to predict users' interests and tendencies towards a third generation *Social Search* engine based on *Trustworthy Implicit Collaboration*. The first-generation ranking engines judged the relevance and quality of a page considering its content. Second-generation ranking metrics started exploiting the link structure of the Web [15]. Our approach try to further improve the ranking metrics by reasoning on users' behaviour while consuming activity over Web-pages and considering the collective intelligence emerged from the community.

As this paper represents the first of its kind in the area, many future works are left. These will be focused on the preservation of the accuracy, of the overall algorithm, in malicious and potential harmful environments. New reasoning techniques have to be investigated in depth to better evaluate digital entities and to extend our model not only to recommender systems but also to the field of informational queries. An important issue will be focused on understanding how to semantically connect searching queries to relevant sets of URLs generated by our *Social Search* schema. Privacy issues must be investigated further in order to guarantee the anonymity of Web-users in providing implicit feedback.

References

1. Agichtein, E., Brill, E., Dumais, S.: Improving Web Search Ranking by Incorporating User Behavior Information. In: SIGIR 2006, Seattle, USA (2006)
2. Agichtein, E., Zheng, Z.: Identifying Best Bet Web Search Results by Mining Past User Behavior. In: Kdd 2006, Philadelphia, Pennsylvaia, USA (2006)

3. Atterer, R., et al.: Knowing the User's Every Move - User Activity Tracking for Website Usability Evaluation and Implicit Interaction. In: WWW 2006, Edinburgh, May 23-26 (2006)
4. Buskens, V.: The Social Structure of Trust. Social Networks 20, 265–298 (1998)
5. Celentani, M., Fudenberg, D., Levine, D.K., Psendorfer, W.: Maitaining a reputation Against a Long-Lived Opponent. Econometria 64(3), 691–704 (1966)
6. Chi Ed H.: Information Seeking Can Be Social. Computer 42(3), 42–46 (2009)
7. Dondio, P., Barrett, S., Weber, S., Seigneur, J.M.: Extracting trust from domain analysis: a study on Wikipedia. In: IEEE ATC, Wuhan, China (2006)
8. Gambetta, D.: From the book Trust: Making and Breaking Cooperative Relations. In: Can we trust trust?, pp. 213–237 (2000)
9. Golder, S.A., Huberman, B.A.: Usage Patterns of Collaborative Tagging Systems. Journal of Information Science 32(2), 198–208 (2006)
10. Hume, D.: A Treatise of Human Nature. Clarendon Press, Oxford (1737) (1975)
11. Karlins, M., Abelson, H.I.: Persuasion, how opinion and attitudes are changed. Crosby Lockwood & Son (1970)
12. Kelly, D., et al.: Reading Time, Scrolling and Interaction: exploring Implicit Sources of User Preferences for Relevance Feedback During Interactive Information Retrieval. In: SIGIR 2001, New Orleans, USA (2001)
13. Abdi, H.: Kendall Rank Correlation. In: Salkind, N.J. (ed.) Encyclopaedia of Measurement and Statistics, Sage, Thousand Oaks (2007)
14. Kitajima, M., Blackmon, M.H., Polson, P.G.: Cognitive Architecture for Website Design and Usability evaluation: Comprehension and Information Scent in Performing by Exploration. In: HCI, Las Vegas (2005)
15. Kleinberg, J.: Authoritative sources in a hyperlinked environment. Journal of the ACM 46(5), 604–632 (1999)
16. Longo, L., Barrett, S., Dondio, P.: Toward Social Search: from Explicit to Implicit Collaboration to Predict Users' Interests. In: WebIST 2009 (2009)
17. Longo, L., Dondio, P., Barrett, S.: Temporal Factors to evaluate trustworthiness of virtual identities. In: IEEE SECOVAL 2007, Third International Workshop on the Value of Security through Collaboration, SECURECOMM 2007, Nice, France (September 2007)
18. Longo, L., Dondio, P., Barrett, S.: Information Foraging Theory as a Form Of Collective Intelligence for Social Search. In: 1st International Conference on Computational Collective Intelligence Semantic Web, Social Networks & Multiagent Systems, Wroclaw, Poland, 5-7 October (2009)
19. Luhmann, N.: Book Trust: Making and Breaking Cooperative Relations. In: Familiarity, confidence, trust: Problems and alternatives, pp. 213–237 (2000)
20. Marsh, S.: Formalizing Trust as Computational Concept. PhD, Stirling (1994)
21. Miller, C.S., Remington, R.W.: Modeling Information Navigation: implications for Information Architecture. In: HCI (2004)
22. Montaner, M., Lopez, B., De La Rosa, J.: Developing Trust in Recommender Agents. In: Proceedings of the First International Joint Conference on Autonomous Agents and Multiagent Systems, AAMAS 2002, Bologna, Italy, pp. 304–305 (2002)
23. Morita, M., Shinoda, Y.: Information Filtering Based on User Behavior analysis and Best Match Text Retrieval. In: 17th ACM SIGIR (1996)
24. Page, L., Brin, S., Motwani, R., Winograd, T.: The PageRank Citation Ranking: Bringing Order to the Web. Standford University, Standford (1999)

25. Pirolli, P.: Information Foraging Theory. Adaptive Interaction with Information. Oxford University Press, Oxford (2007)
26. Pirolli, P., Fu, W.: SNIF-ACT: A Model of Information Foraging on the World Wide Web. In: 9th International Conference on, User Modeling 2003 (2003)
27. Robu, V., Halpin, H., Shepherd, H.: Emergence of consensus and shared vocabularies in collaborative tagging systems. ACM Transactions on the Web (TWeb), 3(4) article 14, (September 2009)
28. Stephens, D.W., Krebs, J.R.: Foraging Theory. Princeton, NJ (1986)
29. Velayathan, G., Yamada, S.: Behavior-based Web Page Evaluation. In: WWW 2007, Banff, Alberta, Canada, May 8-12 (2007)
30. Viégas, B.F., Wattenberg, M., Kushal, D.: Studying Cooperation and Conflict between Authors with history from Visualizations, MIT Media Lab. and IBM Research
31. Weiss, A.: The Power of Collective Intelligence. Collective Intelligence, 19-23 (2005)

Group-Oriented Services: A Shift towards Consumer-Managed Relationships in the Telecom Industry

Luka Vrdoljak[1], Iva Bojic[2], Vedran Podobnik[2], Gordan Jezic[2], and Mario Kusek[2]

[1] Erste & Steiermärkische Bank, Croatia
lvrdoljak@erstebank.com
[2] University of Zagreb, Faculty of Electrical Engineering and Computing, Croatia
{iva.bojic,vedran.podobnik,gordan.jezic,mario.kusek}@fer.hr

Abstract. Today, telecom operators face a threefold challenge: a social challenge dealing with the evolution of the consumer lifestyle, a technological challenge dealing with ever changing ICT trends and a business challenge dealing with the need for innovative business models. This paper introduces an idea of group-oriented services, a special type of personalized telecom services, as a possible solution for all three of these challenges. A proof-of-concept service, called Agent-Based Mobile Content Brokerage, is presented and elaborated with the aim to demonstrate a shift towards consumer-managed relationships, a novel provisioning paradigm within the telecom industry.

Keywords: Telecom Value Chain, Consumer-Managed Relationship, Group-oriented Services, Ontology-Based Consumer Profiles, Semantic Clustering.

1 Introduction

Telecom operators are turning towards new business opportunities in a global multi-service and multi-provider market. With consumers typically having several multi-purpose end-user devices and striving for making the most of pervasive Internet access, telecom operators will have to base their operations on new, consumer-centric business models. These new market demands and technological developments have led to the convergence of different domains (i.e. telecommunications, Information Technology (IT), the Internet, broadcasting and media) all involved in the telecommunications service provisioning process.

The evolution of the New-Generation Mobile Network[1] (NGMN) [1] is aimed at taking changing consumer demands into account and at creating spontaneous, adaptive services that can be delivered anytime, anywhere, to any device the consumer prefers. Therefore, the realization of the full potential of convergence will make it necessary for telecom operators to deploy a dynamic, cooperative and business-aware consistent knowledge layer in the network architecture in order to enable ubiquitous personalized services. Providing such personalized services to the consumer transparently is not only challenging from a technical point of view, but also imposes severe requirements on the telecom operator's business policies.

---

[1] Use Cases related to Self Organizing Network, Overall Description (New-Generation Mobile Networks Alliance Report): http://www.ngmn.org/

N.T. Nguyen and R. Kowalczyk (Eds.): Transactions on CCI II, LNCS 6450, pp. 70–89, 2010.
© Springer-Verlag Berlin Heidelberg 2010

This paradigm shift towards Consumer-Managed Relationships (CMR) in the telecom industry should include innovative services and create added value for consumers, considering every consumer as a specific individual. The challenge for telecom operators is twofold: the first is how to "profile" the mobile consumer; and second is how to include these consumer profiles into the new telecom value chain. In this paper, we first address the latter issue by explaining the structure of the new telecom value chain (Section 2) and then solve the former challenge by proposing ontology-based consumer profiles (Section 3). In Section 4 we conduct an evaluation of our ideas on a special type of personalized telecom service, a group-oriented service called Agent-Based Mobile Content Brokerage (ABC-Broker). Section 5 concludes the paper.

2 The New Telecom Value Chain

Consumers no longer buy products and services - they buy value, i.e. the total package of product performance, access, experience and cost [2]. Yoon in [3] introduces a novel concept for the NGMN called Telco 2.0, based on:

- the evolution of the consumer lifestyle;
- new Information and Communication Technology (ICT) trends and
- the need for novel business models in the telecom industry.

Telco 2.0 presents the telecom operator's new role and business models in the Internet Protocol (IP) world, introduced in order to create added value for consumers. In the NGMN, a consumer's value depends on her/his preferences (i.e. preferred service delivery type, preferred genre of music or movies). A new lifestyle will lead individual consumers to be interested in "personalized", "intelligent", "mobile", "fun", and "sensible" services [3]. In order to make the necessary enhancements, telecom operators are confronted with a new telecom value chain[2].

Fig. 1 a) illustrates the concept behind the new telecom value chain that we firstly introduced in [4], while Fig. 1 b) compares it to the traditional one. In the traditional telecom value chain, the greatest value is comprised in the network infrastructure – i.e. hardware entities and technologies which enable communication. Therefore, introduction of new services affects only the internal telecom operators' value chain. Moreover, the traditional telecom value chain usually has no external components at all. Nowadays, with the growth of service complexity, telecom operators should not only provide a medium for communication, but added value for consumers as well. Therefore, the provisioning of new services requires changes in both the internal and external value chains of telecom operators. The new telecom value chain consists of three entities:

- consumers;
- telecom operators and
- storage providers

described in the following three subsections.

---

[2] In this paper we assume that telecom operators are at the same time service and infrastructure providers. Here we do not analyze scenarios where services are provisioned by 3rd party businesses.

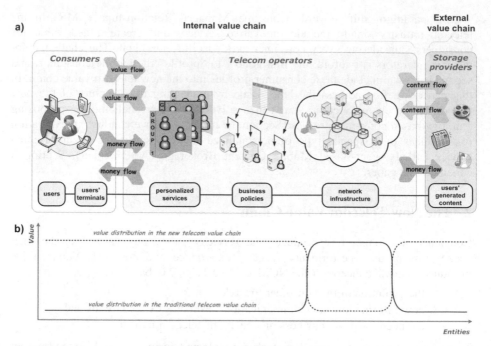

Fig. 1. The new telecom value chain

2.1 Consumers

In 1991, Mark Weiser introduced his vision for the 21st century: a concept of *ubiquitous computing* (now also called *pervasive computing* or *ambient intelligence*). "The most profound technologies are those that disappear", he wrote. "They weave themselves into the fabric of everyday life until they are indistinguishable from it" [5]. With these words, Weiser envisions computers as invisible tools that are quickly forgotten but always with us, while effortlessly used throughout our lives [6]. It is important to note that computers are not physically invisible, but as a part of the context of use. At that time Weiser also identified three main eras of computing [7]:

- *The First Era* – the era of *mainframes* (one computer, many people);
- *The Second Era* – the era of *personal computing* (one person, one computer);
- *The Third Era* – the era of *ubiquitous computing* (one person, many computers).

Continuous advances in wireless technologies and mobile telecommunication systems, along with the rapid proliferation of various types of portable devices, have advanced Weiser's vision towards technical and economic viability [8]. His ideas are becoming a reality with the new generation of mobile communication systems [9, 10].

In [3], Yoon defines the *evaluation of the consumer lifestyle* as digital humanism which satisfies a human's five senses and allows real life-like experiences. Everyday activities are becoming more digitized, intelligent and easier to use, enabling people to create their own context. By taking active part in the creation of content (e.g. text blogging, mobile blogging, video, podcasting, mobile phone photography and "wikis") consumers are becoming *prosumers* [11]. Prosumer content (i.e. consumer-generated content) is becoming more appreciated than company advertisements (i.e. business-generated content). Namely, content recommended by friends is more often trustworthy than content generated by companies whose main goal is to make a profit. Due to the content generated by prosumers, *value* and *money* flows go in both directions between consumers and telecom providers.

2.2 Telecom Operators

Yoon in [3] defines *new ICT trends*, explaining how it is no longer enough to only deliver voice and data to consumers, but also deliver broadcasting (e.g. Internet TV and radio), computing power, storage, entertainment, etc. Nowadays, consumers demand a certain Quality of Service (QoS) for the price they pay to the telecom. QoS is no longer considered merely good mobile signal coverage and good signal quality, but personalized services as well. The infrastructure and servers of telecom operators do not suffice to gratify the QoS demands of today's consumers. Therefore, they change their own business policies in order to provide *personalized services*.

Personalized Services

Most personalization systems are based on some type of consumer profile where collected information can represent the interests or preferences of either a group of consumers or a single consumer. The connection between consumers and personalized services is shown in Fig. 2 [12]. In order to construct such a profile, information can be collected *explicitly* (i.e. with consumer intervention), or *implicitly* (i.e. without any knowledge of the consumer). Information stored in such profiles can be *dynamic* (i.e. can be modified) or *static* (i.e. maintains the same information over time).

After information is gathered, different technologies and/or applications are used to create consumer profiles. *Keyword profiles* are the simplest to build, but they require large amounts of feedback in order to learn the terminology behind them. The same problem exists with most *semantic network-based profiles*. In order to compare the compatibility of a consumer profile with other consumers or services, semantic matchmaking must be performed. Unlike keyword or semantic-net profiles, *concept profiles* are trained on examples for each concept *a priori* and, thus, begin with an existing mapping between vocabulary and concepts. Building concept profiles requires less feedback from the consumer and they are more robust to variations in terminology.

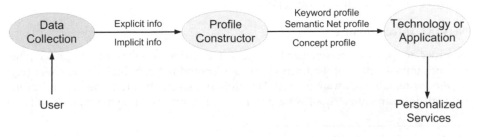

Fig. 2. An overview of consumer-profile-based personalization [12]

Business Policies

Modern companies, such as financial institutions, insurance companies and telecom operators, have begun collecting large amounts of information regarding their customers. They use such information to achieve a more proactive and personalized approach to service provisioning. Such an approach is commonly referred to as Consumer Relationship Management (CRM). The CRM paradigm is currently one of the basic tasks of Business Intelligence (BI).

The logical next step towards a higher level of service provisioning is introducing the Consumer-Managed Relationship (CMR) paradigm. A CMR is a relationship in which a company (i.e. a telecom operator) uses a methodology, software and perhaps Internet capabilities to encourage the customer (i.e. a telecom service consumer) to control access to information and ordering (Table 1).

Table 1. CRM to CMR comparison[3]

CRM	CMR
The company is in control.	The consumer is in control.
Makes business better for the company.	Makes business better for the consumer.
Tracks consumers by transaction needs.	Understands each consumer is unique.
Treats consumers as segments.	Treats consumers as individuals.
Forces consumers to do what the company cares about.	Lets consumers express what they believe they will want.
Consumers feel stalked.	Consumers are empowered.
Organized around products and services.	Organized around consumers.

When a company applies the CMR paradigm, its consumers gain control of information pertaining to them (i.e. their profiles, transaction history). Moreover, a company should model its business policy in such a way that consumer needs and feelings have priority, or are at least of equal weight as company needs and desires. Additionally, the CMR paradigm encourages customers to specify the way in which they wish to communicate with the company, claim their interest in services or products, and modify the charging policy.

Network Infrastructure

In order to provide personalized services for different types of consumers, the network infrastructure of the telecom operator should not only include hardware (e.g. servers, wires), but software as well. We propose using software agents as part of the network infrastructure. A software agent is a program which autonomously acts on

---

[3] Differences between CMR and CRM:
http://e-articles.info/e/a/title/Differences-between-CMR-and-CRM

behalf of its principal, while carrying out complex information and communication tasks that have been delegated to it. The concept of software agents appeared in the mid-1990's [13] and resulted in the application of an agent-based computing paradigm in various research domains [14, 15, 16, 17]. A system composed of several software agents, collectively capable of reaching goals that are difficult to achieve by an individual agent or a monolithic system, is called a Multi-Agent System (MAS).

2.3 Storage Providers

A *need for novel telecom business models* [3] requires expansion of the telecom value chain. While consumers and network operators are in the internal part of the new telecom value chain, storage providers are in the external part. Yoon in [3] predicts that the boundaries of existing business domains will disappear, leading towards the promotion of higher convergence between different industries.

Storage providers are used as "extended storages" for large amounts of telecom operator data. They do not provide content, but only store it. Consequently, there is no *value* flow between telecom operators and storage providers. Telecom operators define available services, but they do not own the required technology for content storage (e.g. data disaster recovery, safe copies). Therefore, they must purchase the required space and services from storage providers (i.e. the *money* flow goes from telecom operators towards storage providers).

When new content is generated, it needs to be stored. Therefore, the *content* flow is also directed from telecom operators towards storage providers. On the other hand, when a consumer wants to purchase certain content stored at such a storage provider, the content flow then goes from the storage provider towards the telecom operator.

Generally, telecom services consist of content which can be *consumer-generated* or *business-generated*. In this paper, we propose usage of User-Generated Content (UGC) (also known as Consumer-Generated Media (CGM) or User-Created Content (UCC)[4]). UGC refers to various kinds of media content, publicly available, that is produced by end-users and delivered over network resources.

3 Consumer Profiling

Traditional IT solutions must be upgraded with mechanisms which enable *advanced consumer profile management*. Such management includes creation, storage and continuous updating of consumer profiles, as well as autonomous analysis and matchmaking of those profiles with service/product descriptions. When a company which introduces the CMR paradigm acts on the market as a telecom operator, it needs an integrated IT system which does not support just traditional telecom operations, but also enables advanced consumer profile management. Such an approach has recently been introduced in the market by some service providers (e.g. the iPhone App Store[5]).

---

[4] User-Created Content: http://www.oecd.org/dataoecd/57/14/38393115.pdf

[5] iPhone App Store:
http://www.apple.com/iphone/iphone-3gs/app-store.html

The innovation in our proposal is that it gives a solution grounded on Semantic Web technologies and software agent paradigm. This novel solution should therefore enable telecom operators to transform their business models from CRM to CMR.

3.1 Semantic Technologies

We use Semantic Web technologies for dynamic mobile service consumer clustering and group-oriented service provisioning. These technologies are used to model a system based on consumer and service profiles, semantic reasoning and clustering. We consider semantic markup to be a very efficient method for resource matchmaking and ultimately better recognition of consumer needs.

The Semantic Web is a vision in which knowledge is organized into conceptual spaces according to meaning, and keyword-based searches are replaced by semantic query answering [18]. Semantic Web languages, such as Resource Description Framework[6] (RDF), RDF Schema[7] (RDFS) and the Web Ontology Language[8] (OWL), are used to provide structure for resource description (i.e. service and consumer profiles).

Using various query languages, based on Structured Query Language (SQL) syntax, it is possible to perform semantic data extraction, thus enabling efficient matchmaking for consumer and service profiles once they have been created according to a certain standard. Such matchmaking enables consumer clustering to be performed according to true, semantic similarities, rather than keyword matchmaking. Semantic query languages possess a number of features in which they differ from SQL queries due to Semantic Web knowledge. These queries can be either *asserted* (explicitly stated) or *inferred* (implicit), and are *network structured,* rather than *relational.* Also, the Semantic Web assumes an Open World Model (OWM) in which the failure to derive a fact does not imply the opposite [19], as opposed to *closed world* reasoning where all relations that cannot be found are considered false [20].

In our implementation, information was retrieved by means of RDF Data Query Language (RDQL) and Sesame RDF Query Language (SeRQL) queries. A Sesame [21] repository with OWL support [22] was utilized to store the required knowledge.

3.2 Consumer Profiles

Mobile consumers are represented through their semantic profiles. Additionally, telecom operators maintain profiles of all available services. Each consumer and service profile can be described using static and dynamic attributes.

The World Wide Web Consortium (W3C) is working on the Composite Capabilities/Preferences Profile[9] (CC/PP), an RDF-based specification which describes device capabilities and consumer preferences used to guide the adaptation of content presented to that device. It is structured to allow a client to describe its capabilities by reference to a standard profile, accessible to an origin server or other sender of resource

---

[6] RDF specifications: http://www.w3.org/RDF/
[7] RDFS specifications: http://www.w3.org/TR/rdf-schema/
[8] OWL specifications: http://www.w3.org/TR/owl-features/
[9] CC/PP specifications: http://www.w3.org/Mobile/CCPP/

data and a smaller set of features that are, in addition to, or different than the standard profile. A set of CC/PP attribute names, permissible values and associated meanings constitute a CC/PP vocabulary.

Open Mobile Alliance's (OMA) User Agent Profile[10] (UAProf) specification, based on the CC/PP, is concerned with capturing classes of mobile device capabilities which include the hardware and software characteristics of the device. Such information is used for content formatting, but not for content selection purposes. The UAProf specification does not define the structure of consumer preferences in the profile.

Our implementation extends the CC/PP and UAProf specifications and maps them to an OWL ontology in order to create mobile consumer profiles, as shown in Fig. 3. The opening and the closing rows must be defined according to EXtensible Markup Language (XML) and RDF specifications, while the remaining rows contain information about the consumer. We distinguish between five different types of consumer information:

- *identification* (i.e. International Mobile Equipment Identity (IMEI));
- *consumer preferences* (i.e. *preferred service delivery type*, *preferred genre* for music or movies);
- *mobile device hardware* (i.e. *screen resolution*, *available memory*);
- *software capabilities* (i.e. *Java version*, *Web browser*, *operating system*);
- *business information* (i.e. download and upload ratio).

Identification and mobile device hardware are both fairly static components which change quite rarely (e.g. when a consumer purchases a new mobile device). Software capabilities are somewhat more dynamic and can be changed depending on consumer actions (e.g. a consumer can install additional software). Consumer preferences and business information are highly dynamic and can change after each service consummation (e.g. consumer preference discovery is based on most recent services the consumer has consumed).

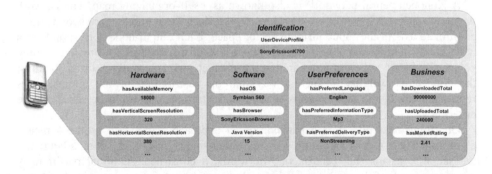

Fig. 3. An example of a consumer profile

---

[10] UAProf specification: http://www.openmobilealliance.org/

3.3 Consumer Clustering

Clustering is a process that results in the partitioning of a set of objects, depending on a set of attributes, into clusters. Clustering algorithms rely on distance measures that describe the similarity between the objects that need to be grouped. Consequently, objects in common clusters are more similar to one another than to those in other clusters. In our case, we compare consumer profiles to partition consumers into groups. Such partitioning enables telecom operators to enhance the provisioning of group-oriented services. Common clustering methods include *partition-based* and *hierarchical* approaches, as well as *Kohonen neural networks*, all of which use specific distance measures.

A partition-based approach includes *k-means* and Partitioning Around Medoids (PAM). The idea is to partition a set of objects into multiple non-overlapping clusters. A partition-based technique creates an initial partition depending on a specific number of clusters and then attempts to improve the partition iteratively by moving objects between or among clusters.

The hierarchical clustering approach starts by building a binary clustering hierarchy (i.e. a tree). Each leaf node represents an object to be clustered. Hierarchical clustering methods can be further classified into *agglomerative* or *divisive*, depending on whether the clustering hierarchy is formed in a bottom-up or top-down fashion. The Hierarchical Agglomerative Clustering (HAC) algorithm uses a bottom-up strategy, starting with as many clusters as there are objects. Based on an inter-cluster similarity measure of choice, the two most similar clusters then merge to form a new cluster. This process is continued until either a hierarchy emerges, where a single cluster remains at the top of the hierarchy containing all the target objects, or the process reaches a specified termination condition (e.g. inter-cluster similarity less than a specified threshold). In contrast, the Hierarchical Divisive Clustering (HDC) algorithm employs a top-down strategy, starting with all the objects in a single cluster. The cluster is then divided into its two most distinct clusters. The division process is repeated until either each object is part of a distinct cluster or the process reaches a specified condition (e.g. intra-cluster similarity greater than a specified threshold).

A Kohonen neural network[11] is also known as a self-organizing map. The network is an unsupervised two-layer neural network. Each input node corresponds to a coordinate axis in the input attribute vector space. Each output node corresponds to a node in a two-dimensional grid and the network is fully connected. During the training phase, all objects to be clustered are fed into the network repeatedly in order to adjust the connection weights in such a way that the distribution of the output nodes represents that of the input objects. The input vector space distribution serves as the criterion.

Our implementation uses a partition-based approach referred to as the k-means algorithm. The k-means algorithm starts by initializing (randomly or using a heuristic) the set of k means (i.e. centroids). Afterwards, it constructs an initial partition by associating each of the n objects with the closest of k centroids: as a result, k clusters are generated. Next, the k-means algorithm recalculates the centroids of each cluster based on objects currently associated with that particular cluster: a new centroid is

---

[11] Kohonen neural network: `http://mlab.taik.fi/~timo/som/thesis-som.html`

calculated as the mean of all objects in the cluster. The algorithm alternates between these two steps until they converge, i.e. when the points no longer switch clusters, centroids are no longer changed or a certain criterion is reached.

Partitioning consumers into groups by comparing consumer profiles enables the mobile operator to enhance the provisioning of group-oriented services. In our implementation, we do not use standard distance measures to compare profiles, but rather take advantage of a novel approach based on semantic matchmaking [23, 24].

Even though the k-means algorithm is quite intuitive and can be used in different environments, there are certain disadvantages. The most obvious is the predefined number of groups. Without sufficient analysis, it is difficult to predict the optimal number of groups. Another shortfall of the k-means algorithm is the random centroid selection at the beginning of the clustering procedure. This can result in different object partitions for the same set of objects. These shortcomings can be resolved by implementing additional clustering analysis algorithms, as described in the following paragraph.

In order to optimize clustering, we extend the k-means algorithm with the *constructive clustering analysis* method that determines the quality of the partition [25]. The main task of the constructive clustering analysis method is finding the optimal number of clusters for a given set of objects. This method uses the so-called *silhouette measure* to determine the optimal number of clusters. To perform constructive clustering, it is necessary to use one of the non-constructive analysis algorithms (e.g. k-means) to perform clustering for a given number of clusters. The silhouette measure is calculated for each object in the given set, taking into account the resulting partition. It is calculated as follows:

$$
s(i) = \begin{cases} 1 - \dfrac{a(i)}{b(i)} & \text{if } a(i) < b(i) \\ 0 & \text{if } a(i) = b(i), \text{or the object is the only object in cluster } \mathcal{A} \\ \dfrac{a(i)}{b(i)} - 1 & \text{if } b(i) < a(i) \end{cases}
$$

where $s(i)$ is the silhouette measure of object o_i, cluster $\mathcal{A}$ is the cluster containing object o_i, $a(i)$ is the average distance of object o_i to all other objects in cluster $\mathcal{A}$, and $b(i)$ is the average distance of object o_i to all other objects in cluster $\mathcal{B}$, which is the *neighbor* of object o_i. The neighboring cluster is the cluster closest to the observed object, different from cluster $\mathcal{A}$. Usually it is the second best choice for o_i. The next step is calculating the *average silhouette width* for the object set, calculated as the average value of the silhouette measures of all objects in the given partition. When we obtain the average silhouette widths for all sets of k clusters, where k is between 2 and $n - 1$ (and n denotes the total number of objects to be clustered), the highest one is deemed the *silhouette coefficient*. The value of k yielding this silhouette coefficient is the optimal number of clusters.

Consumer clustering is a process that can become highly time-consuming in a realistic environment. Our implementation was tested on a small number of profiles (up to fifty) in order to determine the dependency between the number of consumers and the necessary time to perform the clustering described earlier in this section. The results are presented in Fig. 4.

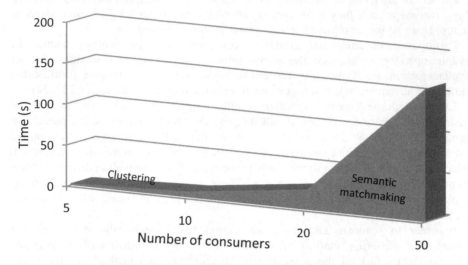

Fig. 4. Correlation between execution time and the number of consumer profiles

In Fig. 4, we can see that semantic matchmaking takes significantly more time than clustering (i.e. clustering takes less than two percent of the execution time for fifty consumer profiles). The time correlation for clustering is nearly linear, but for semantic matchmaking it is nearly quadratic. Such a correlation presents a great optimization challenge, indicating that the entire clustering process is not a task that can realistically be performed on a day-to-day basis, but periodically or when necessary (i.e. when a large number of consumers enter the system in a short period of time, or when there is a critical number of profiles changes).

Therefore, it is necessary to implement an algorithm which enables classification of new consumers into existing clusters depending on their profiles. We propose using the *k-Nearest Neighbors* (*k-NN*) algorithm, a machine learning-based classification method. *k-NN* is one of the most thoroughly analyzed algorithms in machine learning, partly due to its age and partly to its simplicity [26]. It is a classification algorithm grounded on the preposition that the similarity of target function values of instances corresponds to their relative nearness. This algorithm assumes all instances correspond to vectors in an n-dimensional Euclidean space, where their attributes are represented by their coordinates. However, due *k-NN*'s heuristic nature, the classification of a number of new examples into clusters may not comprise instances that are the most similar to each other. Therefore, semantic clustering should be performed every time a predefined number of new profiles has been reached.

4   Agent-Based Mobile Content Brokerage

Group-oriented services are a novel approach to *non-linear* service provisioning. Clustering consumers with similar preferences and mobile devices into groups can automate service advertising and the provisioning processes. This section provides more detailed insight into why and how we propose to introduce group-oriented services into the business policies of telecom operators.

4.1 Telecom Service Provisioning

The Consumer Buying Behaviour (CBB) model introduced in [27] explains the need for the introduction of group-oriented services (see Fig. 5). In our work, this CBB process is strictly linear, and we do not use more than one iteration to complete it (i.e. the purchase and delivery phases do not affect the negotiation phase). Fig. 5 shows this general simplification of CBB processes.

In our system, consumers are represented by their agents (see paragraph 4.4) that act in five stages: *need identification*, *product brokering*, *buyer coalition formation*, *merchant brokering* and *negotiation*. During these phases, the consumer agent must first detect a consumer's need for a certain service, then form a group of consumers with similar preferences and finally purchase it.

In [28] we discussed how software agents can automate product brokering, merchant brokering and negotiation. In this paper, we propose forming buyer coalitions through group-oriented services. Semantic profiles and matchmaking are used for identification of consumer needs and group formation. Afterwards, a group of consumers has to act as one consumer. Group coordination can be achieved using self-organization mechanisms [29].

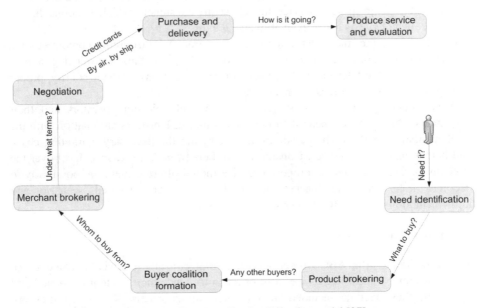

Fig. 5. The Consumer Buying Behavior model [27]

4.2 Group-Oriented Services

Group-oriented services for mobile consumers are a special type of *personalized services* which the future of mobile communications is evolving towards. We define a group-oriented service as a telecommunication service that is provisioned to a group of consumers with certain similarities (e.g. similar preferences, devices and/or context).

The main idea behind group-oriented services is grouping consumers into clusters by taking into account consumer interests, characteristics of their devices and the context in which they find themselves when requesting a service. To achieve this, it is necessary to introduce a rather new approach in the service provisioning process: building implicit social networks of mobile consumers. Unlike explicit social networks (e.g. Facebook[12], MySpace[13] or LinkedIn[14]), implicit networks are built autonomously, based on similarities of consumer profiles, without the interference of the consumers themselves and in order to provide useful information for telecom operators. Such a novel approach enables telecom operators to predict the future interests of consumers based on information gained by tracking the behavior of a group of consumers.

In order to examine the benefits and shortcomings of such an approach, we introduce a proof-of-concept group-oriented service called Agent-Based Mobile Content Brokerage (ABC-Broker). The basic idea of the proposed service is for telecom operators to take on a non-traditional role in the value chain. Instead of generating value and content, these tasks are shifted towards the consumers (i.e. the realization of the evolution of the consumer towards the prosumer).

The role of telecom operators in the ABC-Broker service is content brokerage and implementation of business policies. Such an approach, described in section 2, encourages consumers to generate innovative content (e.g. audio, video, information). Additionally, we propose a service model where consumers which generate highly popular content have a chance even at financial gain.

In addition to the traditional value chain, we propose outsourcing content storage services to specialized companies (as shown in Fig. 1), thus, introducing a new stakeholder into the telecom market. Such companies can ensure data security, proper storage volume and the necessary bandwidth.

This model is expected to be beneficial for both telecom operators and their consumers. Operators will benefit from business and ICT process automation with the implementation of the CMR paradigm, thus reducing the necessary marketing costs, and human and ICT resources. Consumers will benefit with a greater control over the telecom market and from the proposed service model offering them the possibility to become more important market stakeholders. A more detailed scenario and implementation of the ABC-Broker service follows.

4.3 Proof-of-Concept Scenario

The main idea of the ABC-Broker service is that consumers generate content that other consumers might like to see, read or listen to. Once their content is created and uploaded, they become included in a market rating system. Their activities are measured according to multiple attributes: downloaded and uploaded content, market success, granted revenue, etc. Consumer ratings grow as they accumulate downloads

---

[12] Facebook: http://www.facebook.com
[13] MySpace: http://www.myspace.com
[14] LinkedIn: http://www.linkedin.com

of their own generated content. Once a consumer reaches a certain market rating, she/he can start sharing profit with the telecom operator (i.e. the ABC-Broker service provider). Consequently, consumers remain motivated to upload further content.

Consider the following example. A consumer uploads a video of a certain size and is charged x money units for the generated traffic. This fee can be considered as a form of investment. Each consumer that downloads that movie is also charged x money units, but a part of the download fee becomes revenue for the author (e.g. 1% of the fee). This revenue can then be used to gain a discount when consuming other services. When the video reaches a certain number of downloads (e.g. 100 downloads), the author will have repaid her/his upload fee in its entirety and will start earning money. Also, by accumulating more downloads, her/his market rating becomes higher. Implementing the CMR paradigm in such an environment brings consumers and telecom operators closer to a business partner relationship.

If consumers of the ABC-Broker service want to download certain video, audio or any other content, they can browse available content in three categories:

1) the optimal content for the group they belong to;
2) the most recent content uploaded by someone in the same group, and, finally;
3) the most popular content overall.

Consumer groups and content compatibility are calculated using semantic matchmaking as described in section 3.3. Such an approach enables better understanding of consumer preferences and improves service personalization.

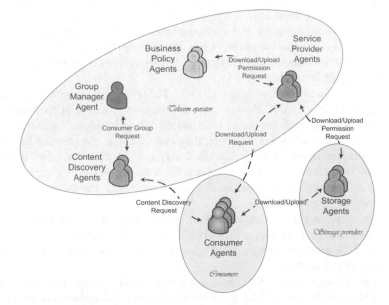

Fig. 6. Multi-agent system implementation

4.4 Proof-of-Concept Implementation

The ABC-Broker service is implemented as a MAS which consists of six types of agents, shown in Fig. 6:

- *The Consumer Agent* (CA): Each consumer is presented by her/his Consumer Agent. The CA is activated on the consumer's mobile device. This agent is in charge of maintaining the consumer profile and communicating any preference or device changes to the telecom operator. Furthermore, this agent manages the consumer's service negotiation process starting with the request, through service discovery and selection, and finally the decision whether or not to download or upload certain content.
- *The Group Manager Agent* (GMA): The GMA is a single agent active on the telecom operator's server. It performs periodic consumer clustering using the *k-means* and *constructive clustering analysis algorithms,* and new consumer classification using a selected algorithm (i.e. *k-NN* [30]). The GMA also provides, on request, a list of members in each group.
- *The Content Discovery Agent* (CDA): In cooperation with the GMA, CDAs provide a list of the most popular content, the most recently uploaded content, and/or a list of content most likely to be interesting to consumers in a certain group. The last one is obtained through semantic matchmaking of consumer and service profiles (i.e. ABC-Broker service description of certain content). This process is very similar to semantic matchmaking of consumer profiles during clustering. The basic difference is that consumer profile matchmaking is symmetric, whilst consumer and service profile matchmaking must have a reference value. For example, if one consumer's screen has a resolution of *5 megapixels*, and another's has *3 megapixels* their similarity is *0.6*. However, when comparing the first consumers screen resolution to that of a movie that has a resolution of *3 megapixels*. The result of the matchmaking is *1*.
- *The Business Policy Agent* (BPA): These agents represent the telecom operator in the ABC-Broker service purchase process. BPAs keep track of consumer-related business information (i.e. business information in a consumer profile). For example, they can calculate the revenue based on the consumer market rating, download and upload ratio, or other information describing consumer activity. Also, BPA agents perform charging tasks. In general, these agents are in charge of enforcing the business policies of telecom operators.
- *The Service Provider Agent* (SPA): SPAs perform the final step in content download from storage providers. Once the negotiation process is finished, an SPA grants or denies the consumer's request to download or upload the associated content.
- *The Storage Agent* (SA): SAs are active at the storage provider's servers. They handle requests from telecom operators and consumers by providing Uniform Resource Identifiers (URI) with information as to where the consumer can upload the proposed content. Furthermore, they validate the

existing content before download, and verify the consumer's identity before download or upload. The authentication and authorization security mechanisms for storage are not a part of the proposed MAS.

Agent-based communication between the telecom operator, storage provider and consumers is based on the following three basic processes: *Content Discovery*, *Download Request* and *Upload Proposal*. Besides these three basic processes, there are certain problems that should also be addressed. The service model must encourage mobile consumers to post and download content. This can be achieved by granting revenue to those consumers who post the most popular content, arranging discounts for consumers with high download or upload rates, etc. Additionally, the telecom operator must ensure that the disclaimer content is genuine and non-offensive during the sign-up process. A similar policy has already been introduced by some Web sites that present mainly consumer-generated content (e.g. *Triond*[15]). Additionally, the telecom operator should identify non-popular content since such content costs the telecom operator much more than the value of the revenue it generates from consumer downloads, and as such should be removed. The *"popularity threshold"* should be defined in agreement between the telecom operator and consumers (i.e. if a movie has less than a certain number of downloads it should be regarded as non-popular and removed).

Content Discovery

A consumer (CA_i) can request a list of content from the telecom operator (see Fig. 7). The list can be comprised of the content that is optimal for her/his group (*list (Optimal)*), the most recently posted content (*list (Recent)*), or the most popular content overall (*list (Top)*). The *optimal list* is obtained by semantic matchmaking of consumer profiles in a consumer group and available service profiles (i.e. ABC-Broker service description of certain content). The *recent list* is a list of content most recently posted by members of the consumer group. On the other hand, the most popular content list is not restricted to the consumer group, i.e. it contains the most popular content overall.

Download Request

A download starts with a request from the consumer agent, which is then acknowledged by the telecom operator (see Fig. 8). The telecom operator (ABC-Broker service provider) then checks the availability of the content with the storage provider. If the content is not available, the consumer is informed. If the content is available, the SPA must check with the BPA whether there are any financial obstacles for the download to commence. If not, the consumer is informed she/he can initiate the download by accessing the given content URI. If the consumer decides not to go through with the download, the storage provider will inform the telecom operator that no download initiation has occurred in a given period of time. If the consumer initiates the download, it begins after the storage provider has acknowledged the

---

[15] Triond: http://www.triond.com/

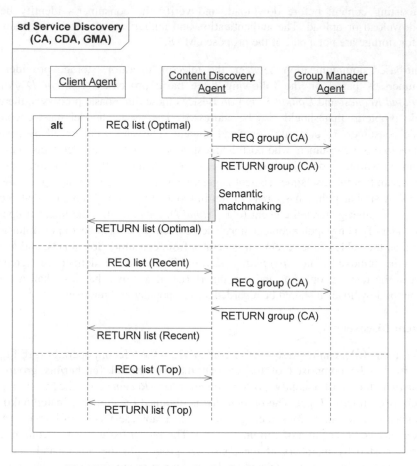

Fig. 7. Sequence diagram for the *Content Discovery* process

request. Once the download is finished, the storage provider informs the service provider who then updates the business information in the consumer profile.

Upload Proposal

This process is very similar to Download Request handling. The difference is that the telecom operator must assess the content and place it in right place in the ABC-Broker service ontology. This process is perhaps too complex to be performed autonomously by software agents, and too delicate to be shifted to mobile consumers. We propose that this process be done manually, with a slight delay after upload. This would slightly postpone introduction of content to potential consumers, but is essential for maintaining the proper QoS.

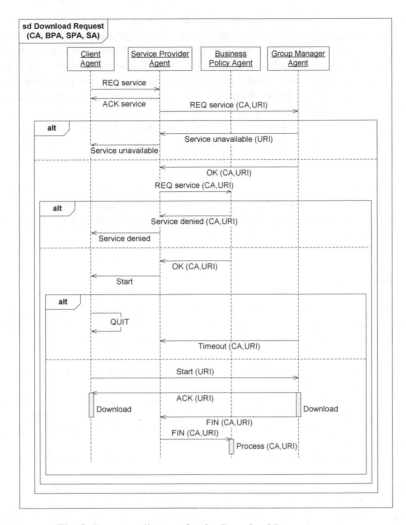

Fig. 8. Sequence diagram for the *Download Requests* process

5   Conclusion and Future Work

In this paper, we describe how ontology-based and agent-supported consumer profiling can affect the course of telecom service provisioning, enabling its personalization. The CC/PP and UAProf schemas are mapped to an OWL ontology, and features for consumer preferences and business-related information are added. Furthermore, a semantic clustering algorithm was implemented, enabling the grouping of consumers according to their profiles. Finally, a proof-of-concept group-oriented service, demonstrating the advantages of combining the semantic and agent technologies, is presented.

Our future research will be focused on the following three challenges. The first challenge is in the technical domain based on how to improve the proposed semantic clustering feature. In particular, we will place emphasis on implementation of a solution which is suitable for dealing with multidimensional data sets, such as consumer profiles, both with respect to scalability and computational-efficiency. The second challenge is the problem of placing new content into an existing ontology. We will analyze the possibilities for automating this process with software agents or additional software tools. Third, we will further analyze the economic viability of our proposed group-oriented service, with the aim of creating a general business policy framework for group-oriented services in the NGMN.

Acknowledgements. This work was carried out within research project 036-0362027-1639 "Content Delivery and Mobility of Users and Services in New Generation Networks", supported by the Ministry of Science, Education and Sports of the Republic of Croatia.

References

1. Knightson, K., Morita, N., Towle, T.: NGN architecture: generic principles, functional architecture, and implementation. IEEE Communications Magazine 43(10), 49–56 (2006)
2. Kothari, A., Lackner, J.: A value based approach to management. Journal of Business and Industrial Marketing 21(4), 243–249 (2006)
3. Yoon, J.-L.: Telco 2.0: A New Role and Business Model. IEEE Communications Magazine 45(1), 10–12 (2007)
4. Podobnik, V., Trzec, K., Jezic, G.: Context-Aware Service Provisioning in Next-Generation Networks: An Agent Approach. In: Alkhatib, G., Rine, D. (eds.) Agent Technologies and Web Engineering: Applications and Systems, pp. 19–38. Information Science Reference, Hershey (2009)
5. Weiser, M.: The Computer for the 21st Century. Scientific American 265(3), 94–104 (1991)
6. Weiser, M.: The World is not a Desktop. ACM Interactions 1(1), 7–8 (1994)
7. Weiser, M., Brown, J.S.: The Coming Age of Calm Technology. In: Dening, P.J., Metcalfe, R.M., Burke, J. (eds.) Beyond Calculation: The Next Fifty Years of Computing, pp. 75–86. Springer, New York (1997)
8. Saha, D., Mukherjee, A.: Pervasive Computing: A Paradigm for the 21st Century. IEEE Computer 36(3), 25–31 (2003)
9. Dumic, G., Podobnik, V., Jezic, G., Trzec, K., Petric, A.: An Agent-Based Optimization of Service Fulfillment in Next-Generation Telecommunication Systems. In: 9th International Conference on Telecommunications (ConTEL), pp. 57–63. IEEE, Zagreb (2007)
10. Ljubi, I., Podobnik, V., Jezic, G.: Cooperative Mobile Agents for Automation of Service Provisioning: A Telecom Innovation. In: 2nd IEEE International Conference on Digital Information Management (ICDIM), pp. 817–822. IEEE, Lyon (2007)
11. Medman, N.: Doing your own thing on the net. Ericsson Business Review 1, 49–53 (2006)
12. Gauch, S., Speretta, M., Chandramouli, A., Micarelli, A.: User Profiles for Personalized Information Access. In: Brusilovsky, P., Kobsa, A., Nejdl, W. (eds.) Adaptive Web 2007. LNCS, vol. 4321, pp. 54–89. Springer, Heidelberg (2007)
13. Nwana, H.S.: Software Agents: An Overview. Knowledge and Engineering Review 11(3), 205–244 (1996)

14. Trzec, K., Lovrek, I., Mikac, B.: Agent Behaviour in Double Auction Electronic Market for Communication Resources. In: Gabrys, B., Howlett, R.J., Jain, L.C. (eds.) KES 2006. LNCS (LNAI), vol. 4251, pp. 318–325. Springer, Heidelberg (2006)
15. Petric, A., Podobnik, V., Jezic, G.: The CrocodileAgent: Designing a Robust Trading Agent for Volatile E-Market Conditions. In: Nguyen, N.T., Grzech, A., Howlett, R.J., Jain, L.C. (eds.) KES-AMSTA 2007. LNCS (LNAI), vol. 4496, pp. 597–606. Springer, Heidelberg (2007)
16. Bojic, I., Podobnik, V., Kusek, M.: Agent-enabled Collaborative Downloading: Towards Energy-efficient Provisioning of Group-oriented Services. In: Jędrzejowicz, P., Nguyen, N.T., Howlet, R.J., Jain, L.C. (eds.) KES-AMSTA 2010. LNCS, vol. 6071, pp. 62–71. Springer, Heidelberg (2010)
17. Podobnik, V., Matijasevic, M., Lovrek, I., Skorin-Kapov, L., Desic, S.: Agent-based Framework for Personalized Service Provisioning in Converged IP Networks. In: Kowalczyk, R., et al. (eds.) SOCASE 2009. LNCS, vol. 5907, pp. 83–94. Springer, Heidelberg (2009)
18. Antoniou, G., van Harmelen, F.: Semantic Web Primer. MIT Press, Cambridge (2004)
19. Walton, C.: Agency and the Semantic Web. Oxford University Press, New York (2007)
20. Grimm, S., Motik, B.: Closed World Reasoning in the Semantic Web through Epistemic Operators. In: 1st OWL: Experiences and Directions Workshop (OWLED), Galway (2005)
21. Broekstra, J., Kampman, A., van Harmelen, F.: Sesame: A Generic Architecture for Storing and Querying RDF and RDF Schema. In: Horrocks, I., Hendler, J.A. (eds.) ISWC 2002. LNCS, vol. 2342, pp. 54–68. Springer, Heidelberg (2002)
22. Kiryakov, A., Ognyanov, D., Manov, D.: OWLIM - A Pragmatic Semantic Repository for OWL. In: Dean, M., Guo, Y., Jun, W., Kaschek, R., Krishnaswamy, S., Pan, Z., Sheng, Q.Z. (eds.) WISE 2005 Workshops. LNCS, vol. 3807, pp. 182–192. Springer, Heidelberg (2005)
23. Grimnes, G.A., Edwards, P., Preece, A.: Instance based clustering of semantic web resources. In: Bechhofer, S. (ed.) ESWC 2008. LNCS, vol. 5021, pp. 303–317. Springer, Heidelberg (2008)
24. Dietze, S., Gugliotta, A., Domingue, J.: Conceptual Situation Spaces for Semantic Situation-Driven Processes. In: Bechhofer, S. (ed.) ESWC 2008. LNCS, vol. 5021, pp. 599–613. Springer, Heidelberg (2008)
25. Wei, C.P., Hu, P.J.-H., Kung, L., Tan, J.: E-Health Intelligence: A Multiple-Level Approach for E-Health Data Mining. In: Tan, J. (ed.) E-Health Care Information Systems: An Introduction for Students and Professionals, pp. 330–351. Wiley, San Francisco (2005)
26. Mitchell, T.: Machine Learning. McGraw-Hill, New York (1997)
27. He, M.: Designing Bidding Strategies for Autonomous Trading Agents. PhD thesis, University of Southampton, Southampton (2004)
28. Podobnik, V., Petric, A., Trzec, K., Jezic, G.: Software Agents in New Generation Networks: Towards the Automation of Telecom Processes. In: Jain, L.C., Nguyen, N.T. (eds.) Knowledge Processing and Decision Making in Agent-Based Systems, pp. 71–99. Springer, Heidelberg (2009)
29. Vrdoljak, L., Bojic, I., Podobnik, V., Kusek, M.: The AMiGO-Mob: Agent-based Middleware for Group-oriented Mobile Service Provisioning. In: 10th International Conference on Telecommunications (ConTEL), pp. 97–104. IEEE, Zagreb (2009)
30. Mitchell, T.: Machine Learning. McGraw-Hill, New York (1997)

The Semantic Web:
From Representation to Realization

Kristinn R. Thórisson[1,2], Nova Spivack[2], and James M. Wissner[2]

[1] Center for Analysis & Design of Intelligent Agents
and School of Computer Science, Reykjavik University
Menntavegur 1, 101 Reykjavik, Iceland
[2] Radar Networks, Inc.
410 Townsend Street, Suite 150, San Francisco, CA 94107 USA
thorisson@ru.is, {nova,jim}@radarnetworks.com

Abstract. A semantically-linked web of electronic information – the Semantic Web – promises numerous benefits including increased precision in automated information sorting, searching, organizing and summarizing. Realizing this requires significantly more reliable meta-information than is readily available today. It also requires a better way to represent information that supports unified management of diverse data and diverse Manipulation methods: from basic keywords to various types of artificial intelligence, to the highest level of intelligent manipulation – the human mind. How this is best done is far from obvious. Relying solely on hand-crafted annotation and ontologies, or solely on artificial intelligence techniques, seems less likely for success than a combination of the two. In this paper describe an integrated, complete solution to these challenges that has already been implemented and tested with hundreds of thousands of users. It is based on an ontological representational level we call *SemCards* that combines ontological rigour with flexible user interface constructs. SemCards are machine- and human-readable digital entities that allow non-experts to create and use semantic content, while empowering machines to better assist and participate in the process. SemCards enable users to easily create semantically-grounded data that in turn acts as examples for automation processes, creating a positive iterative feedback loop of metadata creation and refinement between user and machine. They provide a holistic solution to the Semantic Web, supporting powerful management of the full lifecycle of data, including its creation, retrieval, classification, sorting and sharing. We have implemented the SemCard technology on the semantic Web site *Twine.com*, showing that the technology is indeed versatile and scalable. Here we present the key ideas behind SemCards and describe the initial implementation of the technology.

Keywords: Semantic Web, Ontologies, Knowledge Management, User Interface, SemCards, Human-Machine Collaboration, Twine.com, Metadata.

N.T. Nguyen and R. Kowalczyk (Eds.): Transactions on CCI II, LNCS 6450, pp. 90–107, 2010.

1 Introduction

Intelligent automated retrieval, manipulation and presentation of information defines the speed of progress in much of today's high-technology work. In a world where information is at the center, any improvement is welcomed that can help automate even more of the massive amounts of data manipulation necessary. In many people's vision of the Semantic Web machines take center stage, based on a deeper knowledge of the data they manipulate than currently possible. To do so calls for metadata – data about the data. Making machines smarter at tasks such as retrieving relevant information at relevant times automatically from the vast collection, even on today's average laptop hard drive, requires much more meta-information than is available at present for this data.

Accurate metadata can only be derived from an understanding of content; classifying photographs according to what they depict, for example, is best done by a recognition of the entities in them, lighting conditions, weather, film stock, lens type used, etc. Authoring metadata for images by hand, to continue with this example, will be an impossible undertaking, even if we limited the metadata to surface phenomena such as the basic objects included in the picture, as the number of photographs generated and shared by people is increasing exponentially. Powertools designed for *manual metadata creation* would only improve the situation incrementally, not exponentially, as needed.

Although text analysis has come quite a long way and is much further advanced than image analysis, artificial intelligence techniques for analyzing text and images have a long way to go to reliably decipher the complex content of such data. The falling price of computing power could help in this respect, as image analysis is resource-intensive. This will not be sufficient, however, as *general-purpose* image analysis (read: software with "common sense") is needed to analyze and classify the full range of images produced by people based on content. On the one hand, achieving the full potential of a semantic web, leaving metadata creation to current AI technologies, will not be possible as these technologies are simply not powerful enough. This state of affairs may very possibly extend well beyond the next decade. On the other hand, because the growth of data available online is rising exponentially, and can be expected to continue to do so, manual metadata entry will never catch up to the extent necessary for significant effect. Creating the full set of ontologies by hand required for adequate machine manipulation would be a Herculean effort; waiting for the adequate machine intelligence could delay the Semantic Web for decades.

Does this mean the semantic web is unrealizable until machines become significantly smarter? Not necessarily. While we believe that neither hand-crafted ontologies nor current (or next wave) artificial intelligence techniques alone can achieve a giant leap towards the Semantic Web, a clever combination of the two could potentially achieve more than a notable improvement. The idea is that if online manual labor could somehow be augmented in such a way that it supported automatic classification, making up for its weak points, this could help move the total amount of semantically-tagged data closer to the 100% mark and help automatic processes get over the well-known "90% accuracy brick wall".

For us the question about how to achieve the vision of the Semantic Web has been, *What kind of collaborative framework will best address the building of the Semantic Web?* Most tools and methodologies designed for automating data handling are not suitable for human usage – the underlying data representations is designed for machines in ways that are not meant for human consumption. Data formats designed exclusively for human usage, such as e.g. HTML, are not suitable for machine manipulation – the data is unstructured, the process is slow, error prone and ultimately, to make it work, calls for massive amounts of machine intelligence that are well beyond today's reach.

This line of reasoning has resulted in our two-prong approach to the creation of the Semantic Web: First, we develop a system for helping people take a more structured approach to their data creation, management and manipulation and second, we develop automatic analysis mechanisms that use the human-provided structured data and framework to expand the semantic classification beyond what is possible to do by hand. We have already achieved significant progress on the first part of this approach; the second part is also well under way. Our method facilitates an iterative interaction loop between the user's information input, the automated extension of this work and subsequent monitoring of feedback on the extensions from the user.

Semantic Cards, or *SemCards*, is what we call the underlying representation of our approach. It is a technology that combines ontology creation, management/usage with the user interface in a way that supports simultaneously (a) human metadata creation, manipulation and consumption, (b) expert-user creation and maintenance of ontologies, and (c) automation services that are augmented by human-created meaningful examples of metadata and semantic relationship links, which greatly enhances their functionality and accuracy. SemCards provide an intermediate ontological representational level that allows end-users to create rich semantic networks for their information sphere.

One of the big problems with automation is low quality of results. While statistics may work reasonably in some cases as a solution to this, for any single individual the "average user" is all too often too different on too many dimensions for such an approach to be useful. The SemCard intermediate layer encourages users to create metadata and semantic links, which provides underlying automation with highly specific, user-motivated examples. The net effect is an increase in the possible collaboration between the user and the machine. Semi-intelligent processes can be usefully employed without requiring significant or immediate leaps in AI research.

From the users' perspective what we have developed is a network portal where they can organize their own information for personal use, publish any of that information to any group – be it "emails" addressed to a single individual or photo albums shared with the world – and manage the information shared with them from others, whether it is documents, books, music, etc. Under the hood are powerful ontology-driven technologies for organizing all categories of data, including access management, relational (semantic) links and display policies, in a way that is relatively transparent to the user. The result is a system that offers improved automation and control over access management, information organization and display features.

Here we describe the ideas behind our approach and give a short overivew of a use-case on the semantic Web site Twine.com. The paper is organized as follows: First we review related work, then we describe the technology underlying Sem-Cards and explain how the are used. We then describe our Web portal Twine.com, where we have implemented various user interfaces for enabling the use of Sem-Cards in a number of ways, including making semantically rich Web bookmarks, notes, blogs and semantically-annotated uploads.

2   Related Work

The full vision of the Semantic Web will require significant amounts of metadata, some of which describes entities themselves, other which describes relationships between entities. Two camps can be seen proposing rather different approaches to this problem. One extreme claims that manual creation of metadata will never work as it is not only slow and error-prone, the level to which it would have to be done would go well beyond the patience of any average user – quite possibly all. To this camp the only real option is automation. The other camp points out that automation is even more error-prone than manual creation, as current efforts to automatic semantic annotation on massive scales produces only moderate results of between 80% and 90% correct, at the very best [1]. They claim that the remaining 10% will always be beyond reach because it requires significant amounts of human-level intelligence to be done correctly. Further, as argued by Etzioni and Gribble [2], metadata augmentation has quite possibly not been done by the general user population because they have seen no benefits in doing so. Lastly, this camp points to the massive amounts of tagging and data entry done on sites such as Wikipedia, Myspace and Facebook as a proof of point that end-users are quite willing to provide (some amount of) metadata. Giving them the right tools might change this. Applications that connect casual end-users with ontologically-driven content and processes are, nevertheless, virtually non-existent.

Many efforts have focused on building digital content management with a focus on the object. Of these, our technology bears perhaps the greatest resemblance to the *Buckets* of Maly et al. [3] which are "self-contained, intelligent, and aggregative ... objects that are capable of enforcing their own terms and conditions, negotiating access, and displaying their contents". Like SemCards, Buckets are fairly self-contained, with specifications for how they should be displayed. Buckets grew out of Kahn and Wilensky's [4] proposed infrastructure for digital information services. Key to their proposal was the notion of digital object, composed of essentially the two familar parts, data and metadata. The subsequent work on FEDORA [5] saw the creation of an open-source software framework for the "storage, management, and dissemination of complex objects and the relationships among them" [6]. Buckets represent a focus on storing content in digital libraries, most likely manipulated by experts. In contrast, SemCards aim at enabling casual end-users to create metadata. Buckets are targeted to machime manipulation; SemCards are aimed at machine *manipulation* as well, but more importantly at supporting *automatically generated* meta-information. SemCards also differ from Buckets in that they are especially designed to be sharable between multiple users over mixed-architecture networks.

The Haystack [7] and Chandler[1] projects were efforts to create new user interfaces for wiewing and working with semantic objects. While this work was important – and in many ways still is – it also shows how difficult it is to lead such efforts to ultimate fruition while addressing all the key issues that must be solved. Our work on PersonalRadar followed a similar path[2], albeit always with the ultimate objective of solving the hard problems related to deployment over a WAN.

The separate representation layer provided by SemCards is a key difference between prior efforts and ours. They enable ontologically-driven constructs to be collaboratively built by ontology specialists, algorithms and end-users, encouraging them to provide examples to improve the automation. Because of this, SemCards are tolerant to end-user mistakes; the casual Internet user is not initiated to invest a lot of time in understanding the intricacies of the kinds of advanced ontologies required. Separating the two makes the automation systems more robust to manual input errors.

Other important differences between our approach and prior work are an integrated ability to share data between individuals and groups of users over a network, with complex policy control over access and sharing, and the flexible use of SemCards to represent metadata for real-world objects and hypothetical constructs - as "library index cards for digital content, physical things and abstract ideas".

Although current enterprise portals are capable of organizing group or team information, they are often inaccessible to the public or to individuals, and they are expensive as they are highly monolithic. Even less utilitarian and intelligent with respect to organizing information are the popular online search engines which are deisgned for largely unstructured data. Furthermore, these typically organize information and data by relevance to keywords. We have built a network portal, *Twine.com*, for deploying the SemCard technology. Twine.com provides a test of the strength of our semantic object framework when deployed over the Internet and working in an integrated, coordinated manner. Our work sets itself apart from prior work on the Semantic Web in that it has already been tested with a relatively large number of end users, with measurable results.

---

[1] http://chandlerproject.org

[2] PersonalRadar was a desktop application that we developed around the same time that Chandler became public, and in some ways it presented similar solutions to the semnatic interface; the semantic search/filtering interface for PersonalRadar was, however, vastly superior to anything we have seen so for proposed for that purpose. Unfortunately the numerous excellent interface ideas developed for PersonalRadar are still not supported by Twine as it is virtually impossible to implement these methods over a standard network link.

3   SemCards: Semantic Objects for Collaborative Ontology-Driven Information Management

A single *SemCard* can be characterized as an intuitive user interface construct that bridges between a user and an underlying ontology that affords all the benefits of a Semantic Web such as automatic relationship discovery, sorting, data mining, semantic search, etc. Together many SemCards form semantic nets that are in every way the embodiment of what many have envisioned the Semantic Web to be. Instead of being complex, convoluted and non-intuitive as any machine-manipulatable ontology will appear to the uninitiated (c.f. [8]), SemCards provide a powerful and intuitive interface to a unified framework for managing information.

As mentioned above, SemCards form an intermediate separation layer between ontologies and the user interface. By isolating the stochastic nature of end-user activity from underlying semantic networks built with ontological rigour, two important goals are achieved. First, end-users are encouraged to create meta-data for their content, as the input methods are familiar and straight-forward. SemCards shield the deep ontology from being affected by end-user activity. This does not only help stabilize the system, it also helps the automation processes from having to deal with the "ground shifting from underneath". Second, the automation processes are provided with manually-created semantic nets, created directly and continuously by end-users, that serve as examples and can be used to improve the automatic metadata creation. The net result of this is a significant improvement in automation quality and speed, including automation of many tedious details of information management such as data sharing policy maintenance, indexing, sorting – in fact, the of the full data management lifecycle.

3.1   Structure of a SemCard

In its simplest version a SemCard will appear to the user as a form with fields or slots. A SemCard has one template and one or more instances, corresponding roughly to the object-oriented programming concepts of object template/class, and object instance, respectively. Under the hood their slots are ontologically defined; however, the end user normally does not see this. To take an example, a SemCard for holding an e-mail message may look exactly like any interface to a regular email program. However, the slots ("To:", "From:", etc.) reference an ontology that defines what kinds of data each slot can take, what type of information that is, etc. The e-mail SemCard, when created, will contain information about who authored which part of the content and when. Additionally, the author will not simply be a regular "From" but have a link to the SemCard representing the author of the email SemCard.

No executable code. An important feature of SemCards is that they are completely passive – they do not carry with them any executable code: We have entirely separated the services operating on the SemCards from the SemCards

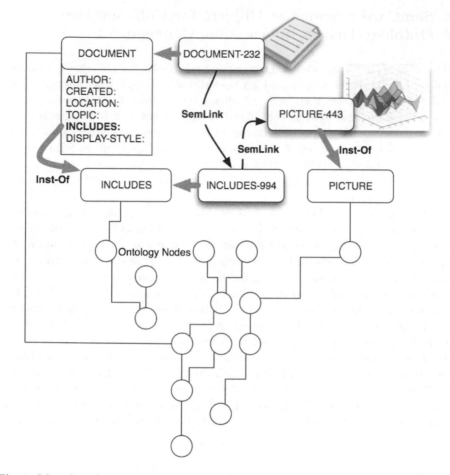

Fig. 1. Metadata for entities, digital or physical, is semantically defined by an underlying ontology that appears to the user as (networks of) SemCards

themselves, leaving only a specification for the desired operations (named processes) to be done on a SemCard in the SemCard itself. This has many benefits, the most important of which is simplicity in usage and ease of maintaining compatibility between systems that use SemCards.

Unique ID. Every SemCard instance has a global, unique identifier (GUID), timestamps representing time of creation and related temporal aspects such as times of modification, as well as a set of policies. Its author is also represented, and any authors of modifications throughout the SemCard's lifetime. The SemCard's policies allow it to be displayed, shared, copied, etc. in predescribed ways, through the use of rules.

Representing any entity. Any type of digital object or information can be pointed to with a SemCard, e.g. a Web page, a product, a service offer, a data record in a database, a file or other media object, media streams, a link to a remote Web service, etc. A SemCard can thus represent any digital item, like a *png* image or *pdf* document, *physical entities* such as a person, building, street, or a kitchen utensil, *as well as immaterial things* like ideas, mythologicical phenomena and intellectual creations. A SemCard can also represent collections, for example a SemCard representing a group of friends would contain links to the SemCards representing the individuals of that social group. Equally importantly, SemCards can represent relationships between SemCards, for example, that a person is the author of an idea.

Display rules. SemCard can carry display rules that dictate how the SemCard itself (as well as its target reference - the thing it represents) should be displayed to the user. These can describe, for example, its owner's preferences or the display device required. As SemCards carry with them their own display specifications their on-screen representation can be customized by their userss; the same SemCard can thus be displayed differently to two different users with different preferences. The rules can specify how metadata and slot values in the SemCard should be organized and what human-readable labels should be used for them, if any, as well as what aspects of the SemCard appear as interactive elements in the interface, and the results of specific interaction with those elements.

3.2   Using Semcards

Creating an instance of a SemCard involves simply selecting the appropriate SemCard template ("template") from a menu or via a search-enhanced selector interface. To fill out the SemCard instance, one or more slots are filled with values – these could be semantic links to other SemCards, typed entities or unclassified content. Each SemCard instance, its semantic dimensions and their values, can be stored as an XML (extensible Markup Language) object, using e.g. the RDF (Resource Description Framework) format [9].

While SemCards could be invisible to users, hidden underneath the standard applications they use, typically a user will want to view and manipulate the information they represent directly, especially for linking them together. For example, a document authored by David, a non-SemCard user, is received by Kris' SemCard system. When received, a SemCard of type "SemDocument" is *automatically* created. Kris links the SemDocument SemCard to his SemCard representing the document's author, David, using an instance of the SemCard type *Authored-By*. This instantly puts the received document in a rich semantic context of the network of all SemCards that link, in one way or another, the document-author pair to a lot of metadata as to who created what at what time, and who shared it with whom, how, and so on.

For viewing and manipulating SemCards we have developed both client-based editors in the spirit of Haystack [10] and Web-based interfaces. Our PersonalRadar desktop application, of which there were made several prototypes, made SemCards actively usable on personal computers, expanding the reach of Twine.com down to personal data, via semantically rich networks. SemCards can be created in many ways; doing so manually from scratch involves selecting a SemCard template type, making an instance of it and customizing its slots using typed entities from an underlying ontology.

SemCards templates are ideally fully defined by one or more ontologies. However, the case could arise where a user wants to represent an entity for which no template exists. A user can create free-form slots and collect them into a new SemCard (that has no template). As long as the type of the SemCard – or at least one slot in it – has a connection to a known ontology (it will always have its author and date of creation), the automation mechanisms can use this information to base further automatic refinement of the SemCard instance, like linking it to (what are believed to be) related SemCards. Man-

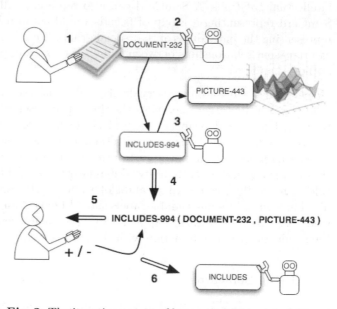

Fig. 2. The iterative nature of human-machine metadata annotation. (1) User creates digital document, (2) a SemCard instance is automatically created; the automation infers that a particular image is included in the document and (3) creates a SemCard for it and a SemCard of type *Includes* that links the two; (4) relationship between the SemCards now forms a triplet that the user can inspect (here shown in prepositional form, but is typically graphical); (5) user modifies the results (+/-) from which (6) the automation processes generalizes to improve own performance.

aging such automatic semantic links becomes akin to unstructured database managment; it will of course never be as good as that for fully-specified SemCards, but because these SemCards live in a rich network of other SemCards, this problem is typically not as large as it may seem.

3.3   End-Users Versus Ontology Experts

In our system expert designers create basic SemCard templates for all major entities such as digital documents, presentations, video files etc., where a template's meta-tags are hand-picked and surface presentation defined (see 3). Importantly, non-experts can then create derivative SemCards by modifying these, adding or removing pre-assigned slots in the SemCards, or making new ones from scratch, using either completely new ones or pre-existing ontologically defined slots (e.g. by copying slots from other SemCards or from a library). All underlying ontological relationships are maintained in the new SemCard; a modified SemCard will store the specifics of its creation history (and can either carry that data around as metadata or link to it in an online database via a GUID). This history information, and its subsequent use and further modification of hundreds or thousands of users, can be used by the automation system to infer about the semantics of the new SemCard and its relation to the underlying ontology, which was not modified in the process.

As SemCards isolate the user from the related ontologies, classificatory mistakes in their creation does not destroy the underlying ontologies. This results in a kind of graceful degradation; instead of breaking the system such mistakes only make the automated handling of information in the system slightly less accurate. The relationship between SemCards and the unerlying ontology can be likened to non-destructive editing for video: As the creation history (original data, i.e. ontologies) are not changed but rather represented in a separate intermediate layer, the edit history of any SemCard can be traced back and reverted, if need be, with no change to the underlying ontologies.

Behind each SemCard is thus an ontology that defines the meaning of the SemCard slots, specifies valid values and relations between slots (see Figure 1). An ontology like FOAF (c.f. [11]) or the Dublin Core [12] can be used with SemCards, as each SemCard carries with it a reference to the ontology it is based on. Thus, networks of ontologies can be used with SemCards, whether they use a basic, simple and singleton ontology like the Dublin Core or are definded more deeply in e.g. foundational ontologies such as DOLCE, SUMO [13] [14], or OCHRE [15].

In our current implementation we have created a fairly extensive ontology for important digital data types including Web page, 2-D image, URL, text document, as well as for physical entities such as person, place, organization, etc. The idea is to make this ontology open-source to encourage linking of other ontologies to it, extending its reach and improving its utility, and ultimately bringing the Semantic Web to maturity sooner.

4 Collaborative SemCard Creation by Man and Machine

Through the iterative addition and editing of SemCards by users and the automation mechanisms, a positive feedback loop of iterative improvement on the network is created through such collaboration (Figure 2); initial example networks provide a model for the automation. Reasoning mechanisms are used to infer the implications of corrections to automatically-created data, based on original manual creation. When the initial manual data entry and corrections reaches a critical point the automation starts to provide significant and noticable enhancements to the user. Increased manual input, especially in the form of additions to automatically generated semantic links, allows the automation system also to make inferences about the quality of the data entry, not just for a single user but for many. This allows it to improve the accuracy of its own automation

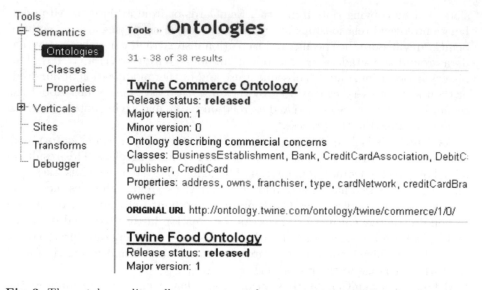

Fig. 3. The ontology editor allows expert ontology creators to quickly create, manage, connect and extend the multitude of ontologies underlying Twine.com

even further, and suggestions to users about related data will be more relevant and targeted.

An important feature of SemCards is that they record significant amounts of metadata about themselves, including their own genesis. This makes automatic creation of SemCards much more flexible as the automation process can make inferences about the quality of the SemCards (based on e.g. edit history). Because the same representational framework - SemCards - can be used for *all* data, including friend networks, author-entity relationships, object-owner, etc., inferencing can use the multiple SemCard relationship types (e.g. not only who created it but also who the creator's friends are) to decide how to perform automatic relationship creation, data-slot filling, automatic correction or deletion. Moreover, as the SemCard stores its edit history, including who/what made the edits, any such changes can be undone with relative ease. Since this history is stored as semantic information, it can be used to sort the SemCards according to their history. This makes managing SemCards over time much more flexible than if they were history-scarce, like e.g the losely-defined metadata of most data on people's hard drives. For example, caching, compressing or any other processes can be made history-sensitive to a high level of detail.

As an example of collaborative automatic/ manual creation of SemCards, Nova, a SemCard end-user, finds a useful URL and creates a SemCard for it of type "bookmark for a Web-page" (see Figure 4). He makes personal comments on the Web page's contents by making a "Note" SemCard and linking it to the Webpage SemCard. Nova's automation processes, running on the SemCard hosting site, add two things: They fill the Webpage SemCard with machine-readable metadata from the Web page, and they also link these SemCards to a new

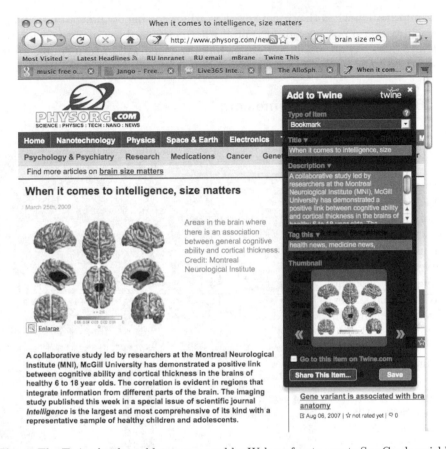

Fig. 4. The Twine bookmarklet popup enables Web surfers to create SemCards quickly. The system automatically fills in relevant information ("Title", "Description", "icon", etc.).

SemCard that *it* created, containing further information mined from the Web site. Now Nova shares (a copy) of the SemCard with Jim (it gets saved in his SemCard space), who may add his own comments and links to related Sem-Cards; the fact that the SemCard was shared with Jim by Nova is automatically recorded as part of the SemCard's metadata. Thus, events, data and metadata are created seamlessly and unobtrusively through the collaborative paradigm.

As their authorship is automatically recorded in the SemCards, this can be later used to e.g. exclude all SemCards created by particular automation processes, should this be desired. Proactive automatic mining of a user's SemCards can reveal implicit relationships that the system can automatically make explicit, facilitating faster future retrieval through particular relationship chains in the resulting relationship graphs.

As a users's SemCard database grows user-customized automation becomes more relevant; in the long run, as the benefits of automation become increasingly obvious to each user, people will see the benefits of providing a bit of extra meta-information when they create e.g. a word processing document or an image. This will trigger a positive upward spiral where increased use of automation will motivate users to add more pieces of metadata, which will in turn enable better automation.

5   Deployment on Twine.com

We have implement the SemCard technology and deployed it on the *Twine.com*, an online Semantic Web portal where people can create accounts and use a SemCard-enabled system to manage their online activities and information, including bookmarks, digital files, sharing policies, and more.

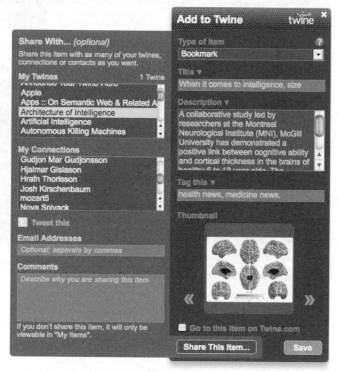

As of summer 2009 there were well over 4 million SemCards on Twine.com. At that time Twine.com had around 250 thousand registered users and over 2 million unique visits montly,[3] using the interface developed for the Website. The rate of new SemCard creation had grown to 3K per day, created by an esti-mated 10% of the users. So far, users seem to rarely correct the automatically-generated SemCards, but a relatively small subset of Twine power users add extensive additional information to them.

Fig. 5. Upon creation of the bookmark, SemCard users can choose to share it (left side of popup) with users via Twines they have created or subscribed to ("My Twines"), or directly with people they have connected with ("My Connections")

We will now detail an actual example of making a SemCard for a Web page, a short article on the Physorg.com Web site.[4] As can be seen in Figure 4, when a user comes to a Web page of interest they can click on the bookmarklet "Twine

---

[3] According to compete.com

[4] http://www.physorg.com/news157210821.html

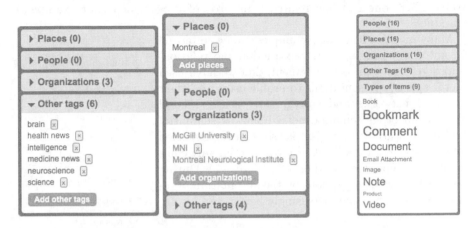

Fig. 6. *Left and center:* Two snapshots of the same dropdown box are shown; automatic processing of a bookmarked Web page can detect places, people organizations and various named entities ("tags"). The user can then modify these by deleting (clicking on the [x]) and adding new ones. The left image shows its "other tags" that were auto-recognized, the middle image showing "organizations", as well as one user-added "place" ("Montreal"). *Right:* Automatic pop-up of items in various categories such as "people", "places", etc., related to a SemCard.

This", which brings up a simple menu with a few information fields. Parts of the SemCard slots have been filled in; the user can choose to edit these, overwrite them with her own information or to leave them as-is. When the user clicks "save" a SemCard for this Web page is created in their Twine account. The user can choose to share this item with users and/or *twines* (see Figure 5) – a twine is a SemCard that can be described as "a blog with controlled access permissions" – in other words, a SemCard for a set of SemCards with particular visual presentation and adjustable viewing permissions.[5] The twine SemCard shows the dynamic properties of SemCards for specifying dynamic processes, e.g. calling on services from mining, inferencing, etc.

When the "bookmark" SemCard is saved, using the "Save" button on the lower right on the bookmarklet popup, the SemCard is stored on Twine.com. Any sharing selection that the user had made during the creation will make the bookmark SemCard available to the users who have permissions to read those twines; for example, sharing it with the twine *Architecture of Intelligence* (Figure 5) will enable everyone who has been invited to subscribe to this twine to see it. In their home page on Twine.com this SemCard will now additionally bring forth a lot of information, including auto-tagging (recognized entities, relationships, etc.).

As seen in Figure 6 a cross next to auto-generated tags allow the user to delete the ones that they don't agree with. Further related information is automatically pulled forward, sorted into "places", "people", "organizations", "other tags" and "types of items": The last one is interesting as it is a unique feature of semantic

---
[5] We will use "twine" with a lower case "t" to refer to a SemCard of type "twine".

Webs – here one can find related SemCards of type "video", for example, or "product".

Many machine learning techniques can be employed for automatic tagging, entity extraction and relationship detection – in our implementation we have used vector space representations to profile users and their semantic networks and subsequently select related items from other semantic nets. Using a (semantic) drill-down search mechanism a user can further keep refining a search for a SemCard, by selecting any combination of type, tags, author, etc. (Figure 7). During such drill-downs, suggestions by the automation of related material become increasingly better.

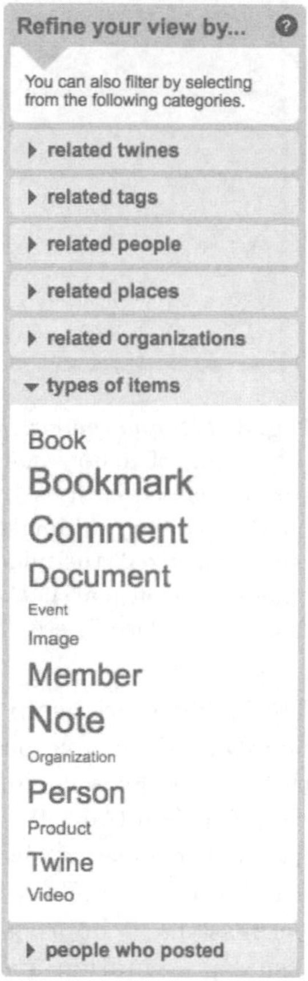

6   Future SemCard-Driven Automation Services

As already mentioned, the system we have developed enables automatic semantic mining of content sent by a user. Using existing semantic networks created manually and automatically by the system, this mining can be done without requiring any actions or special editing by the user, such as inserting special characters or identifying terms or phrases as potential semantic objects. We will now provide a few examples of future automation services enabled by the SemCard technology. These have not been implemented as services yet, but prototypes already exist.

Intelligent E-Mail/Sharing. An example of a potential future use of the SemCard technology is for email-like purposes. In this example the user has a semantic email account with a semantic service provider (or the user keeps the same normal non-semantic email account but adjusts mailbox settings so that mail received and sent are processed by the provider). The semantic service provider processes all incoming and outgoing e-mail, automatically creating Sem-Cards representing the e-mail itself and concepts referenced in the email and identified by entity detection algorithms [16]. No intervention would be required of the user, other than initial set-up. When the SemCards have been created they are automatically linked to other previously defined semcards in the user's account, enlarging the user's knowledge network. Now the user can for example find all emails "sent by Jim to Nova about Semantic Web technologies regarding the PersonalRadar product" – a perfectly valid search using semantic relations built from information readily available in the user's account.

Refine your view by... ❓

You can also filter by selecting from the following categories.

▶ related twines

▶ related tags

▶ related people

▶ related places

▶ related organizations

▼ types of items

Book

Bookmark

Comment

Document

Event

Image

Member

Note

Organization

Person

Product

Twine

Video

▶ people who posted

Fig. 7. One type of semantic search box on *Twine.com*

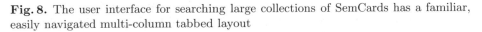

Fig. 8. The user interface for searching large collections of SemCards has a familiar, easily navigated multi-column tabbed layout

Because the underlying representation for this sharing of text messages is the SemCard, this activity constitutes *semantic sharing*. Its principles can be applied to *any* digital object – with a SemCard client the same sharing method used for the email SemCards can be used for sharing any digital object; there is no need to use "attachments" for sharing such entities as they are first-class objects with full meta-data about their history including creation, manipulation and sharing events.

Semantic social networks from emails. Another important feature enabled by SemCards is the creation of semantic relationship networks, where a user's relationships is automatically mapped based on email correspondence. Such a network will be most useful if the correspondence is also based on SemCard technology, as described above, but regular email can also be used to form the basis for this technology. To move to this technology from their current software, users provide their private and business contacts in their account, for example by uploading their address book into the system.

Depending on various factors, including the content and number of the emails exchanged, these relationship link types include types such as "friend", "colleague", "relative", "conversants", with the last type being the most generic. To take the example of the "conversants" link type: The link is created between the user and another person when they have exchanged at least two emails, where the second email was a response to the first. The link contains the time of the exchange (time of sending, time of reading, both emails), as well as who made the link, and when (even when automatically created). As before, the user can set a preference for minimal, medium, or heavy mining of her email.

The system processes the addressees of all emails to infer who is communicating with the user about what, as in the above email example, as well as inferring with whom the user has relationships, what kind of relationships those are, and what projects they relate to. Emails are then linked to those inferred projects. This enables very powerful personalization of information displaying: For example, sets of different preference settings can be associated with separate (named or unnamed) groups of contacts, enabling differential treatment depending on who the user communicates with. A group called "friends" may have certain settings for how entries from/to them should be formatted for viewing; a "personal Facebook-like service" with a corresponding look could be set up by a user for one of her groups, while using a vastly different display setup for others.

7   Conclusions

To realize the full potential of the Semantic Web vision, several challenges must be met. One of these is the unreliability of automated metadata creation systems, another is the lack of a strong and flexible framework for representing data and metadata. We have developed SemCards, which solve these challenges in a way that takes advantage of current technologies while allowing for future growth in the foreseeable future. We have implemented this technology on the desktop as well as on the Web, showing it to scale to hundreds of thousands of users.

The technology presents a powerful representation scheme that enable collaborative human-machine and human-human creation of Semantic Web information. SemCards achieve this by separating hard-core ontologies from the end-user, mediating these via graphical information structures, represented under the hood using RDF and OWL, while supplying their own visual representation schemas for on-screen viewing. The SemCard framework allows better sharing, storing, annotating, enhancing and expanding semantic networks, creating true knowledge networks through a collaboration between people and artificial intelligence programs.

The Semantic Web site *Twine.com*, which has well over 2 million monthly unique visitors, has demonstrated the usefulness and extensibility of the technology. In close collaboration with automation processes, these users have created over 5 million SemCards to date. Our results so far show that SemCards can support all of the features described in this paper for over 300 thousand users and we have good reason to believe that the technology will scale well beyond this.

Other proposed approaches for realizing the Semantic Web vision have fallen short on one or more of the key features that SemCards address and solve. We believe that as a uniform standard for representing data and metadata on the World Wide Web, SemCards, or a related technology, could very well be the missing glue that is needed to link together the forces – natural and artificial – that are needed to propel the Web forward to the next level, the semantic level.

Acknowledgments. The work was supported by Radar Networks, Inc., by Reykjavik University, Iceland, and by the School of Computer Science at Reykjavik University. The authors would like to thank the Twine team for the implementation of the SemCard technology on Twine.com, as well as the funders of Radar, Vulcan Ventures Inc., Leapfrog Ventures Inc. and the angel investors.

References

1. Dill, S., Eiron, N., Gibson, D., Gruhl, D., Guha, R., Jhingran, A., Kanungo, T., Rajagopalan, S., Tomkins, A., Tomlin, J.A., Zien, J.Y.: SemTag and Seeker: Bootstrapping the Semantic seb via automated semantic annotation. In: Proceedings of the World Wide Web Conference (2003) doi: 10.1145/775152.775178
2. Etzioni, O., Gribble, S.: An evolutionary approach to the Semantic Web. Poster presentation at the First International Semantic Web Conference (2002)
3. Maly, K., Nelson, M.L., Zubair, M.: Smart objects, dumb archives: A user-centric, layered digital library framework. D-Lib Magazine, 5 (1999)
4. Kahn, R., Wilensky, R.: A framework for distributed digital object services. International Journal on Digital Libraries 6, 115–123 (1995)
5. Payette, S., Lagoze, C.: Flexible and extensible digital object and repository architecture (FEDORA). In: Nikolaou, C., Stephanidis, C. (eds.) ECDL 1998. LNCS, vol. 1513, pp. 41–59. Springer, Heidelberg (1998)
6. Lagoze, C., Payette, S., Shin, E., Wilper, C.: Fedora: An architecture for complex objects and their relationships. Journal of Digital Libraries - Special Issue on Complex Objects (2005) doi: arXiv:cs/0501012v6
7. Karger, D.R., Bakshi, K., Huynh, D., Quan, D., Sinha, V.: Haystack: A general-purpose information management tool for end users based on semistructured data. In: CIDR, pp. 13–26 (2005)
8. Drummond, N., Jupp, S., Moulton, G., Stevens, R.: A practical guide to building OWL ontologies using the Protégé 4 and CO-ODE tools, 1.2. edn. (2009)
9. Decker, S., Melnik, S., Harmelen, F.V., Fensel, D., Klein, M., Erdmann, M., Horrocks, I.: Knowledge networking in the Semantic Web: The roles of XML and RDF (2000)
10. Huynh, D., Karger, D.R., Quan, D.: Haystack: A platform for creating, organizing and visualizing information using RDF. In: Semantic Web Workshop, WWW 2002 (May 2002)
11. Ding, L., Zhou, L., Finin, T., Joshi, A.: How the Semantic Web is being used: An analysis of FOAF documents. In: Proceedings of the 38th International Conference on System Sciences, p. 313.3 (2005) doi: 10.1109/HICSS.2005.299
12. Sutton, S.A., Mason, J.: The Dublin Core and metadata for educational resources. In: International Conference on Dublin Core and Metadata Applications, pp. 25–31 (2001)
13. Varma, V.: Building large scale ontology networks. In: Language Engineering Conference (LEC 2002), Hyderabad, India, p. 121 (2002)
14. Hong, J.F., Li, X.B., Huang, C.R.: Ontology-based predication of compound relations: A study based on SUMO. In: Proceedings of PACLIC18, Waseda University, Japan, pp. 151–160 (2004)
15. Schneider, L.: Designing foundational ontologies: The object-centered highlevel reference ontology OCHRE as a case study. In: Song, I.-Y., Liddle, S.W., Ling, T.-W., Scheuermann, P. (eds.) ER 2003. LNCS, vol. 2813, pp. 91–104. Springer, Heidelberg (2003)
16. von Brzeski, V., Irmak, U., Kraft, R.: Leveraging context in user-centric entity detection systems. In: Proceedings of the 16th Conference on Information and Knowledge Management (2007)

Decision Support System Based on Computational Collective Intelligence in Campus Information Systems

Yoshihito Saito and Tokuro Matsuo

Graduate School of Science and Engineering, Yamagata University,
4-3-16, Jonan, Yonezawa, Yamagata, Japan
saito2007@e-activity.org, matsuo@yz.yamagata-u.ac.jp

Abstract. Education institutions such as universities have a lot of information including book information, equipment administrative information, student information, and several others. The institutions also have multiple information in time series. As collective intelligence in campus, integrating and reusing these preserved information regarding career and taking a class, university can effectively support students' decision making of their getting jobs and subjects choice. Our purpose of support is to increase student's motivation. In this paper, we focus on course record and job information included in students' information, and propose the method to analyze correlation between a pattern of taking class and job lined up. Afterwards, we propose a support system regarding getting a job and taking class by using our proposed method. For a student who has his/her favorite job to get, the system supports his/her decision making of lecture choice by recommending a set of appropriate lecture groups. On another hand, for a student who does not have favorite job to get, the system supports his/her decision making of getting job by presenting appropriate job families related with lecture group in which he/she has ever taken. The contribution of this paper is showing a concrete method to reuse the campus collective information, implementing a system, and user perspectives.

Keywords: Collective Campus Information, Computational Collective Intelligence, Career Support System, Services in University.

1 Introduction

Educational institutes including universities have huge amount of information and recognize the importance of reuse and integration them to enhance rationality of educational activities [4]. Campus information contains internal information in university, uses and books information in university library, facility and equipment information, publication and ability information of faculties and students, student individual information, and several others. In this paper, we focus on a decision support system for students by using such multiple information. Student information is one of high frequency of update in campus information because it should be updated with each semester. Further, newly-enrolled students enter the university and students who earned required credit graduate the university. Thus, university preserves a lot of cumulative students information every year.

N.T. Nguyen and R. Kowalczyk (Eds.): Transactions on CCI II, LNCS 6450, pp. 108–122, 2010.
© Springer-Verlag Berlin Heidelberg 2010

In many universities, students information are mainly managed in student section and are referred by students, faculties and staffs [1][11][19]. However, since students generally belong the university over a protracted period of time, their information are preserved a lot of sections cumulatively. Further, students information are not always reused to make effective instructions and tutoring. On the other hands, every year, universities have multiple information of former student (alumnae and alumni). The information include the scenario of taking classes, place of employment of job family after their graduation, purchasing information at the university coop (shop), and other information. From a point of collective intelligence research view, collective information provides averagely rational activities of the students [2][6]. If these former students' and current students' information can be reused and integrated, university can help student learn and live by campus information system [3][5]. The information can be used in decision making for students regarding getting jobs and finding appropriate classes for their purposes and intentions.

In this paper, we propose a new campus information support system by collected information in campus to support students' decision-making. The system provides useful information for students about pattern and scenario to take lecture based on student's goal and job family in which he/she want to get by using computational analysis of collective information. Further, our system realizes to support the student by providing appropriate candidates of job families from students' career, pattern and order of taking classes.

Concretely, first, a student can serve a service from the system if he/she already determined the job family he/she wants. There are a lot of paths of scenario to take classes based on the job families. The system puts two and two together based on a lot of preserved former students data, opinions from companies and other factors. Some students have determined job families they want before their entrances to the university, but others start to find and know about jobs after entrances through guidance provided by the university, experiences, and other activities. The system finds and detects relationships between the scenario and job family. Then, the system computes the advantages of lecture families for each job family. The computation is based on the survey what each former student feels useful knowledge for his/her job in which he/she study in the university. The system also refers circulation information in library. Namely, students groups can be classified in the information and current job.

Second, the system can provide a service to students who hesitate and are negative for finding jobs. The system proposes some appropriate jobs and job families based on a history of taking classes and several other data. For example, there is a desirable pattern and scenario of lecture sets for a job. The system provides the job information and the lecture information in which a student can take rest lectures. Also, if students hesitate and do not have any ideas to choose jobs, the system provides a career service to enhance students' knowledge of jobs, to show schedule planning to successfully find jobs, to enhance the motivation of getting jobs after their graduations, and to take lecture seriously because it is related with their future. Thus, the system becomes a part of education support system.

Advantages of our proposed method and system are as follows. First, collecting campus intelligence and knowledge, the system detects a rule and provides useful information to help students make their decisions regarding how they choose classes and jobs. Second, students enhance their motivation regarding lecture choice and finding jobs.

The rest of this paper consists of the following six parts. In Section 2, we explain career service and job assistance and its guidance in a university. In Section 3, we propose a method to analyze relationships between lectures and job families. Section 4 shows a computational method based on proposed method and preserved data. Then, Section 5 explains our system architecture implemented the proposed method. After that, we discuss effectiveness of our proposed method and system. Finally, we give our concluding remarks.

2 Career Service Systems

The word "Career" is widely used and has a lot of concepts [13][14]. The viewpoints between company and university are different regarding a career education and guidance [15][16]. Generally, career education and guidance in company is mainly to develop engineering techniques. On the other hands, the contributions report that career education and guidance in university is mainly to make students' motivation rise up. It is important for students to cultivate a view of a career and work. In some developed and developing country, even though people have with high educational background, the rate of turning over due to a separation between their career view and the facts in their jobs. If students have a lot of experience and take deep consideration in their school days, they would make more successful decision to choose jobs. To decrease the gaps between view of career and the fact in a job, university provides multiple career services for students.

2.1 Career Service Center in a University

Most of Japan's university has a career service section in the university. As same as other countries, each university is concerned about many issues of students including finding jobs [8][9][10]. The services mainly include providing guidance for a seminar, providing an opportunity of internship, and enhancing student's job-interviewing skill. Some universities call such section as the Career Service Center. When students go into a huddle of their jobs and abstractly ask the center staff, they provide some candidates of job family. However, it is strongly limitation because the staff sometimes changes a section due to conversion of work-position. Further, it is not easy to handle and analyze the former students experiences. Thus, the guidance and instruction becomes ambiguous and cannot be provided for individualized treatment. Since the staffs of career service center do not grasp rich knowledge of specialized technologies, it may be suspicious whether they can provide an effective guidance or not. They actually cannot instruct what the students need further knowledge to make successful decision finding job and taking classes.

2.2 Survey

We surveyed to know the students' intentions in school days. We ask two questions shown in Table 1 for 154 students.

For question 1, 141 students out of 154 want that the computer system recommend it. Further, 79 students (including some of the above 141 students) also want to have an advices from a staff of the support section.

Table 1. Questions for preliminary survey

	Questions
Question 1	Do you want to receive a recommendation of lectures related with a job you want ?
Question 2	Do you want to have an advice about job candidates based on the relationship between their getting credits, preferences, reasoned scenario, and appropriate job with former students' information ?

For question 2, most of students answered that they want to know about it. Particularly, 125 students out of 154 want to have an advice from the computer system.

From the above investigation, we give preliminary discussion what our system need to provide an effective services.

2.3 Collective Intelligence in Campus

There are a lot of collective intelligence research [12][17]. Based on them, to develop to the computational collective intelligence, we give the following two definitions to put common concept in this paper.

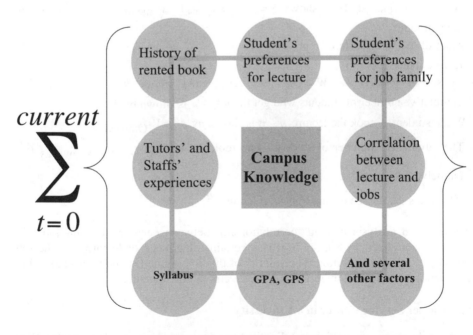

Fig. 1. Campus Collective Intelligence

Definition 1. Collective intelligence = Synthetic-Organic Knowledge to be made a good decision making for people.

Definition 2. Collective knowledge is derived, educed, and elicited set of information from people belonging in the university. Further, that includes historical meaning, that is, preserved data of former users, facts, and events.

Namely, in university, a lot of useful information exist and make cumulative history. Campus collective intelligence are synthesized by cumulative and current data form multiple sections but mining current data. Figure 1 shows the concept of the campus collective intelligence.

3 Scenario Analysis

In this section, we propose a method to analyze collected information of former students and job family in which they work after their graduation. The analysis is used by preserved data in each section of the university. We show a model including definitions.

3.1 Definitions

- A set of former students shows $S = \{s_1,...,s_i,...,s_n\}$. s_i means i th student in the student index.
- A set of available lectures represents $A = \{a_1,...,a_j,...,a_m\}$. a_j is j th lectures in the lecture index.
- A set of jobs shows $W = \{w_1,...,w_h,...,w_l\}$. w_h shows h th job index. The cumulative number of students who get the job w_h is shown by WN_h.
- When student s_i took the lecture a_j, it is shown as $s_i^j = 1$. Otherwise, $s_i^j = 0$.
- The cumulative number of students who took the lecture a_j, it is shown as T_{all}^j. Namely, $T_{all}^j = \sum_{i=1}^{n} s_i^j$.
- G_h^j means the degree of importance of lecture a_j for job w_h.

We show an analysis method for relationship between each lecture and job. If a lecture is correlated with the job, it is a certain importance of lectures for the job. Otherwise, it is not important. The validity of this importance is known because of an assumption of collective intelligence by huge amount of students.

3.2 Career Service Center in a University

In this subsection, we explain a following concrete process to analyze relationships between a job found by former students and a lecture taken by them.

Step 1. The system collects the information of the number of students T_{all}^{j} where the lecture a_j is taken by the students.

Step 2. The system collects the information of number of students T_h^{j} where the students both got job w_h and took the lecture a_j.

Step 3. The system computes the importance of lecture with each job. It is computed by using the following equation.

$$G_h^{j} = (T_h^{j}/WN_h)/(T_{all}^{j}/n) \tag{1}$$

Step 4. When the importance value G_h^{j} is higher, the correlation between the lecture and job is strong.

Most of Japan's university has a career service section in the university. The services mainly include providing guidance for a seminar, providing an opportunity of internship, and enhancing

Equation (1) is used to investigate the correlation between the job and lecture.

Denominator T_{all}^{j}/n at the right side member in the equation (1) shows the rate in which the number of n former students took a lecture a_j.

The numerator T_h^{j}/WN_h at the right side member in the equation (1) shows the rate how many former students took a lecture a_j and got the job w_h.

Namely, the right side member $(T_h^{j}/WN_h)/(T_{all}^{j}/n)$ of equation (1) shows the rate of the students who both took the lecture and chose the job and the students who took the lecture. In the computation G_h^{j}, if $T_h^{j}/WN_h < T_{all}^{j}/n$ and $(T_h^{j}/WN_h)/(T_{all}^{j}/n) < 1$ are, it has not correlations between the job and contents of the lecture. On the other hands, if $T_h^{j}/WN_h > T_{all}^{j}/n$ and $(T_h^{j}/WN_h)/(T_{all}^{j}/n) > 1$ are, it probably has correlations between the job and contents of the lecture.

For example, suppose that 100 students out of 1000 get a job w_h and 80 students take a lecture a_j. By intuition, we feel that there is a certain correlation between the lecture a_j and job w_h since 80 percent of students take a lecture. However, if 900 students out of 1000 takes the lecture, it does not always have a relationship. Such lecture may be taken by students because it is easy or popular for the student to get the credit. Thus, the system can detect the intentions of students why they take the lecture.

When a new-opened lectures are provided, the feature of the equation (1) sometimes becomes $T_h^{j} \ll WN_h$ and $T_h^{j} = T_{all}^{j}$ because total number of students who take the lecture and get the job w_h is not so many. In this case, the value G_h^{j} becomes quite high. On the other hands, in same situation, when the feature becomes $T_h^{j} \ll WN_h$ and $T_h^{j} = T_{all}^{j}$, the reliability of the relationship is not so high because the parameter is less although every students get a job w_h after taking the lecture. However, for a student in actual use of the system, it is useful for his/her if the system displays the total years of the lecture since it has opened. Thus, the system provide the history information of each lecture for students.

Only using the equation (1), it is difficult to compare for the analysis because the value G_h^j becomes small when the number of students increases and the denominator becomes T_{all}^j/n large. To solve the problem, the system normalizes the importance value between 0 to 10 by using the following normalized algorithm. Most important lecture for a job indicates 10 and Most unimportant lecture indicates 0. If it is necessary, the system manager (university) sets up the importance value as 100, 1000, and other number. The normalized importance value is shown G'^j_h. If the rate of G'^j_h increases, the importance of the lecture for the job also increases.

```
begin
for(h = 1; h ≤ l; h + +){
    Tmax = maxGh
    Tmin = minGh
    temp = (Tmax − Tmin)/C
    for(j = 1; j ≤ m; j + +){
        for(X = 0; X ≤ C; X + +){
            if(Tmin + temp ∗ X ≤ G_h^j < Tmin + temp ∗ (X + 1)){
                G'_h^j = X
            }
        }
    }
}
end
```

Fig. 2. The normalization algorithm

The concrete algorithm for the normalization is shown in the Figure 2. *Tmax*, *Tmin*, *temp*, and *X* are variable preserved temporary. *maxG_h* is the largest importance value for the job w_h. *minG_h* is the smallest importance value for the job w_h. Normalized criterion *C* is a parameter to set up by a system manager. When it is large number, the reliability of analysis becomes precise.

When there is available other information to compute, the method is essentially same with the analysis in above. To refer multiple information, each collected data is multiplied with control value of each valuation. Namely, the synthetic value is shown as *CollectiveIntelligence* $= F(c_1 V_1, c_2 V_2, \cdots, c_{10} V_{10})$ like MAUT [7] when there are 10 sorts of data sets. The function includes logical expression. For example, in simple case, the value becomes an arithmetic average value or a geometric average value. Each university has specific conditions and situations about career problem. The computation method should be determined with survey and investigation in the university, where the system is employed.

3.3 Example

We show a concrete simple example by using the correlation analysis method. Suppose that former 10 students exist and 3 students out of 10 get same job. We assume that 10 lectures are provided by university. Table 2 shows the number of

Table 2. Number of Students

a_j	T_{all}^j	T_h^j	a_j	T_{all}^j	T_h^j
a_1	7	3	a_6	5	1
a_2	6	0	a_7	7	3
a_3	9	3	a_8	5	0
a_4	6	2	a_9	4	1
a_5	8	3	a_{10}	4	3

Table 3. Important Lecture for a Job

a_j	G_h^j	$G_h'^j$	a_j	G_h^j	$G_h'^j$
a_1	1.4	6	a_6	0.6	2
a_2	0.0	0	a_7	1.4	6
a_3	1.1	4	a_8	0.0	0
a_4	1.1	4	a_9	0.8	3
a_5	1.3	5	a_{10}	2.5	10

students who take each lecture. The importance of lecture a_1 for the job w_h is computed as $G_h^1 = (3/3)/(7/10)$. The result of other lectures is calculated the importance G_h^j shown in Table 3. Table 3 shows the most important lecture for the job w_h is a_{10}, and lectures a_1 and a_7 also has weak importance for the job.

4 Actual Example by Using Former Student Data

In this section, we explain an actual example by using the collected information from student section and each department in a university. The set of lectures includes classes opened as complementary lectures in the informatics course in the university where authors are belonging. The number of lectures is 29. Each student need to take these sort of lectures more than 15 for a graduation requirement. In our example, we classify 7 job families. These data are integrated to compute the correlation between the classes and jobs.

Table 4 shows a result of computation by using former students data. The result shows relationships between the job w_1 and lectures. When the importance degree G'^j_h becomes large, the degree of correlation is strong. The strongest relationship with the job is lecture a_5. Second strongest relationship of the job is lectures a_{22} and a_{13}. Figure 3 shows the sorted result of computation. Lectures shown the importance between 3 and 5 are taken by the reason, which is popular for students.

Table 4. Actual Data of Former Students in Small Class

a_j	$G_1'^j$	a_j	$G_1'^j$	a_j	$G_1'^j$	a_j	$G_1'^j$
a_1	3	a_9	3	a_{17}	5	a_{25}	4
a_2	2	a_{10}	5	a_{18}	0	a_{26}	4
a_3	5	a_{11}	5	a_{19}	5	a_{27}	6
a_4	4	a_{12}	4	a_{20}	4	a_{28}	3
a_5	10	a_{13}	8	a_{21}	3	a_{29}	5
a_6	3	a_{14}	7	a_{22}	9		
a_7	2	a_{15}	7	a_{23}	3		
a_8	3	a_{16}	4	a_{24}	3		

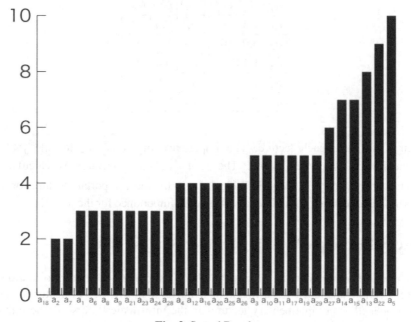

Fig. 3. Sorted Result

5   Career Service System

In this section, we show system architecture of career service system. In addition to the computation method shown in Section 3, some other collective information are used in developing case. The system includes analysis module of library, university coop, distribution of credit and several others. In concrete synthetic computation, each analysis is essentially same with the analysis method shown in Section 3. Thus, we omit the analysis method in other collective information in the university.

Our proposed system has three sorts of supports for students. First, the system recommends appropriate candidate of lectures related with jobs in which student wants. Second, the system provides appropriate lecture information based on previous lecture in which student has taken. Finally, the system suggests appropriate jobs for students based on the credit in which student has gotten. For these services, students can understand what is lack for their goal. Figure 4 shows the system architecture of our proposed career support system. The followings are explanation of each component.

- DB-UL is a library's database system. The system preserves all users information including their preferences.
- DB-SS is database system preserved students data. The data include former students' credit information and history of order of getting credit.
- DB-CS is database preserved job information. The database include the data when and who obtained employment for each company.
- DB-IM is database including using history for students. When staff of career service section advices students, he/she refers when the data are updated and students use the system.
- Lecture Recommendation Part (LRP) is a system to compute appropriate candidates of lectures as scenario.
- DB Access Part (DBAP) is a system to access to each database and search data. Also, this system temporarily preserves the result of search.
- Job Recommendation Part (JRP) is a system to compute appropriate jobs based on history of getting credit for current students.

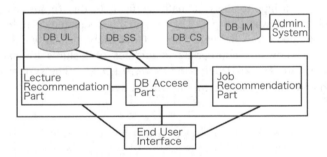

Fig. 4. System Architecture of Career Support Systems

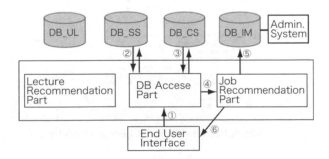

Fig. 5. Process of Job Search

5.1 Lecture Recommendation

Figure 5 is data flow of a process of lecture recommendation for student related with job in which he/she wants. When students use this function for the first time, they need to input job in which they want to get. The followings are concrete flow.

- Student input job information where he/she wants to get. When student continues to use, student's credit, preference, and some other available information form each section in the university.
- DBAP module searches for the information through DB-CS. Also, it preserves matching data (A) in the database DB-CS.
- DBAP searches for the information though DB-SS and DB-UL based on the preserved data (A). Also, it preserves matching data (B) in the database DB-SS and DB-UL.
- DBAP sends the data (A) and (B) to the LRP system. LRP system analyzes the correlation based on the method shown in the Section 3.
- LRP system sends and preserves the result of computation and user data to DB-IM. The data are changed by a time-oriented network graph.
- LRP recommends a result of computation as candidates of lectures.

The result of computation is visually shown as Figure 6. Solid lines indicate the relationship between lectures that is already taken by the students. Broken lines indicate the relationships to the candidate lectures. In this figure case, the student declares a job he/she wants to get. The broken lines squared lecture complements between the job and classes he/she attended. Concretely, he/she wants to get the job w_1 and want to know the appropriate candidates of lectures to make successful decision. He/she already took lectures $a_3, a_8, a_9, a_{11}, a_{13}, \ldots$. The system supposes that the student should take lectures $a_7, a_{17}, a_{23}, a_{26}, \ldots$.

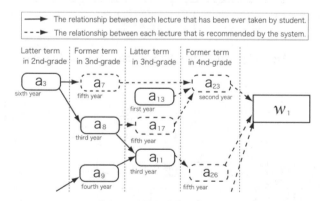

Fig. 6. Reasoned Path and Lecture Candidates

5.3 Job Candidates Presentation

Figure 7 shows the data flow to reason the appropriate candidates of jobs. The process of data flow is shown as follows.

- The lecture in which a student gets a credit is referred from the system in the student section.
- DBAP preserves data (C) searched from DB-SS based on the information collected from the student section.
- DBAP searches for the information based on the data (C) through DB-CS. And also it preserves a matched data (D).
- DBAP sends the JPR system the preserved data (C) and (D). The JRP system computes relationships between the job, lectures and other factors based on the method shown in the Section 3.
- The JRP system preserves the result of computation and user data to DB-IM. Also, the JRP suggests the appropriate candidates of jobs to the student.

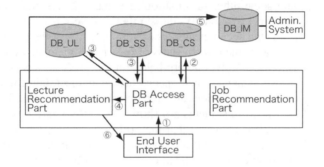

Fig. 7. Data flow in Lecture Recommendation

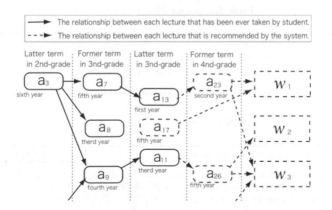

Fig. 8. The path to candidates of jobs

The result of computation of correlations is visually shown as in Figure 8. The meaning of solid lines and broken lines is same with the previous explanation shown in subsection 5.2. In this case, the student has already finish to take the credits of lectures $a_3, a_7, a_8, a_9, a_{11}, a_{13}, \ldots$. The result of computation shows that the job $w_1, w_2, w_3, \ldots$ is related with the input data and the lectures. Further, the system shows that lectures a_{17}, a_{23} are related with w_1, lecture a_{26} is related with w_2, and lectures $a_{23}, a_{26}, \ldots$ are related with w_3.

6 Evaluation

To show the effectiveness of the proposed system, we show the result of evaluation by students. There are a lot of researches including the book and web page recommendation. In each research, users preferences are not always detected and matched with requests like the information input by users. As same as them, it is not easy for our proposed method to match with students' preference perfectly. However, interestingly, our system collects information from former students behavior, their decision-making, and some other information in campus. For some literatures, even though some of people act irrationally, the synthetic society becomes comparatively rationally. Namely, it is the decision support system based on collective intelligence.

To make sure and clarify the effectiveness of our shown method, we had evaluation by 34 students selected randomly who are belonging in graduate students, senior year students, and junior year students. Their special area is in electronics, informatics, and bio-system engineering. Two questions are prepared shown in the Table 5.

The results of answer from students are shown in Table 6 and 7. As shown in the Table 6, students over 80% answered that they refer the suggestion from the system. Also, in Table 7, about 58 % students answered the recommendation result make them enhance the motivation to take lectures and find jobs. From these evaluations, our system achieves some positive results.

Table 5. Questions for the Evaluation

	Questions
Question 1	How do you use the recommendation as result of computation ?
Question 2	Are you motivated your taking classes and finding job by the system ?

Table 6. Answers for the Question 1

How do you use the recommendation ?	Recommendation	
	Lecture	Job
Making a decision based on the recommendation	1	1
Making a decision using as reference	28	27
Making a decision without the reference	2	3
No idea	3	3

Table 7. Answers for the Question 2

Did you have motivation after the recommendation ?	Recommendation	
	Lecture	Job
Yes	20	20
No	1	1
No idea	13	13

7 Conclusion

In this paper, we proposed a method to detect campus collective intelligence and the career service system. When a student uses the system, three sorts of services are provided. First, when a student does not have any idea to choose appropriate lectures, the system suggests the sets of lectures if he/she has a favorite job to get and other factors. Second, If he/she does not have favorite job and other factors, the system suggests the candidates of job based on their experiences including lectures in which he/she has already get credits. Finally, even though student does not want to know the candidates of jobs, the system can show some related lectures based on his/her history, preferences, and several other conditions. In the evaluation of our method and system, students answer that they want to refer the suggestions and use them for subsequent decision making. Further their motivations to take lectures and get jobs are increased.

Future work includes that we insert score data (each score of learning issue for student), period data (synthetic grade calculation of a lecture for student) for analysis. Further, we try to develop the career support system based on a campus collective intelligence in difference between departments and special area of research and to integrate the system with lecture allocation systems [18].

References

1. Glatthorn, A.A.: Developing A Quality Curriculum, ASCD (1994)
2. Pentland, A.: Collective intelligence. IEEE Computational Intelligence Magazine 1(3), 9–12 (2006)
3. Couros, A.: Open, connected, social - implications for educational design. Campus-Wide Information Systems 26(3), 232–239 (2009)
4. Cox, A., Emmott, S.: A survey of UK university web management: staffing, systems and issues. Campus-Wide Information Systems 24(5), 308–330 (2007)
5. Miller, D.B.: Professional development-a program to stimulate personal growth. IEEE Transactions on Education 19(1), 15–19 (1976)
6. Jung, J.J., Nguyen, N.T.: Collective Intelligence for Semantic and Knowledge Grid. Special issue in Journal of Universal Computer Science 14(7), 1016–1020 (2008)
7. Hammond, J., Keeney, R., Raiffa, H.: Smart Choices. Harverd Business Press, Boston (1999)
8. Judge, T.A., Bretz, R.D.: Effects of work values on job choice decisions. Journal of Applied Psychology 77(3), 261–271 (1992)

9. Mitchell, K.E., Alliger, G.M., Morfopoulos, R.: Toward an ADA-appropriate job analysis. Human Resource Management Review 7(1), 5–26 (1997)
10. McGovern, T.V., Barbara, J.W., Susan, M.E.: Comparison of professional versus student ratings of job interviewee behavior. Journal of Counseling Psychology 26(2), 176–179 (1979)
11. Negnevitsky, M.: A knowledge based tutoring system for teaching fault analysis. IEEE Transactions on Power Systems 13(1), 40–45 (1998)
12. Nguyen, N.T.: Inconsistency of Knowledge and Collective Intelligence. Cybernetics and Systems 39(6), 542–562 (2008)
13. Ismail, N.A.: Activity-based management system implementation in higher education institution: Benefits and challenges. Campus-Wide Information Systems 27(1), 40–52 (2010)
14. Butz, P.B., Duarte, M., Miller, M.S.: An intelligent tutoring system for circuit analysis. IEEE Transactions on Education 49(2), 216–223 (2006)
15. Lunneborg, P.W., Wilson, V.M.: Job Satisfaction Correlates for College Graduates in Psychology. Teaching of Psychology 9(4), 199–201 (1982)
16. Saleh, S.D., Hosek, J.: Job Involvement: Concepts and Measurements. The Academy of Management Journal 19(2), 213–224 (1976)
17. Jones, S.K.: Collective Intelligence: It's All in the Numbers. IEEE Intelligent Systems 21(3), 64–65 (2006)
18. Matsuo, T., Fujimoto, T.: A New Lecture Allocation Support System based on Users' Multiple Preferences in Campus Information Systems. International Journal of Computational Intelligence and Applications (IJCIA) 6(2), 245–256 (2007)
19. Chu, W.R., Mitchell, M.C., Jones, M.P.: Using the operator function model and OFMspert as the basis for an intelligent tutoring system: towards a tutor/aid paradigm for operators of supervisory control systems. IEEE Transactions on Systems, Man and Cybernetics 25(7), 1054–1075 (1995)

Fuel Crime Conceptualization through Specialization of Ontology for Investigation Management System

Jolanta Cybulka

Poznań University of Technology,
Institute of Control and Information Engineering,
Pl. M. Skłodowskiej-Curie 5, 60-965 Poznań, Poland
Jolanta.Cybulka@put.poznan.pl

Abstract. We undertook the task of building the conceptual model of a particular economic offense, called "a fuel crime". This model is thought of as a part of a larger conceptualization, which comprises consensual semantics underlying the knowledge base of a system, aimed at supporting the teamwork of investigators of economic crimes. Because such a knowledge-based system represents a perspective on economic crimes, it should be carefully modeled. This can be done with the help of an expressive enough ontology. To achieve our goal we use the *constructive descriptions and situations* (c.DnS) design pattern, which enables us to construct an extensible, layered ontology in a top-down manner: c.DnS top layer is specialized by the reference ontology for investigation management system, that in turn, is specialized by the ontology of the fuel crime.

Keywords: fuel crime ontology, c.DnS design pattern, investigation management system ontology, ontological engineering.

1 Introduction

Intelligent information systems are often equipped with relevant knowledge bases. Creation of such a base is a challenging task, especially when it is intended to communicate with other systems' bases. In such a case the conceptual model of the base should be explicitly given, which additionally can be easily communicated among collaborating systems. One possible way to create the model is to build a relevant ontology, both expressive and extensible. Following this idea, we undertook the task to create the ontological model of the information system intended to support teamwork investigations against economic crimes [2]. Studying the literature regarding criminal analysis, crime detection and investigation or crime prevention, we found several supporting systems meant for criminal analysts. Among them are Analyst's Notebook, COPLINK, FraudFocus and FFPoirot (Financial Fraud Prevention Oriented Information Resources using Ontology Technology). As COPLINK [22] employs workflow technology

N.T. Nguyen and R. Kowalczyk (Eds.): Transactions on CCI II, LNCS 6450, pp. 123–146, 2010.

to support the teamwork, it served as the inspiration for the design phase of our system. The FFPoirot is also worth noticing for it uses an ontology. The most significant difference between FFPoirot's approach and ours concerns the strategy for the ontology building. FFpoirot uses a bottom-up method that results in obtaining a layered ontological structure. Bottom-up approach is based on extracting the basic ontological entities directly from the relevant documents that describe the domain of interest. These entities are called 'lexons' and are elementary conceptual entities representing (from different perspectives) the relationships between semantic types of some domain. It would be difficult to use such elementary entities in applications, thus they are generalized in the form of logical 'commitments' within the next layer. The commitments applied to the lexon base represent some ontological perspectives on a domain. Several such perspectives may be considered, comprising application ontology (application dependent entities), topical ontology (entities connected with some theme) and domain ontology (domain of interest dependent entities). To provide semantic interoperability (between FFPoirot's ontology and others), entities of the considered two layers are embedded in the upper level ontology, namely the SUMO (Suggested Upper Merged Ontology, [15]), which contains the most general semantic categories. The described approach is quite advantageous; however, its essential drawback lies in the necessity of the creation of the huge lexon's universe, many of which may not be useful for any application. We omit this obstacle by employing the top-down strategy of ontology creation. Only necessary semantic entities are carefully derived by humans, going down from the most general (foundational) entities to those constituting core concepts of some domain or task, at last reaching the most detailed concepts of the lowest layer. Roughly speaking, the approach is based on expertise elicitation from humans who have some view on states of affairs and express it by means of a foundational ontology. This ontology is a frame of reference during elicitation of lower layers' semantic entities by the ontologist.

In our previous work [3] we concentrated on the presentation of the the core layer of semantic entities that underly the conceptual model of an information system. As it was mentioned, the system aims at supporting teamwork investigations on economic crimes. There exist many kinds of such crimes, what implies that the system should be able to represent and process knowledge about all of them. Thus, our ontology should be extensible via specializing. An example of such an extension is the conceptual model of a particular case of economic crime – namely, the "fuel crime". Considering this kind of a crime, it is worth noticing that the overall price of fuel in Poland contains several taxes making it significantly higher, except for some cases, such as the heating oil, the fuel used by farmers or on ships, where taxes are lower and so is the price. The only chemical difference between the two "kinds" of fuel is that they are differently dyed. This motivates fraudsters to change "miraculously" the status of fuel by decolorizing it and then re-selling at a higher price, for example, a heating oil as a car fuel. There are also other manifestations of fuel crime, the overview is given in [11]. Here, we concentrate on illegal production and trading of fuel by a business subject that has the infrastructure to do this, but is formally registered as a firm doing other kind of business activity. This illegal fuel is produced via mixing (blending) the somehow obtained fuel components. Such a "production" and trading criminal procedure (a core criminal activity) is an example of the flow of goods and services on the open market. It is accompanied by other kind of transactions that are to mask the whole crime. The first type transactions concern the flow of documents, such as purchase orders, invoices, bills of lading, store documents etc., in which some of documents are true, but some are falsified. The second group of transactions regards the flow of money, especially realized by bank account transfers, using checks, dealing with cash etc., done between many companies, to cover up trails of the core criminal activity. The fraudulent companies are organized in criminal structures, each of which plays a different role (examples are given later on) in the whole crime. Some companies make partially legal business, while some are straw companies only. Every criminal structure has a boss who organizes it. Many other people, who are owners, employees, plenipotentiary, clerks, relatives, straws are engaged in the crime. The fuel crime significantly decreases the taxes. The inquiry and investigation are often initiated after receiving a notification about an offense. The notification may be issued by GIIF (Polish General Financial Information Inspector) or a person who is engaged in the crime but is conflicted with offense bosses.

While creating the ontology, engineering methods of NeOn (Networked Ontology, [7]) and C-ODO (Collaborative Ontology-Design Ontology, [6]) were partially followed. Both of them are suitable to collaboratively design and implement networked ontologies.

The paper is organized as follows. Section 2 is devoted to the ontology for investigation management system that comprises the layer of core concepts. It describes the requirements (subsection 2.1), the content design pattern (subsection 2.2) and the main modules of the core layer (section 2.3). In section 3 the specialization of the core layer is presented, namely the ontology of the fuel crime. At the beginning we mention on the methodology (subsection 3.1), then we give the description of the fuel crime (subsection 3.2) and the specification of the fuel crime ontology that follows the methodology (subsection 3.3). The conclusions are stated in section 4.

2   Ontology for Investigation Management System

The considered ontology serves as the conceptual model of the information system, which aims at supporting teamwork investigations of economic crimes [2]. The requirements for this conceptual model are specified in section 2.1. When designing the model, we have the following general issues in mind:

- the way the ontology supports the implementation of the system's functionality (resulting in the creation of the *task-based* part of the ontology)
- the scope and the method of the domain knowledge conceptualization, i.e. the method of the creation of the *domain-based* part of the ontology and
- the ontology design and engineering pattern.

The first two are described in subsection 2.1 while the content design pattern of the ontology – in 2.2. As it was already mentioned, the applied approach to ontology construction may be considered as a *top-down strategy*. It enables us to create layered, modularized and extensible ontologies, with first specifying the top layer of them. The decision of what top ontology to choose is of great importance. It must provide the modeling means to represent the sufficiently general view on possible states of affairs and should be engineered in a formalized language. The significant expressiveness of the top level guarantees the possibility to model many different semantic aspects of reality and, at the same time, to manage the changes and extensions possibly occurring at lower levels in the life cycle of the ontology. In section 2.2 we give the brief description of the chosen upper layer ontology.

After establishing the top ontology, its specializations (i.e., more specific layers) may be defined, to cover the considered domain- or task-based knowledge. In this proposed solution the lower layers of ontology are created gradually down to the lowest level, which represents the semantics of data in the system's database(s). One such specialization layer is the ontology for investigation management system. It is assumed to comprise core semantic concepts in the domain of economic crimes and their investigation procedures (see section 2.3). These may be further specialized, for instance, to cover the semantics of a fuel crime (section 3).

2.1   Requirements for the Ontology

As to the *task-based* part of the ontology, we expect it to aid the implementation of the workflow-based investigation management system's functions, which fall into the following categories:

a) data acquisition,
b) data extraction (by means of user's queries analysis and answering),
c) data exchange between the system and the environment,
d) representation of the dynamics of processes within a workflow paradigm.

We briefly describe these categories. The system is supplied with data communicated both on-line by the investigation team members and accessed from databases. The on-line methods require the definition of a communication language that should be user friendly and flexible to the greatest extent possible. A relevantly expressive ontology is a good way to represent such language semantics. The data residing in relational databases also profit by their semantics specification. If the meaning of a relational scheme is explicitly stated, it is possible to automate the acquisition of data from documents (or 'motivation scenarios' concerning investigated cases) to a database. This may be done through, at first, the generation of a textual representation of an interesting part of the ontology (an ideal textual paraphrase; several such texts may exist with different syntactic variants of semantic ontological entities). Then, syntax-based tools, which recognize patterns (data) in real documents, may be used to put it into the database.

The system's data extraction process may also profit by the semantics – especially when the data are extracted through 'semantic queries'. In such queries the ontological entities, for example concepts and relations are used.

The ontology also has an impact on the exchange of data (differently formatted in different sources), for the mappings between their sources may be discovered on the basis of semantics attached to data schemas. With mappings it is possible to use semantics-driven translation to convert data forms.

The system manages the work of an investigation team by using workflow technology. Here, the conceptual model may facilitate structuring the management of processes (the static part of the workflow conceptualization) and reasoning about the processes in time (the dynamic part). In this approach our solution shows similarity to the COBRA approach (Core Ontology for Business Process Analysis, [13]).

The *domain-based* part of the ontology currently concerns the two main specializations of the foundational layer. The first one was defined after the analysis of documents concerning both the practical and theoretical (expert) knowledge on economic crimes and methods of their investigation (see [11], [16], [19], [20], [21]). The resulting conclusion was that the ontology should represent the semantics of four interconnected state of affairs types:

- trade/business reality (that is the instrument of criminal activities),
- investigation reality (investigations are carried by the police),
- inquiry reality (carried by prosecutors with the help of the police),
- investigation system's dynamics (a workflow process).

The ontological representation of dynamics is necessary because in practice the analysis of any crime (here, a criminal trade/business activity) is interlaced with the execution of investigative actions: the result of some such action very often has impact on the previously adopted investigative plan.

The second noticed specialization concerns the core conceptualization of law together with the legal qualification of the (suspicious) trade/business situations. This specialization needs elaboration. Fortunately, there exist several ontologies of law, such as CLO (Core Legal Ontology), LKIF-Core (Legal Knowledge Interchange Format-Core ontology), FOLaw (Functional Ontology of Law) or others (see the good review in [1]). With the help of adopted foundational ontology, the first domain-based specialization occurred to be easily expressible. We hope that it will be the case with the second one and others as well.

2.2   c.DnS Content Design Pattern

The choice of a foundational ontology that fulfills the listed requirements is very challenging. Fortunately, there are solutions which can be adopted, for example the ontology of *constructive descriptions and situations*, c.DnS for short [5]. In this conceptual modeling design pattern, two components are considered: a basic ontology of 'what really exists' and the ontologically reified means (called here *schematic entities*) to describe the concepts of the basic ontology from the point of view of some perceiving agent. It may be regarded as the epistemological layering or as the "contextualization" of the basic ontology.

The entities of the basic ontology that are classified by relevant schematic entities are regarded as ontologically "grounded". The advantages of this c.DnS ontology are as follows:

1) its expressive power is very high and therefore it may be easily projected on different subdomains,
2) it is well suited to model domains populated with many non-physical entities,
3) it enables the addition of contextual or epistemic knowledge to the ontology,
4) the simplified version of the ontology is engineered in the OWL language and can be freely accessed [17].

To model something using the c.DnS paradigm, one has to define the relation (1). On this basis some basic binary (or ternary, with the time argument) projections were defined, which specify the relations that hold between the pairs of concepts (their names are given in italics).

$$c.DnS = <S, E, A, D, C, K, I> \tag{1}$$

The S stands for a *Situation*[1], a kind of *Schematic entity* that ontologically reifies the real state of affairs. The S is constituted (in the c.DnS this is done by means of the *set for* formal relation) by the *Ground entity* E, coming from the basic ontology. The *Situation* S is located in time by means of a *Time interval* T_S (we *classify* T_S as a kind of C *Concept*; it is illustrated in the sequel). To be grounded, the S must be described (from some viewpoint) by a *Social agent* A (whom the *Physical agent*, that is to say, some person *acts for*). The *Agent* A, in time T_D (also *classified* as a kind of C) creates a (potentially many) *Description* D of S, which is then *assumed by* A (and may be also *assumed* or only *shared* by other agents). Every such D must be *satisfied* by the S. To make the entities E grounded in the *Description* D, they must be *classified* (named) by some C. The *Agent* A is a *member of* some *Collective* K, every member of which *shares* or *assumes* the *Description* D of the *Situation* S. In the end, D *is expressed by* an *Information object* I (which may be represented by different physical means).

Recalling our ontology, up to now there are four main concepts embedded in the foundational layer. They are the *Situations* representing the four main processes, represented in our system supporting prosecutor inquiries and police investigations: a criminal process[2], an inquiry process, an investigation process and a workflow process. We assume that processes are *Goal-oriented situations* and, in addition, they are executions of special descriptions called *Plans*. The processes are constituted (*set for*) by different real entities, such as persons, objects, real locations, actions, states, social relations, qualities, etc. Processes

---

[1] Words and phrases in italics name ontological concepts and formal relations. These entities have also names in Polish and the so-called "local names", which are concatenations of natural language words, see the OWL version of [18] interpreted by NeOnToolkit [12].

[2] We use here the commonsense meaning of a "process".

are inspected by agents (*Perceiving social agents*) who form their *Descriptions* by means of *Information objects*.

In the phase of formulating a *Description*, *Perceiving social agents* try to recognize and describe the *Plan* of the criminal activity. In the *Plan*, concepts classifying the real entities are either *used* or *defined*. The main concepts are *Tasks* (descriptions of goal-oriented actions), *State descriptions*, *Stative activity descriptions* (e.g. being used to sell some kind of goods, building something, accounting etc.) and *Roles* (classifying detailed functions of different entities involved in actions, states or activities). Besides *Plans*, the *Goals*, *Norms* and *Constitutive descriptions* are the main types of descriptions used in our ontology. We also use different kinds of *Social agents* both individual and collective, such as *Organizations* and *Institutions*. The collections of social agents are associated with *Organizations* and *Institutions*, through the actions done by their members. *Organizations* act through the members of *Intentional collectives*, *unified by a common planned activity*. Similarly, *Institutions* are associated with *Normative intentional collectives*, which are *unified by Norm and plan bundles* (their plans of acting are restricted by some specific regulative norms).

2.3   Ontology of Criminal Processes and Investigation Procedures

In the presented ontological view on reality, four main processes are considered. The first of them is a crime. The next two are an inquiry and an investigation – these processes follow directly from Polish law [10, 12, 14]: an inquiry (in general) is carried by a prosecutor and an investigation is carried by the police. The fourth process, workflow, represents the dynamic aspects of the inquiry/investigation processes. The conceptual scheme relates them and each process is formalized by means of a specialized version of the constructive descriptions and situations relation c.DnS, namely:

- *c.DnSForACriminalProcess*[3]
- *c.DnSForAnInquiryProcess*
- *c.DnSForAnInvestigationProcess*
- *c.DnSForAWorkflowProcess*.

We present the c.DnS structures in more detail using the UML (Unified Modeling Language)[4] graphical notation. Every process is graphically represented by a UML "package" comprising all the concepts and relations belonging to the relevant specialization of c.DnS. In every package the only concepts and relations shown are those by means of which the packages are interrelated. This is depicted in Fig.1. In details, the *classifies* formal ontological relation holds between the *AgentiveInquiryProcessRole* or the *AgentiveInvestigationProcessRole* (for example, *playedBy* the *PublicProsecutor* or the investigating *Policeman*) and the *PerceivingSocialAgent*, who perceives and *re-describes* the reality of a criminal process. A *WorkflowProcess*, representing the dynamics of an *InquiryProcess*

---

[3] From now on we will use the "local names" for concepts and relations.
[4] http://www.omg.org/spoc/UML

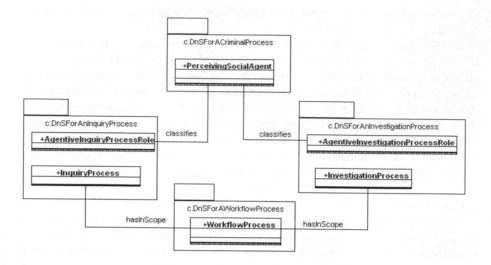

Fig. 1. Connections between the four processes

(or an *InvestigationProcess*) is related to it by the *hasInScope* formal ontological relation.

The c.DnS Structure for a Criminal Process. The structure of the main elements of the *c.DnSForACriminalProcess* is depicted in Fig. 2 and in Fig. 3. The criminal process consists of the actual criminal process (*ActualCriminalProcessSituation*, a specialization of *Goal-oriented situation*) and the inquiry version (*InquiryVersion*, a *RecognizedPlanOfCriminalProcess* situation). There may exist several such versions. The distinction of the two kinds of situations is based on the observation that actual states of affairs of criminal processes (here, *Situation*s), though reified in the ontology, are in most cases "untouchable" except the "in flagranti" circumstances. The *PerceivingSocialAgent* relies only on their trails, trying to recognize the *Plan* of a criminal activity. Thus, in fact, the criminal process reality is represented by a (maybe the set of) special *InquiryVersion* situation that is the realization of a recognized plan. Moreover, every criminal process situation is related to some *InquiryVersion* by means of the *hasInScope* formal ontological relation. The description of a criminal process contains a recognized plan of a criminal process (*RecognizedPlanOfCriminalProcess*) that is satisfied by the *InquiryVersion* situation. Moreover, such a situation is checked for compliance with another description, namely the incriminating norm (*IncriminatingNorm*, formally, the inquiry version situation *fallsUnder* the incriminating norm). Every *Plan* has as a proper part the *Goal* description (*GoalOfRecognizedPlanOfCriminalProcess*), representing its main goal. There are some kinds of *Descriptions* that are not considered yet, for instance the so-called *ConstitutiveDescriptions*, which constitute concepts whose existence is declared only by a definition given via such descriptions. For instance, the "forbidden action" concept exists if it is constituted by a relevant law definition. The

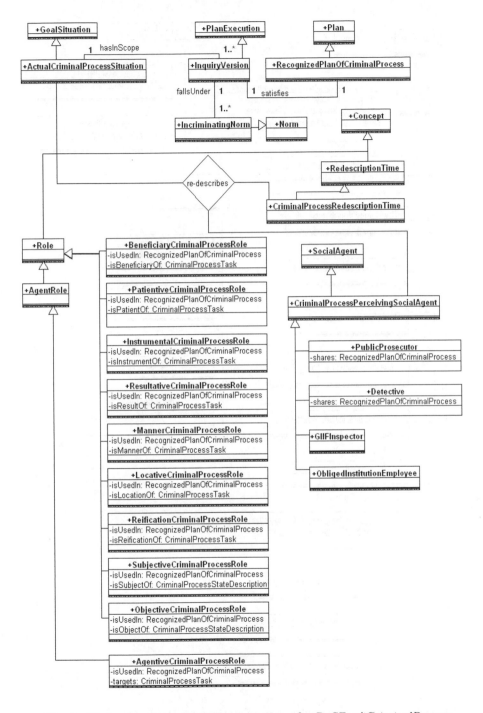

Fig. 2. First part of graphical representation of *c.DnSForACriminalProcess*

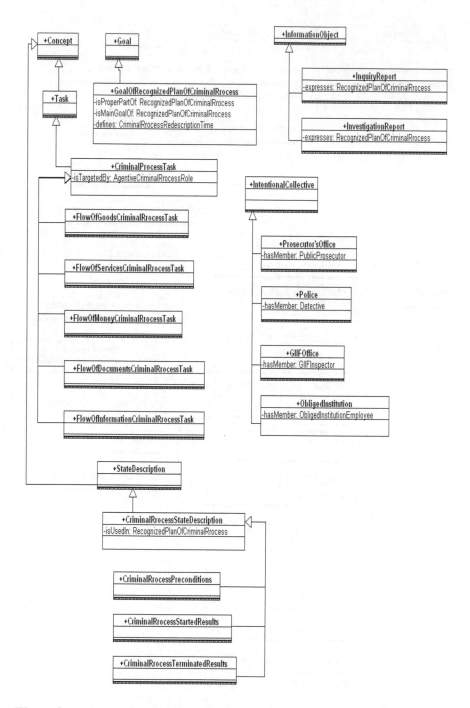

Fig. 3. Second part of graphical representation of *c.DnSForACriminalProcess*

same concerns *Social agents*, such as a *PublicProsecutor*, a *Policeman* or any *Institution* or *Organization* – the law provisions or other regulations constitute their existence.

We propose to introduce, among others, the public prosecutor agent (*PublicProsecutor*) and *Policeman* (for example *Detective*, *CriminalAnalyst*) as the perceiving agents. Both types of agents can perceive (trails of) some actual criminal process situation (*ActualCriminalProcessSituation*) and then *re-describe* it in a form of the mentioned recognized plan. There are other *Social agents* that are classified by (*isClassifiedBy*) *Roles* in a *RecognizedPlanOfCriminalProcess* and in other plans. As it was mentioned in subsection 2.2, we consider a social person, an organization, and an institution. *Organizations* are collective *SocialAgents* that are *actedBy* members (being also social agents) of some *IntentionalCollectives*. Such *Collective* *isUnifiedBy* a common *Plan*. The *Institution* differs from the *Organization* in that it *isActedBy* members of a *NormativeIntentionalCollective*, which is unified by a *NormPlanBundle*. This means that the plans of activity in institutions are constrained by some regulative norms. Among the *PerceivingSocialAgents* we also distinguish the *Institutions* like the General Financial Inspector Bureau (*GIIFInspector*, *GIIF*) and the obliged institution agent (*ObligedInstitution*). The latter means every financial institution that is legally obliged to inform the GIIF bureau about the suspicious financial activities; *Bank* institutions are among them.

Perceiving agents are members of the mentioned social agent collections (*AgentCollection*, in fact, the *NormativeIntentionalCollectives*). They *share* the earlier considered *Description*. Such *Collectives* gather members who *actFor Institutions*, e.g. for a prosecutor's office or for a police investigative team. Other collectives (connected with either institutions or organizations) are also defined in our ontology.

As it was mentioned before, the entities are ontologically grounded only when they are classified by concepts. The considered concepts are *CriminalProcessTask*, *CriminalProcessStateSpecification*, *CriminalProcessActivitySpecification* and *CriminalProcessRole*. *CriminalProcessTask* is meant for classifying these entities which are real (goal-oriented) *Actions*. *Tasks* are used in *Plans* where they are related to another concepts called the criminal process roles. The skeleton typology of *Tasks* is distinguished on the basis of the observation that, to detect and to legally assess the economic offenses, the *Actions* realizing the five flows should be trailed [21]. These are the flow of business documents (*FlowOfDocumentsCriminalProcessTask*, e.g. purchase orders, bills of lading, invoices or tax documents), the flow of goods (*FlowOfGoodsCriminalProcessTask*), the flow of services (*FlowOfServicesCriminalProcessTask*), the flow of money (*FlowOfMoneyCriminalProcessTask*, e.g. bank account transfer, cash transfer), and the information flow (*FlowOfInformationCriminalProcessTask*, e.g. phone billings). Thus, we have five generic types of tasks in every *RecognizedPlanOfCriminalProcess*. It is worth noticing that in general each of such tasks can be legal. But the sequences of them performed in special circumstances (for example, with forging or falsifying some documents) may be discovered as symptoms of a crime. For example, let us assume a chain of purchase orders (in one direction) followed by a sequence of invoices (in the opposite direction). If a relevant money transfers (the invoices payment) in the first direction is not accompanied by a shipment of goods (in the opposite direction), then the considered activity is fraudulent. This should be classified as a forbidden action (see the *CriminalProcessNotion* below) on the basis of some inference rule (programmed in the supporting system). The same concerns criminal roles, which seem to be normal business roles but their engagement in actions being components of criminal sequences enables to classify them as illegal.

CriminalProcessStateSpecification component is used to characterize the entities that are specifications of real states (e.g. being in a relationship or having an attribute of some value). Among such specifications there are *CriminalProcessPreConditions*, *CriminalProcessTerminatedResults*, and *CriminalProcessStartedResults* used to describe the states connected with potential execution of a plan. They also enable to conceptualize the dynamics of a plan execution. The preconditions (*CriminalProcessPreConditions*) are descriptions of states that are necessary to start the execution of a plan, the terminated results (*CriminalProcessTerminatedResults*) describe states that are terminated through the execution of the plan, and the started results (*CriminalProcessStartedResults*), describe states, which are started by the plan execution. The state specifications, similarly to tasks, use some roles (namely the subject being in the state and, possibly, some objects concerning the state).

There are also activity specifications (*CriminalProcessActivityDescription*). They can be useful to describe, for example, the activity category of some business firm. Similarly to tasks and state descriptions, the activity specifications use some roles. The same concerns the event description *CriminalProcessEventDescription*.

The *CriminalProcessRoles* are: *AgentiveCriminalProcessRole*, *PatientiveCriminalProcessRole*, *BeneficiaryCriminalProcessRole*, *InstrumentalCriminalProcessRole*, *ResultativeCriminalProcessRole*, *MannerCriminalProcessRole*, *LocativeCriminalProcessRole*, *ReificationCriminalProcessRole*, *SubjectiveCriminalProcessRole*, and *ObjectiveCriminalProcessRole*. Every role mirrors the thematic roles of arguments of predicates in sentences of a natural language. The reification role serves as a tool to represent tasks concerned with other tasks (the "higher order tasks' can be defined through this ability). For example, let T1 be the task expressed by the sentence 'The subject S does the job J in the place P'. We have here the social agent S classified by the role, say "performer", the job J classified by the patient-object role ("job") and the place P described by the locative role "the place of doing the job". Then the new task T2 appears expressed by the sentence "The subject S2 charges the subject S1 with doing the job J in the place P". Now, the agent S2 is classified by the role "employer" and the only other argument of the predicate "to charge with" is the reference to the task T1. Thus we reify T1 using the reification role R-T1 assigned to the task T2.

Among concepts, the *CriminalProcessSituationTime* and the *CriminalProcessRedescriptionTime* are used to classify real time intervals. The criminal situation descriptions (in fact, the inquiry versions) are expressed by a document that may be an *InquiryReport* or an *InvestigationReport*. It is an *InformationObject*, which may have different *PhysicalRealizations* (i.e. paper or electronic ones, which are kinds of not mentioned up to now entities).

The intended meaning of conceptual elements given in Fig. 2 and Fig. 3 is explicated via the formal relations holding between them. The being a recognized plan of a criminal process description deserves a special attention. This plan can be a complex structure describing the goal-oriented (and compound) action, so it has the main goal (*GoalOfRecognizedPlanOfCriminalProcess*) as a proper part. There may also exist sub-goals that influence the main goal. The plan must use at least one agentive role that is targeted by at least one task. We also assume that plans use state, activity and event specifications (the two latter are not shown in Fig. 2 and Fig. 3). The plan may define the concepts, and use the state, activity and event descriptions.

The c.DnS Structures for an Inquiry and an Investigation. Similarly to a criminal process description, the *c.DnSForAnInquiryProcess* and *c.DnSForAnInvestigationProcess* structures represent the reality of an inquiry and an investigation. We describe them briefly.

The *InquiryProcess* inquiry process situation is described by mans of the *InquiryProcessPlan* inquiry process plan that must be constrained by some *RegulativeNorm* regulative norm, in order to be law compliant (the inquiry process situation executes the regulative norm). The plan goal (*GoalOfInquiryProcessPlan*) represents the main goal of the inquiry process plan.

There exists the inquiry social agent (*InquiryProcessSocialAgent*), the member of the social agent collective (*InquiryProcessSocialAgentCollection*), who perceives the inquiry process. It is mostly a domain of interest of internal intelligence agencies, but among the perceiving agents there may be a prosecutor agent who supervises the inquiry process and in such a position he defines parts of the inquiry process plan.

InquiryProcessTask stands for inquiry process task meant for classifying these entities which are real actions. Tasks are used in plans and are related to another concepts called the inquiry process roles. Analogously to *CriminalProcessRole* the typology of *InquiryProcessRole* is given. Also, the *Concept*s and documents (*InformationObjects*) of *c.DnSForAnInquiryProcess* resemble the elements from *c.DnSForACriminalProcess*. The typology of the subprocesses of the *InquiryProcess* deserves a special attention. It was established on the basis of [16], [19], [20]. A number of subprocesses were distinguished, comprising two important processes of the generation of inquiry versions and the planning of an inquiry. The latter is conceptually interesting since it is the execution of some plan and its result is also a plan. Let us look closer at them. The plan of the generation of inquiry versions defines four tasks, and one agentive role (the leader of an investigation team) that targets these tasks:

1) generation of an inquiry version hypothesis by means of answering the questions about "what had happened?", "where?", "when?", "in what way?", "by means of what?", "why?" and "by whom?",
2) recognition of gaps which potentially exist in all the inquiry version hypotheses,
3) checking for verifiability of every inquiry version hypothesis,
4) ordering of hypotheses according to the degree of their probability.

There are also other *Role*s, and *StateDescription*s and *ActivityDescription*s not mentioned here. The planning of the inquiry is also a process in which the leader of the investigation team *plays* the *AgentiveInquiryProcessRole*. The resulting plan is a description of a planning situation that is *assumed* (formal relation, stronger than *shares*) by a planning agent. Some *Task*s in the inquiry planning process are the following:

1) adoption of one of the inquiry versions (ordered within the previously considered process),
2) definition of the tasks which are connected with the plan describing the adopted inquiry version,
3) definition of the additional tasks enabling to clarify the gaps in the adopted inquiry version,
4) definition of the whole plan with tasks defined in 2) and 3),
5) definition of agentive roles targeting the tasks which are defined in the generated plan.

The third process situation, namely the *c.DnSForAnInvestigationProcess* investigation process, is defined analogously to the inquiry process. The main differences are in the definition of the perceiving social agent (internal Police agencies) and of the types of the subprocesses. The investigation social agent perceives the investigation process (*InvestigationProcess*). The set of subprocesses resembles the similar set defined for the inquiry process except for some types of tasks, to carry which the Police is not allowed [16], [20].

The c.DnS Structure for a Workflow Process. The fourth considered process (Fig. 4) represents the dynamics of inquiries (and analogously, investigations). It was created on the basis of the COBRA solution [13]. This approach requires the modeling of time, so the *TimeInterval* and the *TimeInstant* concepts and the set of temporal relations adopted from Allen and Vilain were introduced (see [13] for references). Also, the temporal entities (that span in *TimeInterval*s or occur at *TimeInstant*s) were to be defined – as such the two specializations of the c.DnS *GroundEntity* were used, namely *Event* and *State*. Please note that in Fig. 4 we considered only the situation element (*WorkflowProcess*) of the whole c.DnS structure, accompanied by the entities that have setting in this situation. The *InquiryProcess* (*InvestigationProcess*) situation is also a setting for temporal *GroundEntit*ies, but for the sake of clarity they are not involved in Fig. 4. The temporal entities set in the *InquiryProcess* (*InvestigationProcess*) are subjects

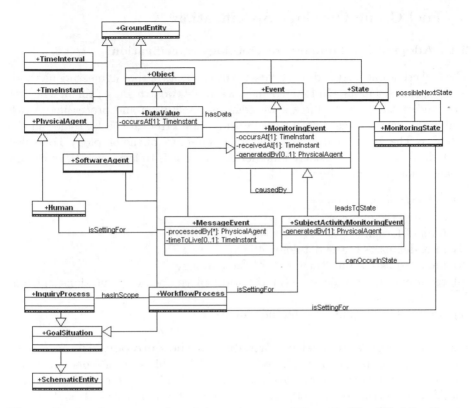

Fig. 4. Graphical representation of the main parts of the *c.DnSForAWorkflowProcess*

to sequences of *MonitoringEvents* of a *WorkflowProcess* that occur at *Time-Instances* and result in *DataValues*. Two types of such monitoring events were distinguished, namely *MessageEvent*, not generated by a *PhysicalAgent* (*Human* or *SoftwareAgent*) but processed by it, and *SubjectActivityMonitoringEvent* that is *generated* by a *PhysicalAgent* and leads to some (possible) *MonitoringState*. The following monitoring states are possible [13]: scheduled, assigned, ready (for not started subject actions or activities), running, suspended (for started subject actions or activities), aborted, terminated (for unsuccessfully finished actions or activities) or completed (for successfully finished actions or activities). The monitoring event can concern either an atomic subject action or activity, or a compound one. The compounds may be monitored as follows: instantiated, started, suspended, resumed, terminated, completed or aborted. For example, if the compound subject activity is in the "ready" monitoring state the "started" monitoring event leads to the "running" state. The atomic subject *Action* or *Activity* is monitored by the following types of *MonitoringEvents* ([13]): assigned, started, reassigned, relieved, manually skipped, scheduled, aborted, completed, resumed, withdrawn, suspended or automatically skipped. For example, the atomic activity that is in "suspended" monitoring state is transferred to the "running" state after the "resumed" monitoring event.

3   Fuel Crime Ontology Specification

3.1   Adopted Methodology of Ontology Specification

The fuel crime ontology is designed using the elements of the engineering method-ologies proposed in [6], [7]. In particular, we apply two features of them. The first one concern the way of source knowledge representation and processing, which enables to separate relevant "pieces of semantics", that are to be reified in the ontology. The second feature regards the architecture of the ontology. Following the indications of the considered methodologies, one is to formulate the ontology specification by expressing:

1) purpose of the ontology,
2) scope of the ontology,
3) level of formality,
4) intended users of the ontology,
5) intended uses ("functionality") of the ontology,
6) requirements specification (in the form of competency questions and an-swers),
7) pre-glossary of concepts and individuals.

Purpose, scope and level of formality of the ontology. The fuel crime ontology aims at providing the knowledge model of this kind of economic crime. During defining phase, it was assumed that it should be compatible with the ontology supporting the investigation management system (see section 2), in the sense of specializing it. The scope is determined by the motivating scenario (see section 3.2), which is a description of one particular case of a fuel crime, which is an instantiation of one scheme of such an offense. The ontology is formalized in OWL-DL (Web Ontology Language, the layer based on Description Logics) language.

Intended users of the ontology. Among the users we distinguish investigation management system implementors, fuel crime domain experts (who create crime scenarios) and also humans and software agents who communicate with the system, using its functionality.

Intended uses of the ontology. Ontology may be used as a semantic reference for domain experts who organize and communicate knowledge concerning new cases of fuel crime. Such a support, based on consensual knowledge model, will ease both describing new scenarios concerned with new cases, and introducing changes to the existing ontology. Another use case of the ontology regards its application to specify the semantics of human-system communication language. Other uses are connected with supporting the implementation of data process-ing tasks within the investigation management system (acquisition, extraction, exchange and inferences).

Requirements specification and pre-glossary of terms. We followed the top-down strategy to identify them. Their creation process was driven by the content pattern of the upper layer ontology for investigation management system. Details are given in section 3.3.

The main impact on the architecture of the ontology has the application of ontology design patterns. The most important one is the content pattern of c.DnS (see section 2.2). With this pattern in mind, the competency questions were formulated, the answers to which, in fact, constitute the layer specializing the c.DnS tuple.

3.2   Motivating Scenario

This scenario is based on the manuscript created by the domain expert [21], and also on its re-worked by a knowledge engineer version, given in [8], [9] and [10]. This scenario serves as the source domain knowledge, based on which the competency questions (see section 3.3) are defined, that are to be answered by the knowledge base of the investigation management system. The scenario of an exemplary fuel crime was revealed by the public prosecutor J. Więckowski [21] several years ago and specified by J. Martinek in [10]. After careful reading, one may divide the whole activity into three phases: obtaining fuel components (to make a blend), trading the blend (to obtain money) and masking the illegal provenance of money. The story goes as follows.

Company Petro-C, owned by I.N. and ruled by A.N., is registered as a heating oil trading company, having a fuel base, equipped in 7 huge containers and a pumping system between them. The company suggests it buys and re-sells the fuel components. It appeared that Petro-C has two methods of obtaining components.

Obtaining components – method I. Petro-C buys components from one of EPSI, N-PLUS, Lament or EPSI-sc companies and fictitiously sells them to the Petro-M company. In details, Petro-C orders the components in one of EPSI, N-PLUS, Lament or EPSI-sc that orders carriage of them from the oil refinery Trzebinia to Petro-C. EPSI or one of the others invoices components for Petro-C and the latter pays them by account money transfers. Then, Petro-C fictitiously sells components to Petro-M, that is, it invoices them for Petro-M but does not ship them. Petro-M compensates the value of "bought" components to Petro-C. After executing these transactions, Petro-C still has the components. Petro-M acts as a professional accountant and collaborates with the group of companies KAPI, MAD, MAD-sc and KOMPOL, to whom it "sells" the "bought" from Petro-C components.

Obtaining components – method II. One of EPSI, N-PLUS, Lament or EPSI-sc orders the components in oil refinery Trzebinia and at the same time it orders their shipment to Petro-C, but invoices them for Petro-M. Then, company Petro-C pays invoices by account money transfers, but entitles payments as fuel, not fuel components (fictitiously, Petro-C obtains fuel). Then, Petro-M pays say, EPSI and EPSI pays the oil refinery Trzebinia for the shipped components, all by account money transfers. In this case, Petro-C also gains components, and claims it has bought fuel.

Actually, Petro-C uses its infrastructure and blends components to obtain fuel. Now, the problem arises, how to sell the illegally produced fuel and mask the criminal procedure.

Selling of blend – method I. The first method consists in shipment of the fuel to one of the companies MT, PETRO, IPETRO or POL without invoicing it. In turn, these companies distribute it, give cash to Petro-C, and legalize the fuel by buying false invoices for it from KRAFTOL or DOMINET. They even pay VAT-7 tax to Inland Revenue for these invoices. KRAFTOL and DOMINET are straw companies, formally owned by strawmen, used to produce false documents (invoices) and facilitate free money transfer in different forms (bank accounts, in blanco checks).

Selling of blend – method II. In the second method, Petro-C indirectly sells fuel with the help of Petro-M. In detail, Petro-C ships the fuel to one of the companies MT, PETRO, IPETRO or POL without invoicing it, but this time, Petro-M invoices the fuel for them. The considered companies pay the invoices to Petro-M that, in turn, transfers money to Petro-C by bank account (for some not known goods).

Selling of blend – method III. Also, Petro-C is engaged as a fictitious intermediary seller of fuel to legal firm PKS. It "buys" fuel from Petro-M, which does not ship it but invoices it and Petro-C compensates this invoice. Then, Petro-C sells the fuel to PKS, shipping it and invoicing. PKS pays invoices by account money transfers.

Activities connected with masking of criminal activity. The process of covering up the trails of illegal production of fuel by Petro-C is continued by further fictitious re-selling of components. At first, Petro-C fictitiously sells them to Petro-M. Then, Petro-M invoices components for KOMPOL that compensates Petro-M for it, but Petro-M never ships them to KOMPOL.

The KOMPOL acts also as a fictitious provider of fuel to Petro-C with intermediary activity of Petro-M. Petro-M fictitiously buys fuel in KOMPOL and "sells" it to Petro-C (no fuel shipment and payment via compensation).

Petro-M acts also as financial intermediary between Petro-C (illegal fuel producer and provider) and several companies (MT, PETRO, IPETRO or POL) that sell it. Petro-C provides these companies with (illegal) fuel without invoicing it. Petro-M fictitiously buys fuel from KOMPOL (no shipment, nothing known about payment) and fictitiously sells it to MT, PETRO, IPETRO or POL (no shipment, payment by account money transfer), and finally Petro-M pays Petro-C for some unknown goods by account money transfer.

Inception of the investigation. The investigation was started after receiving a notification about an offense by GIIF, with suspicion that KRAFTOL does money laundering. It also appeared that money transfers were entitled as payments for fuels, but the company had not relevant infrastructure to deal with fuels. Thus, KRAFTOL was a typical straw company and so was DOMINET that legalized the unknown provenance fuels.

3.3   Competency Questions and Answers

The fuel crime model is a specialization of the *c.DnSForACriminalProcess* relation. Recalling its definition, we assume that there exists a *SocialAgent* (for example, a prosecutor) who perceives a real fuel crime situation and wants to reveal its main *Plan* and to ascribe the main *Goal* to it. Also, the pre- and postconditions (initiated and/or terminated results) of the execution of the *Plan* are specified, on the basis of which the truth of the *Plan* can be verified and also its dynamics can be modeled. Complex *Plan*s are often divided into subplans with subgoals. We adopt the "occurrence-centered" view on reality – thus the main entities connected with *Plan*s are *Description*s of involved *Action*s, *State*s, *Event*s and *Activit*ies. All of the occurrences have *Role*s ascribed to them. *Description*s of *Action*s fall into three categories called "flows" (see section 2.3): of documents, of goods or services and of financial assets. The real criminal situation is a setting for real entities, such as *PhysicalPerson*s, *Substance*s, *Object*s, *SpaceRegion*s etc.

   We specify the elements of the *c.DnSForAFuelCrimeProcess* relation in terms of answers given to manually created competency questions. Questions represent the semantics of queries that may be addressed to the investigation management systems' knowledge base. In answers the specification of both ontological concepts and individuals is given. We distinguished four subplans of the main plan. Due to the lack of space, only one such subplan is described with details, namely "blending components to obtain fuel". The other subplans are also conceptualized giving the whole amount of 39 questions and answers. The scheme of the considered relation is as follows.

$$c.DnSForAFuelCrimeProcess = <FuelCrimeProcess,$$
$$FuelCrimeEnitity,$$
$$FuelCrimePerceivingAgent,$$
$$FuelCrimeDescription,$$
$$FuelCrimeConcept,$$
$$FuelCrimePerceivingAgentsCollective,$$
$$FuelCrimeInformationObject >$$

The answer to the Q1 question specifies the concepts specializing the *FuelCrimePerceivingAgent*. The next two questions (Q2 and Q3) are concerned with *FuelCrimeDescription*, namely the main plan (which is a description of the fuel crime situation) and its main goal. Other parts of this description are subplans and subgoals (Q7 and Q8). The execution of the plan (and its subplans) results in a situation constituting the *FuelCrimeProcess* (particularly, one element of it, namely an inquiry version). This situation is the setting for some real states, actions and activities, and also physical objects subsumed by *FuelCrimeEnitity*. Some of them are explicitly given, as physical persons, substances, physical objects (Q14), places (Q15) and social agents, both individual and organizations (Q13). The occurrents (actions, activities and states) are represented in the way they are perceived by *FuelCrimePerceivingAgent* and classified by him via specializations of *FuelCrimeConcept*. These concepts are: preconditions, initiated-and/or terminated results of the plan execution (questions Q4, Q5 and Q6), tasks that classify actions (Q9), activities descriptions (Q11) and states descriptions (Q12). Occurrents have arguments targeted to them – in our approach they are classified as specializations of roles that resemble thematic roles of predicates in natural language sentences, see question Q10. All the questions accompanied by answers are now given.

Q1. Who perceives and describes the fuel crime? **A1.** The following social agents: GIIF inspector, District Public Prosecutor in K.

Q2. What is the main goal of the fuel crime? **A2.** Obtaining big amount of money (illegally) using the fuel trade market.

Q3. What is the main plan of the fuel crime? **A3.** Producing (without license) fuel by mixing (blending) components, selling it on the market and laundering the illicit gain.

Q4. What are the preconditions to execute the main plan? **A4.** The preconditions are: a) having the infrastructure to blend components, b) carry fuel, c) trade fuel and d) document the trade.

Q5. What are the initiated results of executing the main plan? **A5.** The initiated results are: a) having the big amount of money (by criminal organization), b) having the trade documents legitimizing big amount of money (by criminal organization) and c) not having the big amount of tax income (by Inland Revenue).

Q6. What are the terminated results of executing the main plan? **A6.** The terminated results are: a) having fuel components and b) having (illegally) produced fuel (a "blend").

Q7. What are the criminal subgoals of the fuel crime? **A7.** The criminal subgoals are: a) obtaining fuel, b) masking fuel production trails, c) obtaining money for the fuel and d) laundering the obtained money.

Q8. What are the subplans of the main fuel crime plan? **A8.** The subplans are: a) blending components to obtain fuel (a "blend"), b) *"loosing"* the obtained components, c) trading a blend to obtain money and d) legitimizing the obtained money (money laundering).

Q9. What are the actions (tasks) executed in "blending components to obtain fuel" plan? **A9.** The actions are the following:

1. *Flow of documents actions*:
   a) Obtaining fuel components (I)
      Petro-C orders components in one of EPSI, N-PLUS, Lament or EPSI-sc. One of EPSI, N-PLUS, Lament or EPSI-sc orders components in refinery Trzebinia.
      One of EPSI, N-PLUS, Lament or EPSI-sc charges shipment of components from Trzebinia to Petro-C.

One of EPSI, N-PLUS, Lament or EPSI-sc invoices the components for Petro-C.
   b) Obtaining fuel components (II)
   One of EPSI, N-PLUS, Lament or EPSI-sc orders components in refinery Trzebinia.
   One of EPSI, N-PLUS, Lament or EPSI-sc charges shipment of components from Trzebinia to Petro-C.
   One of EPSI, N-PLUS, Lament or EPSI-sc invoices the components for Petro-M.
2. *Flow of goods actions*:
   a) Obtaining fuel components (I)
   Trzebinia conveys the components to Petro-C.
   b) Obtaining fuel components (II)
   Trzebinia conveys the components to Petro-C.
   c) Obtaining fuel from components
   Petro-C obtains fuel blend from the components.
3. *Flow of money actions*:
   a) Obtaining fuel components (I)
   Petro-C transfers money for the components to one of EPSI, N-PLUS, Lament or EPSI-sc by bank account.
   b) Obtaining fuel components (II)
   Petro-M transfers money for the components to one of EPSI, N-PLUS, Lament or EPSI-sc by bank account.
   One of EPSI, N-PLUS, Lament or EPSI-sc transfers money for the components to Trzebinia by bank account.

Q10. What are the roles used in "blending components to obtain fuel" plan?
A10. The roles are the following:

- *Agentive roles*: components order issuer, components bill of lading issuer, components invoice issuer, components warehouse document issuer, components carrier, components blender, money sender.
- *Patient-beneficiary roles*: components order receiver, components bill of lading receiver, components invoice receiver, components warehouse (Wz) document receiver, components warehouse (Pz) document receiver, components receiver, money receiver.
- *Patient-object roles*: ordered components, conveyed components, transport means, invoiced components, warehoused components, blended components, fuel terminal infrastructure, quote of money, bank account.
- *Locative roles*: components bill of lading issuing place, components order issuing place, components invoice issuing place, components warehouse (Wz) document issuing place, components warehouse (Pz) document issuing place, components carriage starting place, components carriage target place, components blending place, sender account bank, receiver account bank.
- *Resulting roles*: issued components order, issued components bill of lading, issued components invoice, issued components warehouse (Wz) document, issued components warehouse (Pz) document, transporting of components, fuel blend, transferred quote of money.

- *Manner roles*: blending components, transferring money via bank account.
- *Reification roles*: invoicing of ordered components, carriage of invoiced components, payment of invoiced components.

Q11. What are the activities performed in "blending components to obtain fuel" plan? **A11.** The activities are: a) leading of Petro-C group criminal structure by a boss, b) trading components by EPSI, N-PLUS, Lament, EPSI-sc, c) producing fuel blend by Petro-C, d) Petro-M accounting for Petro-C.

Q12. What are the states of agents and objects in "blending components to obtain fuel" plan? **A12.** The states are: a) Petro-C ownership of fuel tanks, b) Petro-C ownership of tankers, c) Petro-C registration as a heating oil trading firm.

Q13. What (social) agents are engaged in "blending components to obtain fuel" plan? **A13.** The agents are the following:

- *Individual social persons*: firm owner, bank account owner, criminal organization boss, employee,
- *Organizations*: Petro-C group criminal structure,
- *Institutions*:
  - *firms*: Petro-C, Petro-M, EPSI, N-PLUS, Lament, EPSI-sc,
  - refinery Trzebinia,
  - bank.

Q14. What physical objects are engaged in "blending components to obtain fuel" plan? **A14.** The objects are the following:

- *Physical persons*: individuals I-N, A-N and others,
- *Substances*: components, fuel (blend),
- *Physical objects*: fuel tank, pumping system, tanker, physical realization of purchase order, physical realization of invoice, physical realization of bill of lading, physical realization of warehouse (Wz) document, physical realization of warehouse (Pz) document.

Q15. What places are engaged in "blending components to obtain fuel" plan? **A15.** The places are the following: firm premises, refinery premises, fuel base premises.

4   Conclusions

We undertook the task of building the presented ontology in order to have a mean to "grasp" the semantics of the being created information system. The presented conceptual scheme is being formalized in OWL ontology language, by using two tools: Protégé 4.0 [14] ontology editor (with the FaCT++ reasoner plug-in) and NeOn Toolkit [12] environment. The working implementation of the ontology is published zipped in [18] (the starting file is PPBW.owl).

This version was created on the basis of a description (made by the expert) of several cases of economic crimes (including the fuel crime) that were legally assessed and sentenced a couple years ago. It occurred that there exists the common template by means of which the cases and their investigations can be modeled. We expressed this template using the constructive descriptions and situations paradigm, because thinking of the semantics of states of affairs in this way appeared to be both compliant with the commonsense and easy. Additionally, within this framework the whole semantics modeling task can be conveniently divided into subtasks (specialization threads) that are modeled separately but at the same time they form a coherent whole. The complete formalization of the whole ontology in an ontology language is an important task to do. To be useful its result ought to be computationally tractable. Also, the ontology should be enriched by new specializations such as the ontology of law.

Acknowledgements. This research is supported by the Polish Ministry of Science and Higher Education, Polish Technological Security Platform grant 0014/R/2/T00/06/02.

References

1. Casellas, N.: Modelling Legal Knowledge through Ontologies. OPJK: the Ontology of Professional Judicial Knowledge, PhD thesis, Spain,
   http://idt.uab.es/~ncasellas/nuria_casellas_thesis.pdf
2. Cybulka, J., Jędrzejek, C., Martinek, J.: Police Investigation Management System Based on the Workflow Technology. In: Legal Knowledge and Information Systems, Frontiers in Artificial Intelligence and Applications, vol. 189, pp. 150–159. IOS Press, Amsterdam (2008)
3. Cybulka, J.: Applying the c.DnS Design Pattern to Obtain an Ontology for Investigation Management System. In: Nguyen, N.T., Kowalczyk, R., Chen, S.-M. (eds.) ICCCI 2009. Lecture Notes in Computer Science, LNAI, vol. 5796, pp. 516–527. Springer, Heidelberg (2009)
4. FFPoirot – Financial Fraud Prevention Oriented Information Resources using Ontology Technology, http://ffpoirot.org
5. Gangemi, A., Lehmann, J., Catenacci, C.: Norms and Plans as Unification Criteria for Social Collectives. In: Proceedings of Dagstuhl Seminar 07122, Normative Multi-agent Systems, pp. 48–87G. Vol. II (2007), ISSN 1862-4405
   http://drops.dagstuhl.de/opus/volltexte/2007/910
6. Gangemi, A., et al.: C-ODO: an OWL Metamodel for Collaborative Ontology Design. In: WWW 2007, Banff, Canada, May 8-12 (2007)
7. Gomez-Perez, A., et al.: NeOn Methodology for Building Ontology Networks: Ontology Specification. NeOn Deliverable D5.4.1, http://www.neon-project.org
8. Martinek, J.: Prowadzenie śledztwa w sprawach nielegalnego handlu paliwem z wykorzystaniem wspomagania informatycznego. In: Wymiar Sprawiedliwości i Administracja Publiczna Wobec Prawa Nowych Technologii, Wrocław, September 21-22 (2009)
9. Martinek, J.: Information Structures of Police Investigation Management System. In: 7th Conference on Computer Methods and Systems CMS 2009, Oprogramowanie Naukowo-Techniczne, Kraków, pp. 49–54 (2009)
10. Martinek J.: Baza danych dużej sprawy paliwowej. Raport techniczny, Polska Platforma Bezpieczeństwa Wewnętrznego (2008)

11. Mądrzejowski W.: Przestępczość zorganizowana. System zwalczania. Wydawnictwa Akademickie i Profesjonalne, Warszawa (2008)
12. Neon Toolkit, http://neon-toolkit.org/wiki/Main_Page
13. Pedrinaci, C., Domingue, J., Alves de Medeiros, A.K.: A Core Ontology for Business Process Analysis. In: Bechhofer, S., et al. (eds.) ESWC 2008. LNCS, vol. 5021, pp. 49–64. Springer, Heidelberg (2008)
14. Protégé Ontology Editor ver. 4.0, http://protege.stanford.edu
15. SUMO – Suggested Upper Merged Ontology, http://www.ontologyportal.org
16. The Code of Penal Procedure (in Polish). Ustawa z 6.06.1997 r. Kodeks postępowania karnego (1997)
17. The OWL Version of c.DnS Ontology, http://www.loa-cnr.it/ontologies/collInt.owl
18. The OWL version of the ontology of criminal processes and investigation procedures, http://www.man.poznan.pl/~jolac/cDnSPL.zip
19. The Penal Code (in Polish). Ustawa z dnia 6 czerwca 1997 r. Kodeks karny (1997)
20. Widacki, J.: Kryminalistyka. C.H.Beck, Warszawa (2008)
21. Więckowski, J.: Private Communication. Public District Prosecutor's Office in Katowice (2008)
22. Zhao, J.L., Bi, H.H., et al.: Process-driven Collaboration Support for Intra-agency Crime Analysis. Decision Support Systems 41, 616–663 (2006)

A Robust Approach for Nonlinear UAV Task Assignment Problem under Uncertainty

Le Thi Hoai An and Nguyen Quang Thuan

Laboratory of Theoretical and Applied Computer Science (LITA)
Paul Verlaine - Metz University, Ile du Saulcy, 57045, Metz, France

Abstract. This paper presents a new robust approach to the task assignment of unmanned aerial vehicles (UAVs) operating in uncertain environments whose the objective is maximizing the target score. The intrinsic uncertainty imbedded in military operations makes the problem more challenging. Scalability and robustness are recognized as two main issues. We deal with these issues by an approach based on DC (Difference of Convex functions) programming and DCA (DC Algorithm). The numerical results show that this approach is efficient.

Keywords: UAV, Task Assignment Problem, Uncertainty, DC Programming, DCA.

1 Introduction

The use of unmanned aerial vehicles (UAVs) for various military missions has received growing attention in the past years. Apart from the obvious advantage of not placing human life at risk, the lack of a human pilot enables considerable weight savings and lower costs. On the other hand, UAVs provide an opportunity for new operational paradigms. Howerver, to realize these advantages, UAVs must have a high level of autonomy and capacity to work cooperatively in groups. In this context, several algorithms dealing with the problem of commanding multiple UAVs to cooperatively perform multiple tasks have been developed. The aim is to assign specific tasks and flyable trajectories to each vehicle to maximize the group performance. The intrinsic uncertainty imbedded in military operations makes the problem more challenging. Scalability and robustness are recognized as two main issues. Also, to allow implementation, the developed algorithms must be solved in real time.

Extensive research has been done recently in this field [1,3,9,10,15,16,17,18]. In [1,10,15], task allocation has been formulated in the form of Mixed-Integer Linear Programming (MILP). In this approach, the problem is solved as a deterministic optimization problem with known parameters. Since the MILP is NP-hard, it suffers from poor scalability although the solutions preserve global optimality [14]. Moreover, military situations are in general dynamic and uncertain because of the UAV's sensing limitation and adversarial strategies. Thus, replanning is necessary whenever the information is updated. Heuristics and ad-hoc methods

N.T. Nguyen and R. Kowalczyk (Eds.): Transactions on CCI II, LNCS 6450, pp. 147–159, 2010.

have been considered during replanning in [10,3]. On the other hand, uncertainty is considered via optimization parameters, and risk management techniques in finance are utilized (see e.g. [16,18]). In [16], a nonlinear integer programming problem is formulated where a risk measure by conditional value-at-risk is considered as constraint. In [18], a robust approach using the Soyster formulation on the expectation of the target scores is investigated. These approaches are based on solving hard combinatorial optimization problems and then scalability is still a big issue. An alternative approach dealing with uncertainties consists of formulating a stochastic optimal control problem by using the method of Model Predictive Control (MPC) [2,17].

In this paper, we are interested in task allocation models where we seek to assign a set of m UAVs to a set of n tasks in an optimal way. The optimality is quantified by target scores. The mission is to maximize the target score while satisfying capacity constraints of both the UAVs and the tasks.

The scoring scheme defining effectiveness in our work is a nonlinear function. More precisely, we consider a model in the form of mixed integer nonlinear programming for which the classical MILP solution method can not be used. We propose an efficient approach based on DC programming and DCA for solving it.

DC programming and DCA were introduced by Pham Dinh Tao in 1985 and have been extensively developed by Le Thi Hoai An and Pham Dinh Tao since 1994. DCA has been successfully applied to real world non-convex programs in different fields of applied sciences (see e.g. [8,11,12] and the references therein). DCA is one of rare efficient algorithms for non-smooth non-convex programming which allows solving large-scale DC programs. Although DCA is a continuous approach, it has been efficiently investigated for solving nonconvex Linear/quadratic programming with binary variables (see e.g. [5,6,13]) via exact penalty techniques [4]. This motivates us to use DCA for this Task Assignment Problem (UTAP). Thank to a new result concerning exact penalty techniques in DC programming we first reformulate the UTAP as a continuous optimization problem which is in fact a DC program. Then, we apply DC programming and DCA for the resulting problem. Despite its local character, DCA with a good initial point (depending on the specific structure of treated DC programs) converges quite often to global solutions in practice. Hence, an important question in the use of DCA is how to find a *good* starting point. For this purpose we combine DCA with a Branch and Bound (B&B) scheme. The use of B&B is twofold: for finding a good starting point to restart DCA, and, by the way, for proving the globality of the solution furnished by DCA.

The rest of paper is organized as follows. The problem statement and its mathematical formulation are described in section 2. Section 3 is dedicated to DC programming and DCA for solving the considered problem. The B&B and the combined DCA - B&B methods are presented in section 4 while the numerical experiments are reported in section 5. Section 6 concludes the paper with some conclusions and perspectives.

2   Problem Statement and Its Mathematical Formulation

Let V and T be the sets of m UAVs and n targets, respectively. The scoring scheme defining effectiveness is based on the definition of target score. Each target j has an associated score based on the task success probability r_j and a weight w_j measuring the importance of the target. The probability that the task will be successfully carried out for that target depends on y_j, the number of UAVs which have been assigned to the target j, in the following way:

$$1 - (1 - r_j)^{y_j}.$$

A target score is computed as the product of the success probability and its weight:

$$g_j(y_j) = w_j(1 - (1 - r_j)^{y_j}), \tag{1}$$

and the UAVs group effectiveness is simply the sum of all individual target scores: $\sum_{j \in T} g_j(y_j)$. Then the goal is to maximize the UAVs group effectiveness.

Let x_{ij}, for $i \in V = \{1, \cdots, m\}$ and $j \in T = \{1, \cdots, n\}$, be the decision variable defined by: x_{ij} is equal to 1 when the UAV i is assigned to the target j and 0, otherwise. An entry of $m \times n$ adjacency matrix A, a_{ij}, indicates which target each UAV can be assigned. So, the number y_j can be computed as $y_j = \sum_{i \in V} a_{ij} x_{ij}, \quad j \in T$.

The mathematical model of the UTAP can be written as follows:

$$(UTAP) \quad \max \sum_{j \in T} w_j(1 - (1 - r_j)^{\sum_{i \in V} a_{ij} x_{ij}}) \tag{2}$$

$$s.t.$$

$$\sum_{j \in T} x_{ij} = 1, \quad i \in V \tag{3}$$

$$x_{ij} \in \{0, 1\}, \quad i \in V, j \in T. \tag{4}$$

The constraints (3) ensure that each UAV i is used for only one task. The problem (UTAP) is an integer nonlinear programming which is known to be very hard.

3   Solution Method via DC Programming and DCA

In this section we will develop DC programming and DCA for solving (UTAP). First, let us give a brief introduction of DC programming and DCA.

3.1   DC Programming and DCA

For a convex function θ defined on $\mathbb{R}^n$ and $x_0 \in dom\theta := \{x \in \mathbb{R}^n : \theta(x) < +\infty\}$, $\partial\theta(x_0)$ denotes the sub-differential of θ at x_0 that is

$$\partial\theta(x_0) := \{y \in \mathbb{R}^n : \theta(x) \geq \theta(x_0) + \langle x - x_0, y \rangle, \forall x \in \mathbb{R}^n\}. \tag{5}$$

The sub-differential $\partial\theta(x_0)$ is a closed convex set in $\mathbb{R}^n$. It generalizes the derivative in the sense that θ is differentiable at x_0 if and only if $\partial\theta(x_0)$ is reduced to a singleton which is exactly $\{\theta'(x_0)\}$. A convex function θ is called *convex polyhedral* if it is the maximum of a finite family of affine functions, i.e.

$$\theta(x) = \max\{\langle a_i, x \rangle + b : i = 1, \cdots, n\}, a_i \in \mathbb{R}^n. \tag{6}$$

DC programming and DCA which have been introduced by Pham Dinh Tao in 1985 and extensively developed by Le Thi Hoai An and Pham Dinh Tao since 1994 (see e.g. [8,11,12]) constitute the backbone of smooth/nonsmooth non-convex programming and global optimization. They address a general DC program that takes the form:

$$(P_{dc}) \quad \inf\{f(x) := g(x) - h(x) : x \in \mathbb{R}^n\}$$

where g and h are lower semi-continuous proper convex functions on $\mathbb{R}^n$. Such a function f is called DC function, and $g - h$ is a DC decomposition of f while g and h are DC components of f. The convex constraint $x \in C$ can be incorporated in the objective function of (P_{dc}) by using the indicator function on C denoted χ_C which is defined by $\chi_C(x) = 0$ if $x \in C$; $+\infty$ otherwise.

Let $g^*(y) := \sup\{\langle x, y \rangle - g(x) : x \in \mathbb{R}^n\}$ is the conjugate function of g. Then the so called dual program of (P_{dc}) is defined by:

$$(D_{dc}) \quad \beta_d = \inf\{h^*(y) - g^*(y) : y \in \mathbb{R}^n\}. \tag{7}$$

The necessary local optimality condition for the primal DC program, (P_{dc}), is

$$\partial h(x^*) \subset \partial g(x^*). \tag{8}$$

The condition (8) is also sufficient for many important classes of DC programs, for example, for Polyhedral DC programs, or when function F is locally convex at x^* ([8,11]).

A point that x^* verifies the generalized Kuhn-Tucker condition

$$\partial h(x^*) \cap \partial g(x^*) \neq \emptyset \tag{9}$$

is called a critical point of $g - h$. It follows that if h is polyhedral convex, then a critical point of $g - h$ is almost always a local solution to (P_{dc}).

The transportation of global solutions between (P_{dc}) and (D_{dc}) is expressed by:

Property 1:

$$[\cup_{y^* \in \mathcal{D}_{dc}} \partial g^*(y^*)] \subset \mathcal{P}_{dc}, \ [\cup_{x^* \in \mathcal{P}_{dc}} \partial h(x^*)] \subset \mathcal{D}_{dc}, \tag{10}$$

where $\mathcal{P}_{dc}$ and $\mathcal{D}_{dc}$ denote the solution sets of (P_{dc}) and (D_{dc}) respectively.

Under certain technical conditions, this property also holds for the local solutions of (P_{dc}) and (D_{dc}). For example (see [8,11,12] for more information):

Property 2: let x^* be a local solution to (P_{dc}) and let $y^* \in \partial h(x^*)$. If g^* is differentiable at y^* then y^* is a local solution to (D_{dc}). Similarly, let y^* be a local solution to (D_{dc}) and let $x^* \in \partial g^*(y^*)$. If h is differentiable at x^* then x^* is a local solution to (P_{dc}).

Based on local optimality conditions and duality in DC programming, the idea of DCA is quite simple: each iteration of DCA approximates the concave part $-h$ by its affine majorization (that corresponds to taking $y_k \in \partial h(x^k)$ and minimizes the resulting convex function).

Generic DCA Scheme
Initialization: Let $x_0 \in \mathbb{R}^n$ be a best guess, $k = 0$;
Repeat
    Calculate $y^k \in \partial h(x^k)$;
    Calculate x^{k+1} by solving the convex problem

$$\min\{g(x) - h(x^k) - \langle x - x^k, y^k \rangle : x \in \mathbb{R}^n\} \quad (P_k); \qquad (11)$$

    $k = k + 1$;
Until convergence of x^k.

Convergence properties of DCA and its theoretical basis can be found in [8,11,12]. However, it is worthwhile to report the following properties that are useful in the next (for simplify, we omit here the dual part of these properties):

i) DCA is a descent method (the sequences $\{g(x^k) - h(x^k)\}$ is decreasing) without line search;
ii) If the optimal value of problem (P_{dc}) is finite and the infinite sequence x^k is bounded then every limit point x^* of $\{x^k\}$ is a critical point of $g - h$.
iii) DCA has a linear convergence for general DC programs.
iv) DCA has a finite convergence for polyhedral DC programs.

The construction of DCA involves DC components g and h but not the function f itself. Hence, for a DC program, each DC decomposition corresponds to a different version of DCA. Since a DC function f has an infinite number of DC decompositions which have crucial impacts on the qualities (speed of convergence, robustness, efficiency, globality of computed solutions, ...) of DCA, the search of a "good" DC decomposition is important from algorithmic point of views. How to develop an efficient algorithm based on the generic DCA scheme for a practical problem is thus a judicious question to be studied, the answer depending on the specific structure of the problem being considered.

3.2   DC Reformulation

First, let us present a new result concerning exact penalty techniques in DC programming developed in [7]. Consider the general zero-one problem (GIP) in the form:

$$(GIP) \quad \min\{f(x) : x \in K, \quad x \in \{0, 1\}^n\}, \qquad (12)$$

where f is a DC function and K is a nonempty bounded polyhedral convex in $\mathbb{R}^n$. Such a combinatorial optimization problem can be reformulated as a continuous one thanks to the next theorem.

Theorem 1. *Let K be a nonempty bounded polyhedral convex set in $\mathbb{R}^n$, f be a finite DC function on K and p be a finite nonnegative concave function on K. Then there exists $t_0 \geq 0$ such that for all $t > t_0$ the following problems have the same optimal value and the same solution set:*

$$(P_t) \quad \alpha(t) = \min\{f(x) + tp(x) : x \in K\} \tag{13}$$

$$(P) \quad \alpha = \min\{f(x) : x \in K, p(x) \leq 0\}. \tag{14}$$

PROOF: The proof of this theorem can be found in [7].

Continuous formulation. We now are able to formulate (GIP) as a continuous optimization problem. Let p be the finite function defined on K by

$$p(x) := \frac{1}{2} \sum_{i=1}^{n} x_i(1 - x_i) \leq 0.$$

It is clear that p is nonnegative and concave on $K' := K \cap \{[0,1]^n\}$. Moreover we have

$$\{x \in K : x \in \{0,1\}^n\} = \{x \in K' : p(x) = 0\} = \{x \in K' : p(x) \leq 0\}.$$

Therefore, the problem (GIP) can be rewritten as

$$\min\{f(x) : x \in K', \ p(x) \leq 0\}.$$

From Theorem 1 it follows that with a sufficiently large number t the last problem is equivalent to

$$\min\{f(x) + tp(x) : x \in K'\}.$$

Now, let us turn back to the original problem (UTAP). By passing the constant terms, (UTAP) is equivalent to the following problem:

$$\min\left\{f(x) := \sum_{j=1}^{n} w_j(1 - r_j)^{\sum\limits_{i=1}^{m} a_{ij}x_{ij}} : x \in K, x \in \{0,1\}^{m.n}\right\} \tag{15}$$

where K is the set of points in $\mathbb{R}^{m.n}$ satisfying (3). Since the convex function $f(x)$ is also a DC function (it is in fact a *false* DC function), applying the above results dealing with (GIP) for (15) we get the following equivalent problem to (UTAP) (with a sufficiently large number t):

$$\min\left\{F(x) := \sum_{j=1}^{n} w_j(1 - r_j)^{\sum\limits_{i=1}^{m} a_{ij}x_{ij}} + tp(x) : x \in K'\right\}, \tag{16}$$

where

$$K' := K \cap \{[0,1]^{m.n}\}.$$

DC formulation. We have transformed the UTAP in the form of a continuous optimization problem. For applying DCA, let us highlight a DC decomposition of F. There are many ways to decompose the DC function F and we wish to choose a DC decomposition such that the convex sub-problem (11) can be easily solved.

In order to employ the efficient commercial software CPLEX for convex sub-problem, we use the following DC decomposition:

$$F(x) = g(x) - h(x) := \frac{\lambda}{2}\|x\|^2 - \left(\frac{\lambda}{2}\|x\|^2 - F(x)\right) \tag{17}$$

where λ is positive number such that the function

$$h(x) := \frac{\lambda}{2}\|x\|^2 - F(x) = \frac{\lambda}{2}\|x\|^2 - f(x) - tp(x)$$

is convex. Since $-p$ is already convex function, h will be convex if the function $\frac{\lambda}{2}\|x\|^2 - f(x)$ is convex, i.e. its Hessian matrix is semi-definite positive (note that f and $-p$ are twice-differentiable, so are the functions $\frac{\lambda}{2}\|.\|^2 - f$ and h).

For notational simplicity, we represent $x = (x_{11}, x_{12}, ..., x_{1n}, ..., x_{m1}, x_{m2}, ..., x_{mn})$ as $x = (x_1, x_2, ..., x_{m.n})$. In other words, an element x_{ij}, for $i = 1, ..., m; j = 1, ..., n$, is presented as x_l with $l = n.(i-1) + j$.

We have $\nabla^2 h(x) = \lambda I - \nabla^2 f(x)$ and the Hessian matrix of f is computed as

$$\left(\nabla^2 f(x)\right)_{ll'} = \frac{\partial f^2}{\partial x_l \partial x_{l'}} = \begin{cases} 0, & \text{if } j \neq j'; \\ a_{ij} a_{i'j'} w_j (1 - r_j)^{\sum\limits_{i=1}^{m} a_{ij}x_{ij}} (\log(1-r_j))^2, & \text{otherwise,} \end{cases} \tag{18}$$

with $l = (i-1).n + j$ and $l' = (i'-1).n + j'$ for $i, i' \in \{1, ..., m\}; j, j' \in \{1, ..., n\}$.

The norm of $\nabla^2 f(x)$ can be calculated:

$$\|\nabla^2 f(x)\|_\infty = \max_{u=1..m,\, v=1..n}\left\{a_{uv}(\sum_{i=1}^{m} a_{iv})w_v(1 - r_v)^{\sum\limits_{i=1}^{m} a_{iv}x_{iv}} (\log(1-r_v))^2\right\}.$$

Since $\sum\limits_{i=1}^{m} a_{iv}x_{iv} \geq 0$ and $(1 - r_v) \leq 1$, we have

$$\|\nabla^2 f(x)\|_\infty \leq \max_{u=1..m,\, v=1..n}\left\{a_{uv}(\sum_{i=1}^{m} a_{iv})w_v(\log(1-r_v))^2\right\}. \tag{19}$$

So, the matrix $\nabla^2 h$ is semi-definite positive when

$$\lambda \geq \max_{u=1..m,\, v=1..n}\left\{a_{uv}(\sum_{i=1}^{m} a_{iv})w_v(\log(1-r_v))^2\right\}. \tag{20}$$

The problem (16) can be now written in the standard form of DC program:

$$\min\{G(x) - h(x) : x \in \mathbb{R}^{m.n}\}, \tag{21}$$

where $G(x) := \chi_{K'}(x) + \frac{\lambda}{2}\|x\|^2$ is clearly convex function.

3.3 DCA for Solving (21)

According to the generic DCA scheme given above, DCA applied on the last problem (21) consists of computing the two sequence $\{y^k\}$ and $\{x^k\}$ such that

$$y^k \in \partial h(x^k); \quad x^{k+1} \in \arg\min\left\{G(x) - \langle x, y^k \rangle : x \in \mathbb{R}^{m.n}\right\}.$$

By the definition of h, y^k can be computed as

$$y_l^k = (\lambda + t)x_l^k - \frac{t}{2} - w_j \log(1 - r_j)a_{ij}(1 - r_j)^{\sum\limits_{i=1}^{m} a_{ij}x_{ij}^k} \tag{22}$$

for $i = 1, ..., m$; $j = 1, ..., n$ and $l = i.(n-1) + j$.

x^{k+1} is in fact an optimal solution of the following convex quadratic problem

$$\min\left\{\frac{\lambda}{2}\|x\|^2 - \langle y^k, x \rangle : x \in K'\right\}.$$

Finally DCA applied to (21) can be described as follows:

Algorithm DCA-UTAP:
Step 1: Choose an initial point x^0 and a small enough $\epsilon > 0$. Set $k = 0$.
Step 2: Compute $y^k = \nabla h(x^k)$ via (22).
Step 3: Solve the convex program to obtain x^{k+1}:

$$\min\left\{\frac{\lambda}{2}\|x\|^2 - \langle y^k, x \rangle : x \in K'\right\}. \tag{23}$$

Step 4: **if** $(\|x^{k+1} - x^k\| \leq \epsilon(\|x^k\| + 1))$ **then** stop, x^k is the computed solution,
  else set $k = k + 1$ and go to Step 2.

The convergence of Algorithm DCA can be summarized in the next theorem.

Theorem 2. *(Convergence properties of Algorithm DCA)*

  i) **DCA-UTAP** *generates the sequence* $\{x^k\}$ *such that the sequence* $\{F(x^k)\}$ *is monotonously decreasing.*
  ii) *The point* x^* *verifies the necessary local optimality condition of Problem (21), say*

$$(\nabla h(x^*) - \lambda\|x^*\|) \in \partial\chi_{K'}(x^*).$$

PROOF: direct consequences of the convergence properties of general DC programs and the fact that h is differentiable.

4   A Combined DCA - Branch and Bound Algorithm

For globally solving (UTAP), we combine DCA with a classical Branch and Bound (B&B) scheme. The lower bounds are computed by solving the relaxed problem while the upper bounds are calculated by applying **DCA-UTAP** to (21). At the beginning, the starting point of **DCA-UTAP** is the optimal solution of the relaxed problem. Furthermore, when a feasible point is found while computing lower bounds, we restart **DCA-UTAP** from this point.

4.1   Lower Bound

We compute a lower bound of α by solving the relaxed problem of (UTAP):

$$\min\{f(x) = \sum_{j=1}^{n} w_j (1 - r_j)^{\sum_{i=1}^{m} a_{ij} x_{ij}} : (x, y) \in K'\}. \tag{24}$$

Since the last problem is convex, we apply DCA once again to solve it.

Like DCA applied to (21), the following DC decomposition is used for (24):

$$f(x) = \sum_{j=1}^{n} w_j (1 - r_j)^{\sum_{i=1}^{m} a_{ij} x_{ij}} = \overline{g}(x) - \overline{h}(x), \tag{25}$$

where

$$\overline{g}(x) := \frac{\lambda}{2} \|x\|^2; \quad \overline{h}(x) := \frac{\lambda}{2} \|x\|^2 - \sum_{j=1}^{n} w_j (1 - r_j)^{\sum_{i=1}^{m} a_{ij} x_{ij}}. \tag{26}$$

Here, λ takes the same value in the formula (20). The DCA applied to (24) is nothing else **DCA-UTAP** with a little modification in the step of computing y^k:

$$y_l^k = \lambda x_l^k - w_j \log(1 - r_j) a_{ij} (1 - r_j)^{\sum_{i=1}^{m} a_{ij} x_{ij}^k} \tag{27}$$

for $i = 1, ..., m \ j = 1, ..., n$ and $l = i.(n - 1) + j$.

4.2   The Combined DCA- B&B Algorithm

Algorithm DCABB

Let $R_0 := [0, 1]^{m.n}$ and ϵ be a sufficiently small positive number. Set *restart* := *true*;

Solve the convex relaxation problem of (24) to obtain a solution x^{R_0} and the first lower bound $\beta_0 := \beta(R_0)$;

Solve (21) by DCA from the initial point x^{R_0} to obtain $x_t^{R_0}$;

If $x_t^{R_0}$ is feasible to (UTAP) **then**

set $\gamma_0 := f(x_t^{R_0})$, $x^0 := x_t^{R_0}$, *restart* := *false* **else** $\gamma := +\infty$;

Endif

If $(\gamma_0 - \beta_0) \leq \epsilon|\gamma_0|)$ **then** STOP, x^0 is an ϵ-optimal solution of (UTAP) **else** set $\Re \leftarrow \{R_0\}, k \leftarrow 0$;

Endif

While (stop=false) **do**

Select a rectangle R_k such that $\beta_k = \beta(R_k) = \min\{\beta(R) : R \in \Re\}$.

Let $j^* \in \{1, ..., m.n\}$ be the index such that $x_{j^*}^{R_k} \notin \{0, 1\}$. Divide R_k into two sub-rectangles R_{k_0} and R_{k_1} via the index j^*:

$$R_{k_i} = \{x \in R_k : x_{j^*} = i; i = 0, 1\}. \tag{28}$$

Solve the subproblems (P_{k_i}) to obtain $\beta(R_{k_i})$ and $(x^{R_{k_i}})$:

$$(P_{k_i}) \quad \beta(R_{k_i}) - \min\{f(x) : x \in K, x \in R_{k_i}\} \tag{29}$$

If either $x^{R_{k_i}}$ is feasible to (UTAP) or restart $=$ true **then**
    - apply DCA to (21) from $x^{R_{k_i}}$ to obtain $x_t^{R_{k_i}}$;
    - **If** $x_t^{R_{k_i}}$ is feasible to (UTAP) **then**
       update γ_k and the best feasible solution x^k;
       set restart := false.
    Endif
Endif
Set $\Re \leftarrow \Re \cup \{R_{k_i} : \beta(R_{k_i}) < \gamma_k - \epsilon, i = 0, 1\} \setminus R_k$.
If $\Re = \emptyset$ **then** STOP, x^k is an ϵ-optimal solution **else** set $k \leftarrow k+1$.
Endwhile

5 Numerical Results

The algorithms were coded in C and run on a Intel Core 2CPU 1.86Ghz of 2GB RAM. The comercial sofwarte CPLEX 11.2 is used as an convex quadratic programming solver (note that we can also resort to other efficient methods for solving the convex quadratic program (23)).

30 test problems are considered with different size: $(m = 10, n = 10)$, $(m = 20, n = 10)$ and $(m = 30, n = 10)$ (10 instances per size). The weights w_j are randomly generated in $[0, 10]$. The probabilities r_j and the matrix A are also randomly generated.

The comparative results between three algorithms **DCA-UTAP**, **DCABB** and **BB** are reported in Tables 1, 2 and 3. The following notations are used in these tables:

- *Pb*: Problem,
- *Bin*: number of the binary variables,
- *Ctr*: number of the constraints,
- *OPT*: value of the objective function obtained by each algorithm,
- *LB*: the best lower bound (given by **BB**),
- *It*: number of iterations of each algorithm,
- *Time*: CPU time in seconds of each algorithm,
- $GAP = \frac{OPT-LB}{OPT} 100\%$,
- *Nb*: number of restart DCA in **DCABB** to get OPT.

Comments on the numerical results

◇ **DCA-UTAP** furnishes a good approximate optimal solution in a short time. For the size $(m = 10, n = 10)$ (100 binary variables) the average gap (between the *optimal value* and the best lower bound) is 6.12% while the average CPU is 0.625 seconds. When $(m = 20, n = 10)$ (resp. $(m = 30, n = 10)$) the average gap is 11.23 (resp. 10.46) and the average CPU is 1.88 (resp. 2.85) seconds. Hence, using **DCA-UTAP** is interesting for the UTAP problem, in particular for the large scale setting. Indeed, with $(m = 30, n = 10)$ **BB** do not work (the algorithm can not furnish a feasible solution after one hour) and **DCABB** improve slightly the solution obtained by **DCA-UTAP** while the time consuming increases dramatically (more than one hour for 7/10 problems).

Table 1. Comparative results with $m = 10$ and $n = 10$

Data			DCA				DCABB					BB			
Pb	Bin	Ctr	It	OPT	Time	Gap	It	Nb	OPT	Time	Gap	It	OPT	Time	Gap
1	100	10	25	33.125266	0.953	11.40	3	5	29.911818	10.562	1.98	59	29.425858	170.890	0.26
2	100	10	3	43.600538	0.125	6.71	5	9	41.502606	5.922	2.03	1276	40.790448	1919.812	0.29
3	100	10	19	31.875111	0.875	6.33	1	1	29.927311	3.000	0.23	158	29.927309	776.766	0.17
4	100	10	13	28.845089	0.641	12.07	187	130	26.106369	723.906	2.99	1147	NA	>1h	NA
5	100	10	9	34.970767	0.500	0.15	1	1	34.964411	0.641	0.13	11	34.964398	8.937	0.06
6	100	10	3	30.422789	0.110	7.95	794	5	28.286803	2896.813	1.03	794	28.286803	2887.265	1.03
7	100	10	8	39.284260	0.375	10.75	40	2	35.454166	48.422	1.15	40	35.454166	47.859	1.15
8	100	10	9	29.738714	0.516	1.03	18	2	29.528116	23.437	0.33	18	29.528116	23.110	0.33
9	100	10	21	19.188294	1.313	0.46	12	2	19.188199	40.063	0.46	12	19.188199	38.578	0.46
10	100	10	21	16.315438	0.844	4.35	299	2	15.761578	816.407	2.08	299	15.761578	797.063	2.08

Table 2. Comparative results with $m = 20$ and $n = 10$

Data			DCA				DCABB					BB			
Pb	Bin	Ctr	It	OPT	Time	Gap	It	Nb	OPT	Time	Gap	It	OPT	Time	Gap
1	200	20	7	25.800585	0.812	8.16	35	69	23.765625	675.485	0.30	218	NA	>1h	NA
2	200	20	26	23.642896	2.985	10.33	85	27	22.784809	>1h	6.95	85	NA	>1h	NA
3	200	20	15	26.760725	1.734	14.99	7	12	22.883666	136.656	0.60	168	NA	>1h	NA
4	200	20	12	25.687555	1.391	10.11	56	7	28.328693	>1h	22.69	58	NA	>1h	NA
5	200	20	3	21.372439	0.375	14.87	33	5	24.216463	>1h	22.09	40	NA	>1h	NA
6	200	20	47	28.852983	5.485	13.97	52	NA	NA	>1h	NA	59	NA	>1h	NA
7	200	20	6	24.942689	0.718	9.71	94	187	23.102439	655.064	2.59	507	NA	>1h	NA
8	200	20	24	21.801630	3.105	11.49	64	NA	NA	>1h	NA	275	NA	>1h	NA
9	200	20	4	14.539893	0.813	12.57	36	1	14.060431	>1h	10.61	37	NA	>1h	NA
10	200	20	12	25.004022	1.391	6.09	878	7	25.418418	>1h	8.25	878	NA	>1h	NA

Table 3. Comparative results with $m = 30$ and $n = 10$

Data			DCA				DCABB					BB			
Pb	Bin	Ctr	It	OPT	Time	Gap	It	Nb	OPT	Time	Gap	It	OPT	Time	Gap
1	300	30	8	16.681124	2.484	14.08	236	471	14.766721	2167.078	3.04	319	NA	>1h	NA
2	300	30	3	15.189069	0.750	9.95	398	NA	NA	>1h	NA	486	NA	>1h	NA
3	300	30	4	15.970833	0.984	7.44	96	35	16.023174	>1h	7.74	112	NA	>1h	NA
4	300	30	26	16.599515	6.343	14.02	630	967	15.400154	>1h	7.91	765	NA	>1h	NA
5	300	30	15	19.453271	3.658	9.41	47	93	18.481463	1619.641	4.87	73	NA	>1h	NA
6	300	30	14	20.639400	3.365	11.36	42	45	20.195123	>1h	10.38	57	NA	>1h	NA
7	300	30	17	26.161186	4.680	6.75	9	17	25.394145	235.125	4.09	139	NA	>1h	NA
8	300	30	4	18.779954	0.969	8.35	197	18	19.256186	>1h	11.89	202	NA	>1h	NA
9	300	30	7	22.471048	1.734	10.77	77	1	25.752417	>1h	28.55	77	NA	>1h	NA
10	300	30	13	20.846978	3.584	12.50	121	13	19.914118	>1h	9.17	126	NA	>1h	NA

◇ The combined **DCABB** is interesting for the problems with medium size. Table 1 shows that, in general, after some times of restarting **DCA-UTAP** the algorithm gives an optimal solution. But, as in any B&B algorithm, we need more time to prove the globality of the solution by improving lower bounds. Here the use of **BB** is twofold: for finding a good starting point to DCA, and, by the way, for proving the globality of the solution furnished by DCA. Thanks to the efficiency of DCA, **DCABB** is much more efficient than **BB**.

◇ **BB** do not work for the problems with more than 100 binary variables.

6   Conclusion

We have developed in this paper an efficient approach based on DC Programming and DCA for the UAVs task assignment problem under uncertainty that is known to be very hard. The original combinatorial optimization problem is reformulated as a continuous one via an exact penalty technique. It turns that the resulting problem is a nice DC program for which several DC decomposition can be exploited. We propose a DCA scheme that solves one convex quadratic program at each iteration. DCA is a continuous approach but its gives integer solutions. The numerical results of several test problems prove the efficiency and the robustness of DCA: it gives an good approximate optimal solution in a short time. Hence, DCA is recommended for this problem, especially for large-scale settings. In addition, for medium-size settings, we suggest the combined DCA-B&B since it can find an optimal solution in a moderate time.

This work suggests that it is interesting to investigate DCA for other non-linear models of task assignment problem that we plan in our future works.

References

1. Chandler, P.R., Pachter, M., Rasmussen, S.R., Schumacher, C.: Multiple Task Assignment for a UAV Team. In: AIAA Guidance, Navigation, and Control Conference, Monterey, CA (August 2002)
2. Cruz Jr., J.B., Chen, G., Li, D., Wang, X.: Particle Swarm Optimization for Resource Allocation in UAV Cooperative Control. In: AIAA Guidance, Navigation, and Control Conference, Providence, RI (August 2004)
3. Le Ny, J., Feron, E.: An Approximation Algorithm for the Curvature-Constrained Travelling Salesman Problem. In: 43rd Annual Allerton Conference on Communications, Control and Computing, Monticello, IL (September 2005)
4. Le Thi, H.A., Pham Dinh, T., Le, D.M.: Exact penalty in d.c. programming. Vietnam Journal of Mathematics 27(2), 169–178 (1999)
5. Le Thi, H.A., Pham Dinh, T.: A continuous approachfor large-scale constrained quadratic zero-one programming. (In honor of Professor ELSTER, Founder of the Journal Optimization), Optimization 50(1-2), 93–120 (2001)
6. Le Thi, H.A., Nguyen, T.P., Pham Dinh, T.: A Continuous DC Programming Approach To The Strategic Supply Chain Design Problem From Qualiffed Partner Set. European Journal of OperationalResearch 183, 1001–1012 (2007)
7. Le Thi, H.A., Pham Dinh, T., Huynh, V.N.: Exact Penalty Techniques in DC Programming. Technical Report, LMI, INSA-Rouen, France (July 2007)
8. Le Thi, H.A., Pham Dinh, T.: The DC (difference of convex functions) Programming and DCA revisited with DC models of real wourd nonconvex optimization problems. Annals of Operations Research 133, 23–46 (2005)
9. Murray, R.M.: Recent Research in Cooperative Control of Multivehicle Systems. Journal of Dynamic Systems, Measurement, and Control 129(5), 571–583 (2007)
10. Papadimitriou, C.H., Steiglitz, K.: Combinatorial Optimization: Algorithms and Complexity. Prentice-Hall, Englewood Cliffs (1982)
11. Pham Dinh, T., Le Thi, H.A.: Convex analysis approach to DC programming: Theory, Algorithms and Applications. Acta Mathematica Vietnamica, dedicated to Professor Hoang Tuy on the occassion of his 70th birthday 22(1), 289–357 (1997)

12. Pham Dinh, T., Le Thi, H.A.: DC optimization algorithms for solving the trust region subproblem. SIAM J. Optimization 8, 476–505 (1998)
13. Pham Dinh, T., Nguyen, C.N., Le Thi, H.A.: An efficient combined DCA and B&B using DC/SDP relaxation for globally solving binary quadratic programs. Journal of Global Optimization, 38 (January 2010) (published online)
14. Protvin, J.Y.: Genetic algorithms for the travelling salesman problem. Annals of Operations Research 63(3), 339–370 (1996)
15. Richards, A., Bellingham, J., Tillerson, M., How, J.P.: Coordination and control of multiple UAVs. In: AIAA Guidance, Navigation, and Control Conference, Monterey, CA (August 2002)
16. Richards, A., How, J.P.: Aircraft Trajectory Planning With Collision Avoidance Using Mixed Integer Linear Progrmming. In: American Control Conference, Anchorage, AK (May 2002)
17. Salman, A., Ahmad, I., Al-Madani, S.: Particle Swarm Optimization for Task Assignment Problem. Microprocessors and Microsystems 26(8), 363–371 (2002)
18. Schumacher, C., Chandler, P., Pachter, M., Pachter, L.: Constrained Optimization for UAV Task Assignmnet. In: AIAA Guidance, Navigation, and Control Conference, Providence, RI (August 2004)

Pricing the Services in Dynamic Environment: Agent Pricing Model

Drago Žagar, Slavko Rupčić, and Snježana Rimac-Drlje

University of Osijek
Faculty of Electrical Engineering
Osijek, Croatia
{Drago.Zagar,Slavko.Rupcic,Snjezana.Rimac}.etfos.hr

Abstract. New Internet applications and services as well as new user demands open many new issues concerning dynamic management of quality of service and price for received service, respectively. The main goals of Internet service providers are to maximize profit and maintain a negotiated quality of service. From the users' perspective the main goal is to maximize ratio of received QoS and costs of service. However, achieving these objectives could become very complex if we know that Internet service users might during the session become highly dynamic and proactive. This connotes changes in user profile or network provider/s profile caused by high level of user mobility or variable level of user demands. This paper proposes a new agent based pricing architecture for serving the highly dynamic customers in context of dynamic user/network environment. The proposed architecture comprises main aspects and basic parameters that will enable objective and transparent assessment of the costs for the service those Internet users receive while dynamically change QoS demands and cost profile.

Keywords: QoS, Price Optimization, Agent architecture, Proactive, QoS management, adaptation.

1 Introduction

In parallel with rise of a confidence in Internet network, also rise the expectations to its reliability which connotes satisfactory level of *Quality of Service* (QoS). These expectations force the Internet users to negotiate with its *Internet Service Providers – ISPs*, about the guaranties required for specific levels of QoS. The price for Internet access is generally the main (but also the easiest) criterion for new customers to compare different ISPs. Very important questions for customers are how to estimate the received quality of service and how to get the optimal service value. This process is obviously very complex and connotes dynamic analyze and adaptation of many different parameters. These parameters can be used to compare the services offered by different ISPs and to inform a price/quality trade-off decision for a consumer. Parameters should be designed to be sufficiently flexible to be used across a mixture of connection technologies. Therefore, some elements of QoS can not always be clearly measurable in a numerical and objective way (security, reliability and ease of

N.T. Nguyen and R. Kowalczyk (Eds.): Transactions on CCI II, LNCS 6450, pp. 160–180, 2010.

billing). Usually, these parameters can be measured only subjectively, and may also not always be a part of price/quality trade-off [2],[13].

A development of recent complex and demanding applications continuously increases the requirements on a quality of service, provided by communication's infrastructure. It is very possible that the same complex applications and the services will be executed by different level of quality that would satisfy every single user. This is much more important if we know that applications and services could, during the communication, require different level of QoS. The variable QoS requirements could become from variable demands of a user and an application and from the variable network characteristics, respectively. Furthermore, variations of QoS as well as the QoS degradations can also be a consequence of using on user's devices with different characteristics, in different networks, or on mobile devices. A proper relation between the quality and the cost of the service will result in adequate user satisfaction.

The variable requirements have to be negotiated between the end system and the network, every time when the user or the network changes the demands on QoS [18]. At the moment there exist several pricing models that could be used for Internet accounting, but not all are generally applicable. This is especially emphasized in dynamic user/network environment in which user and network could change their QoS characteristics and profiles. Dynamic accounting model could be a benefit for the customer, because he will find the appropriate and optimal model of network usage.

This paper presents a new agent based pricing architecture for serving the users in context of dynamic user/application/network environment. The most convenient concept that could comprise highly adaptive and proactive behavior is agent based architecture. The proposed agent based architecture places in context some basic parameters that will enable objective and transparent assessment of the costs for the service those Internet users receive while dynamically change QoS demands and cost profile.

The paper is organized as follows: second section presents different aspects of service price estimation and optimization as a motivation for new proposal, the third section proposes a new agent based architecture for dynamic pricing the services in distributed network environment, the fourth section presents some aspects of price adaptation and optimization procedure for the services with dynamic QoS demands. The last section concludes the paper and discusses some open research issues as well as further research perspectives.

2 Service Price Modeling

The service price on a retail market is established in close connection between service user and service provider. The service providers set and adapt the service price in order to maximize the profit. The service users try to optimize the ratio of received service value and the service price.

Revenue from services can be basically calculated in accordance to different factors (e.g. time, cost, quantity of services). Consumers select the class of service in accordance to their preferences and habits, and compare prices of similar services enabled by the various service providers. The main goal is to maximize the benefits (level of satisfaction) within limited budget [3][4][5].

The stability of market equilibrium is very important issue in every pricing model and therefore has been well studied in economics. The system is globally stable if it is continuous and the supply function is strictly upward sloping and the demand function is strictly downward sloping. This can be illustrated easily using excess demand analysis. When the price is lower than the equilibrium price, the excess demand is positive [9].

There exist many various strategies for optimization of service price from different aspects. They could comprise different pricing architectures, pricing strategies and service models. Flat rate pricing model is stimulant to over use the network, which, especially in relation to increasing number of subscribers, can lead to network congestion. The result is reduction of the quality of service and QoS management. In contrast, usage-based pricing scheme can be a good step to general price/resources optimisation. The QoS architectures that are mostly used and relatively largely implemented (e.g. Diffserv model) deal with this problem in a user oriented manner i.e. a user always chooses the service class providing the best QoS [6],[11],[12],[25].

Classical pricing schemes are becoming outdated because of three major reasons:

i.   Existing simple schemes are not stimulant to improve utilization.
ii.   Some users might wish to pay more than others to avoid congestion and get better QoS.
iii. The current Internet and, even much more, the next-generation Internet has to deal with numbers of applications with very diverse quality of service requirements. If we comprise these requirements in a pricing model, we could improve users' level of satisfaction [8].

Additionally to above reasons we might add the fourth, which is obvious:

iv.   The users could during the session dynamically change their demands in accordance to variable requirements and network condition. In such a way the user can get the improved (optimal) cost per session (service).

2.1 Market Model

Figure 1. depict the structure of network market from different points of view: network domain providers, service providers and service users. This network model consists of tree types of entities: end network users, domain sellers and service providers, as well as two types of market: wholesale and retail. An individual user requires network resources with certain Quality of Service. The service user can start the session anytime; QoS level can change during the session as well as session duration can be variable. Furthermore, the user could require immediate network access (unconditional minimal delay).

The domain seller owns large amount of network resources (or has a rights on resources) and is interested in selling as much of network resources as possible (bandwidth etc.). Internet service providers buy large amount of network resources from network owners on wholesale market and then offer the individual users access to the network on retail market. It is extremely difficult to assure appropriate provisioning of network resources and allocating connections to every individual user in dynamic users/network environment. Therefore, service provider is very important factor in network economy. Service provider acts as middleware broker between domain resource provider and end service users. This is even more complicated by

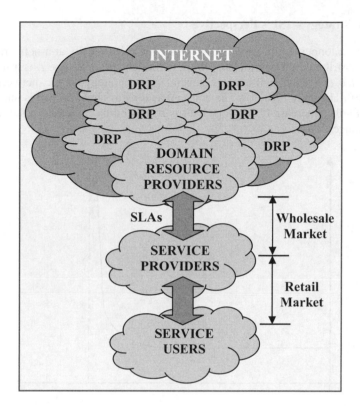

Fig. 1. Network market model

larger deployment of Quality of Service as well as ubiquitous users' mobility. It is very hard question how to determine the optimal amounts of provisioning and proper access distribution. This is difficult problem especially by balancing user requests in short term while ensuring proper network resources for the long term [23].

The price of service on the market and methods for service price modeling could be analyzed from three different aspects:

a) Management of limited resources (Resource value management);
b) Hierarchical market model (Market value management) and
c) End user standpoint (User QoS value management).

The first approach uses modeling for optimization of network resources (network devices, queues, network QoS parameters...) and for calculation of costs for privileged classes of services.

The second approach uses modeling for optimization of profit by using hierarchical market model. The service provider can maximize the profit by using the end user traffic characteristics (ToD demands) and SLA (*Service Level Agreement*) terms.

The third approach uses modeling for achieving the best possible QoS for the end user as maximum *Social Welfare*. The optimal service price will be determinated as maximum QoS for every single user.

2.2 Price Strategy – ISP's Perspective

An iterative tatonnement process is used to set the price locally at a network element in several distributed pricing models. In these models, price at time t_1 is a function of price at time t. Figure 2. illustrates general price strategy of the network service provider [9]. The price is set low and constant as long as network load is under certain value L_i. Further increase of network load is penalized by increased price to prevent network congestion.

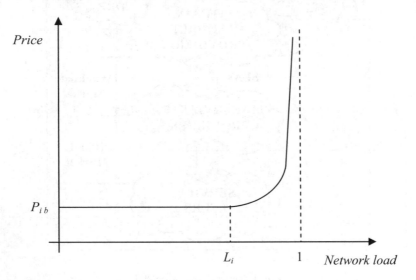

Fig. 2. General pricing strategy

From the Provider's perspective the goal is [9]:

$$\text{Maximize:} \quad \left\{ \sum_{r \in R} (R_r(x) - C_p(x)) \right\} \tag{1}$$

$$\text{Or to assure profit:} \quad \left\{ \frac{\sum_{r \in R} R_r(x)}{\sum_{r \in R} C_p(x)} \right\} > 1 \tag{2}$$

Where:
R – set of users
$R_r(x)$ – revenue generated by user r using x network resources
$C_p(x)$ – cost of service provider providing x network resources
b_r – budget of user r

Subject to: a set of constraints (e.g. capacity constraint $\Sigma(x) \leq C$, QoS constraints, or fairness constraint).

The solution of this kind of model is the optimal price that maximizes the provider's revenue or profit. The optimal amount of necessary network resources to provision as well as the associated prices should be determined by estimating the aggregate user demand. It is obvious that due to dynamic nature of users and networks demand will change over time, implying necessary demand prediction and price estimation as a regulator of available/reserved resources [23].

2.3 Price Strategy – User's Perspective

Users' willingness to pay will simply depend on the type of services offered and on the price charged which could be described by the utility function. This function gives a measure of the user's sensitivity to the perceived QoS level that is to the variations of the network resources allocated to the relevant flow. From an economic point of view, the utility function is strictly related to the users' demand curve, which describes users' willingness to pay as a function of the received QoS level [10].

For this purpose, applications are commonly divided into three classes with different utility functions:

– elastic applications, which do not need guaranteed network services;
– partially elastic applications, which need soft (statistical) QoS guarantees: they can adapt the transmission rate to varying network conditions, up to a certain pre-defined extent.
– inelastic applications, which need hard (deterministic) QoS guarantees, and therefore IP guaranteed services.

Figure 3. shows some typical examples of utility functions for these types of applications [10].

From the User's perspective the goal is to :

Maximize [9]: $$\left\{ \sum_{r \in R} (U_r(x) - C_r(x)) \right\} \tag{3}$$

or: $$\left\{ \frac{\sum_{i=1}^{n} QoS_i}{\sum_{i=1}^{n} p_i} \right\} \tag{4}$$

Subject to: a set of constraints (e.g. budget constraint, application constraint etc.)

Where:
QoS_i – QoS received by user r during price interval i
p_i – price negotiated in price interval i
R – set of users
$U_r(x)$ – utility function of a user r using x network resources
$C_r(x)$ – total capacity

The solution of this kind of model is the optimal price that maximizes the social welfare (or surplus). Quality of Service per cost should be maximized $\Sigma(QoS_i)_{max}$.

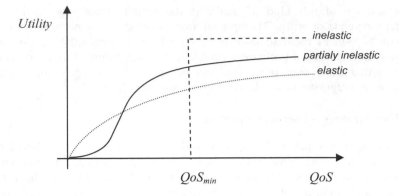

Fig. 3. Examples of utility functions

The user price strategy and own price elasticity can influence the competition among service providers. If the number of service providers is very large, then the retail market is competitive market. In such a model new service providers will enter the market as long as profits are positive. User demands are very elastic if there exist large selection of service providers. In contrast, if the service provider has a monopoly the user elasticity is small and therefore users don't have choice and profits increase. Utility functions of the user and of the network operators can differ and an agent based game approach to Internet pricing may be found appropriate [21],[23].

2.4   Pricing in Dynamic Environment

The study of dynamic pricing a QoS-enabled network environment has become one of the hottest research areas in recent years. Many optimal pricing schemes have been proposed in the past few years. QoS pricing schemes proposed so far often entail either congestion control or admission control or even both. Most of them either assume a well-known user *utility function* or *user demand function* and establish an optimization model to maximize either the social welfare or provider's revenue [9].

Some early versions of congestion-dependent pricing also considered charges per packet. Such approaches often use an auction to determine the optimal price per packet, resulting in *prices that vary with demand*. Several research studies investigate the issue of user behavior after price change [7],[12].

The price of resources will be based on usage and charged to the users. Therefore, time scale associated with the price is also very important issue. The service providers should ensure flexible price estimation based on current users demands and available resources along with some predictability. In dominantly static price scheme with only one service provider (subscriber scheme) the duration of price interval can change from extremely large to very small. Smaller price intervals assures better congestion control since prices can be adjusted based on aggregated user demands. Such flexibility increases profit because prices can be set to encourage usage. The dynamic of price change should be adjusted to changes in demands, while to often price changes will not increase the profit. In relatively static environment (static user/network conditions) users prefer a simpler price structure. Users don't like multiple price changes during the session, even if it could result in a lover cost. The Figure 4. shows the effect of price interval number on ISP's profit. The profit will rise till a value T and after that no further profit increase is present [23], [24] .

However, in dynamic surrounding the changes are unavoidable and if we can implement a reliable agent based QoS/price management system that could assure optimal quality of service together with reasonable cost/revenue it is inevitable.

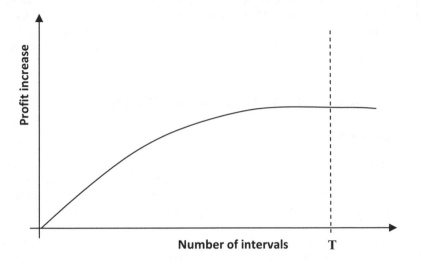

Fig. 4. The effect of price interval number on ISP profit

Some researchers presume that optimal pricing schemes require a centralized architecture to collect all the required information and perform an optimal price setting or resource allocation. From this, very probable point of view, it is obvious that the optimal pricing schemes do not scale well. Also, it is not feasible to adopt a centralized approach when multiple domains/service providers are involved. If the centralized approach is used only within a domain, then it is not clear if the locally optimal solution will lead to a globally optimal solution.

An ideal model for network access would be the continuous accessibility. In every access point we could have defined a price for Internet access, and user willing to pay can approach the network. The price should be set as high as optimal network usability will be achieved. One mechanism for access price estimation could be "Walrasian tatonnement", in which a trial price could be set and the users can decide whether to accept or refuse the offer. If the total amounts of users' requests exceed the network capacity then the price should be set to a higher level. The main problem by this scheme is that user must cautiously monitor the price. If a time of day traffic sample is enough predictive than this scheme could work, but it is well known that Internet traffic will be highly penetrating and unpredictable [1].

However, most of the research has been concentrated on the situations where the requirements of services are determined and all available resources are known in advance. They require a completely specified problem as input and have not been able to adequately deal with uncertainties and dynamics in the environment.

To provide a better QoS guarantees in accordance to service price a proactive approach is preferred to a reactive approach in many cases. This fits dynamic environment much better, especially if we know that users are free to adjust their QoS demands during a service session although this should not be mandatory. One perspective approach to dynamic QoS management is to model the interaction among users and service providers (through pricing and resource allocation) as either a cooperative or non cooperative game and use game theory to analyse the system.

As well as the centralized QoS pricing approach obviously doesn't lead to a general solution our attempt introduces distributed agent based architecture for QoS pricing. It is especially appropriate for dynamic network environment and can proactively lead a system to state which is dynamically optimized.

3 Agent Based Model for Dynamic QoS Pricing

3.1 Agent Model for Dynamic Environment

QoS negotiation process could become a very complex procedure, time wasting, and burden by huge number of the measures to define the quality of service and by shortage of proper definition of applied measures. Furthermore, we often do not have the appropriate methodology to measure and observe the negotiated QoS. If these problems were addressed on an ad-hoc basis, between every single customer and its ISP, the implementation of QoS will lead to big effort and large traffic measurements that don't scale well in general network model. These problems are much more emphasized if we introduce dynamic network environment, which could be lunched by different variations in network surroundings. The dynamic distributed environment could be shown as tight connection between network, user and application (Figure 5.). Variations of QoS as well as QoS degradations are not necessarily caused by overall traffic in the network, but could also be a consequence of using devices with different possibilities, different networks, or mobile devices. We can assume that during the communication new and complex applications and services would require a different level of service quality and would be executed with different level of quality of service. Furthermore, characteristics of services offered in distributed environments are exposed to high variations, from the light quality degradation to a complete loss of

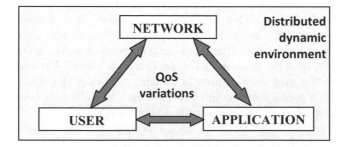

Fig. 5. Distributed dynamic environment

communication link. The end system has to compensate these variations and provide the user with acceptable level of service quality. The proactive applications are predestined for distributed and dynamic environment with limited resources and unpredictable variations in quality of communications [14],[15],[19],[20].

We believe it is necessary, and should be possible, now or in a near future, for all or for some traffic sources (users) to choose between several Internet service providers. This is necessary if we want to achieve optimal (or near optimal) correlation between service users and service providers.

The quality of service processing in distributed dynamic environment includes several coherent activities:

◆ definition of demands on service quality in the form of subjective user wishes or acceptable applications quality; performances, synchronization, costs, etc.;

◆ mapping of obtained results into parameters of service quality for different system components or layers;

◆ negotiation between system components or layers to insure that all components can satisfy the desirable quality of service.

Software agents represent a software development paradigm which is appropriate for distributed problem solving. The term "agent" denotes an encapsulated software-based computer system that has autonomy, social ability, reactivity, and pro-activity. A multi-agent system consists of a number of agents, which interact with one another in order to carry out tasks through cooperation, coordination and negotiation. By modularizing a complex problem in terms of multiple autonomous components that can act and interact in flexible ways, agent technology is well suited for complex, dynamic, and distributed software systems [22].

3.2 Agent Architecture for Dynamic QoS Pricing

The main motivation for proposing new agent based model was a need to improve QoS, user costs and user satisfaction. This is especially request of the applications that could require a different level of QoS during the session. Examples of such applications are distributed multimedia, virtual reality, mobile applications, telemedicine, etc. They all have in common that in order to adapt QoS level could during the session change their requests on QoS and could be executed with variable (acceptable) quality of service.

The architecture proposal should be based on the following three underlying objectives:

• Economic efficiency;
• Simplicity and scalability and
• Optimal revenue from the user's as well as ISP's point of view.

The first goal is to achieve the optimal overall customer value of received services. The second goal is to design a simple and scalable architecture/scheme. The last goal is to provide optimal level of user QoS guarantees and to minimize the cost/service ratio, while ISP's revenue should be based on dynamic open market model.

These objectives are sometimes conflicting or even contradictory. Most researchers believe that optimal pricing solutions are very hard or even impossible to achieve as the scale of the problem is becoming large. Taking into account all measures that should be taken to improve different aspects of service pricing it must be pointed out that in practice, as in many other fields, maximal simplicity is often more important than maximal efficiency [9],[16],[17].

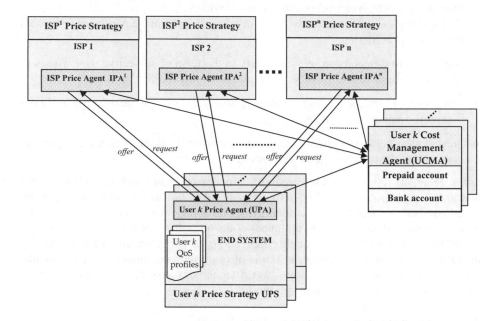

Fig. 6. The architecture for pricing the services in dynamic user/network environment

Figure 6. shows the proposed architecture for pricing the services in dynamic user/network environment. The architecture consists of different service providers competing for users. Every service provider should have its own price strategy that will attract the users to choose it. Every user also should have its own price strategy that will obtain the optimal QoS/price value. If the user changes the ISP during the communication (mobility, QoS request change, device change...) this process should be as transparent as possible. The best way to employ dynamic price system is implementation of price agents by users' and ISPs'. By using predefined price strategies price agents have to dynamically negotiate QoS pricing.

A very important question is how to implement a billing system in dynamic environment in efficient and secure manner. One obvious solution could be a centralized approach by an independent agency that could provide service of cost management. Every user should open a user account which could be managed dynamically by *UCMA User Cost Management Agent. UCMA* could communicate

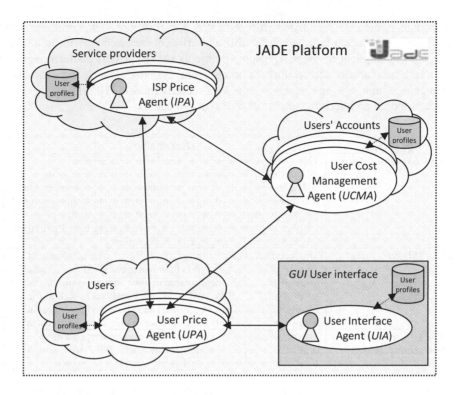

Fig. 7. Architecture of agent system

with *User Price Agent* and *Network Price Agents* as well as user bank account or credit system to arrange independent and transparent billing process.

The centralized accounting system is especially good for dynamic user/network environment. The services which are used in a stable surroundings and with rather static QoS requirements are still better to be realized in a term of SLA with specific service provider. This is especially important if we want to have a hard level guarantees which will not always be possible in dynamic conditions.

During dynamic pricing process decision and coordination among services by agents are modeled as a distributed constraint satisfaction problem in which solutions and constraints are distributed into a set of services and to be solved by the interactions among agents. Finding a global solution to the dynamic surroundings requires that all agents find the solutions that satisfy not only their own constraints but also inter-agent constraints.

The Figure 7. shows the proposed agent architecture system. One of the most appropriate agent platform for distributed and dynamic environment is JADE (Java Agent DEvelopment Framework) platform. JADE is open source (LGPL license), modular and scalable platform that satisfies FIPA standards. JADE is fully implemented in Java language and the minimal system requirement is the version 1.4 of JAVA (the run time environment or the JDK). JADE enables a simple development of multi-agent applications, which is coordinated with the FIPA specifications. The communication architecture offers agent transparent, flexible and efficient messaging by using the best of the FIPA-compliant Message Transport Protocols (MTP). JADE platform has also introduced the support for security of multi-agent systems. The security of agent architecture is built in as an extension of the Java security model [27][28].

The proposed architecture consists of four types of agents:

Agent type	Description
UPA - User Price Agent	This agent takes care of an optimal user's price/value management. The management is based on own price strategy taking into account different parameters as user preferences, QoS requirements, terminal capabilities, system performances, cost and market analyses as well as user account data. According to analyses of parameters included in price strategy *User Price Agent* negotiates with *ISPs* in specific environment.
IPA - ISP Price Agent	This agent takes care of an optimal *ISP's* revenue management. The *ISP* price management is based on specific *ISP* price strategy. Some of parameters incorporated in price strategy could be current traffic load, *ISP* policy, cost and market analyses as well as the current and previous user profile. The *ISP Price Agent* negotiates with *User Price Agents* to achieve a dynamic service agreement.
UCMA - User Cost Management Agent	This agent uses user accounts data to manage user cost in centralized manner. In communication with *ISP Price Agents* and *User Price Agents UCMA* efficiently manages user costs.
UIA - User Interface Agent	This agent is responsible for user-service interaction. It presents the user available services and data important to requested service. According to declared policy built in *User Price Agent* and available providers/services the user decides about acceptable price/QoS ratio as the optimal measure of user satisfaction.

3.3 Agent Interactions by Negotiation

The basic agent interactions (Agent Interaction Protocol - AIP) by initial negotiation process are shown by sequence diagram in AUML (*Agent Unified Modeling Language*) (Figure 8.) [26].

According to analyses of parameters included in user price strategy *User k Price Agent UPA^k* will send same request to all ISPs in specific environment (*ServiceRequest()*). The user price strategy should comprise different aspects of user preferences, QoS requirements, system and terminal capabilities, as well as the data gathered from the current market analyses. The number and the depth of QoS parameters taken into consideration will depend on specific application. By the first use of every application the user agent will take a specific user profile. The user profile should be a base for the user price strategy. The user can anytime change the priority of specific parameters and thus directly influence the user agent price strategy. The main objective of negotiation process from the user side is to obtain an optimal ratio of Quality of Service and service costs which will result in proper user satisfaction. One of the most appropriate methods for user's satisfaction measurement

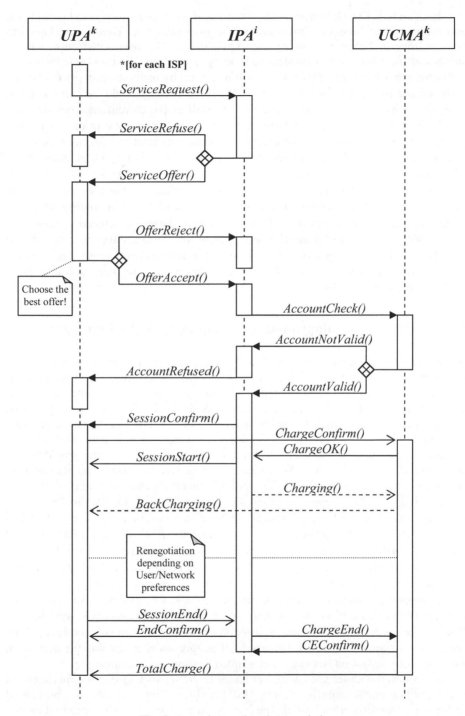

Fig. 8. Agent interactions by negotiation

is a simple interactive GUI provided by *User Interface Agent* which could provide the user with a set of necessary information. The information set should be adapted to user abilities to properly estimate price/QoS value. The user satisfaction has no universal measure and it is dependent on time, space and specific user preferences.

On the other hand, *ISP Price Agent* will negotiate by using its own price strategy. Some of the parameters incorporated in ISP price strategy could be current traffic load, ISP policy, cost and market analyses as well as the current and previous user profile(s). *ISP^i Price Agent IPA^i* processes requests from user price agents and generates QoS/price offers (*ServiceOffer()*) or refuses the requests (*ServiceRefuse()*).

Upon receiving all or some offers (*ServiceOffer()*) *UPA^k* will decide weather offer/s is/are acceptable and will choose the best offer (*OfferAccept()*). Otherwise, *UPA^k* will adjust request according the received offer/s. After checking the user account with *UCMA* (*AccountCheck()*) and positive response (*AccountValid()*) *IPA* confirms (*Session-Confirm()*), the session can start (*SessionStart()*). Otherwise (*AccountNotValid()*), session will be rejected (*AccountRefuse()*). During the session either user or ISP can start the renegotiation (adaptation) process, in accordance to User/Network preferences and specific application policy built in price strategy. The regular session ends by issuing *SessionEnd()* message.

4   Dynamic Price Adaptations in Variable QoS Environment

In order to adapt or optimize a level of QoS the applications and services could, during the communication, require different level of QoS. The variable requirements have to be negotiated between the end system and the network, every time when the user/application or the network changes the QoS demands. The aim of the proposed architecture is very similar to on-line coordination with feedback for large scale adaptation/optimisation problem, on-line adjusted, using real time parameters. This is especially important in situations where the customer and service providers are distributed in different locations. With regard to service requirements, the issues of time, cost, location, etc., are considered to be very important parameters of quality of service.

The Figure 9. shows agent interactions by user initiated adaptation. During the session user agent *UPA^k* could request QoS/price adaptation by issuing *U-Adapt Request()* message. If adaptation is not acceptable the *IPA^i* will reject the offer and send *U-AdaptRefuse()* message. After that, the session will continue till the end of new negotiation process. If adaptation is acceptable the *IPA^i* will check the new user account validity and adapted session will continue (*U-AdaptAccept()*).

The adaptation process can also be initiated by *ISP's* by issuing *I-AdaptRequest()* message (Figure 10.). If adaptation is not acceptable the user agent will send *I-Adapt Refuse()* message and start new negotiation processs. The session will continue till the end of new negotiation process. Otherwise, if adaptation is acceptable the user agent will send *I-AdaptAccept()* message and adapted session will continue.

The proposed architecture enables efficient User/Network QoS/price management in competition market model with many ISP providers. Figure 11. shows a process of QoS/price adaptation/optimisation. The price should be adapted when external factors change. Some of external factors could be user request, application request or changes in network environment. The negotiation strategy is based on price adaptation/ optimisation that is implemented in end system and service providers. In order to improve negotiation the user and ISP (ISPs) could change QoS/price policy. The

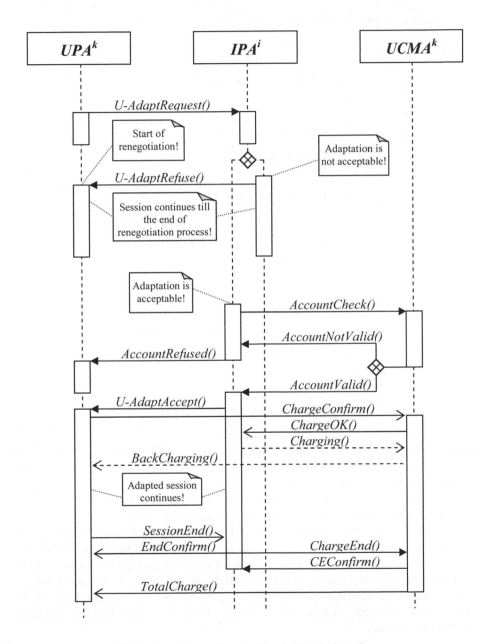

Fig. 9. Agent interactions by User initiated adaptation

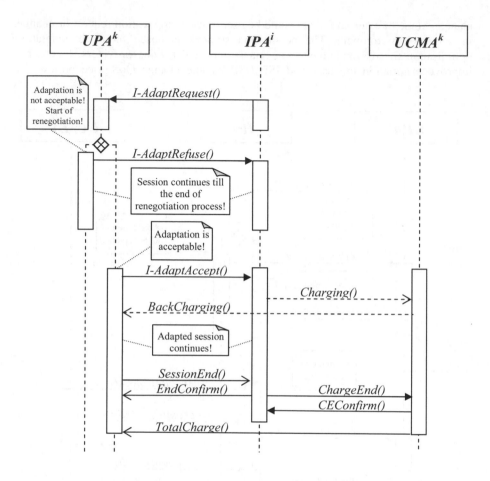

Fig. 10. Agent interactions by ISP initiated adaptation

dynamic result will be QoS/Price working point that will worth till the next QoS change. A very important issue is a granularity level that leads to solution in as small number of negotiation steps as possible. Second important issue is level of linearity in different phases of QoS negotiation process. At the beginning of negotiation process a grid step might be coarser while the final steps could be more refined.

An oftenness of price change is also very important issue. For transparent and continuous QoS providing it is necessary to define the limits (QoS, price...) that will trigger a new negotiation procedure. As a result the negotiation process between network and user could become more efficient. In the Figure 12. is shown the process of QoS adaptation in which the received QoS should be as close as requested QoS. To best meet the QoS requirements the accumulated QoS difference $\Sigma_i \Delta QoS_i$ should be as small as possible.

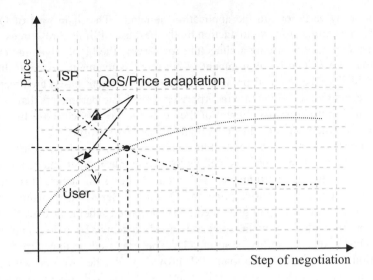

Fig. 11. QoS/Price adaptation/optimisation policy

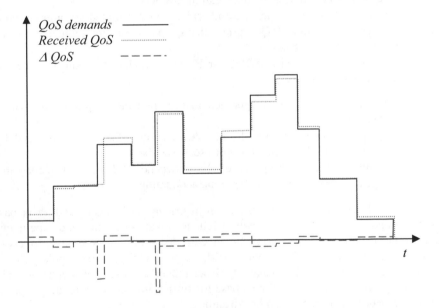

Fig. 12. Dynamic QoS management

5 Conclusions

In response to fluctuations in either end system or network resources the dynamic heterogeneous network environment is desirable to dynamically adapt QoS/Price. Variations that are comprised could be caused by the limited/changed system resources or by variations in the application demands. The main goal of QoS/Price control is to maximise user's satisfaction by the best use of limited resources.

This paper proposes pricing architecture for serving the highly dynamic customers in variable user/network environment. The most convenient concept that could comprise highly adaptive and proactive architecture is agent based architecture. The proposed agent based architecture incorporates some basic parameters that will enable objective and transparent assessment of the costs for the service those Internet users receive while dynamically change QoS demands and cost profile.

The proposed agent based architecture separates the pricing for core networks and the pricing for access networks as well as the wholesale market and retail market in dynamic user/network environment. The architecture is in nature distributed and market-based approach that uses price and Quality of Service as dynamic regulators for traffic load as well as QoS guarantees. The proposed scheme effectively manages ISP's resource availability while comprises user's dynamic behaviour and optimizes ISPs revenue and users utility, respectively. The proposed architecture fits well in competition market model with many ISP providers. We believe that with adequate price setting strategy from sides, ISP's and user's we will obtain a dynamically optimised QoS/price value. The benefit gained from maintaining such distributed agent architecture can overcome the overhead it introduces.

The proposed architecture is flexible and scalable in distributed agent environment and with properly determined QoS/price change per (re)negotiation assures high efficiency with limited overhead.

In the proposed agent based QoS/Price architecture model, the main improvements could be summarised as follows:

- Proactive agent based approach insures transparent pricing in dynamic QoS environment.
- proposed model insures the best level of QoS/Price ratio that end user receives and an optimal level of user's satisfaction;
- centralised accounting served by independent User cost management agent enables transparent dynamic accounting;

This is a good base for further investigation in pricing mechanisms and agent based negotiation processes. Further work will include a formal verification and experimental validation of the proposed agent based architecture for pricing in dynamic user/network environment. Another possible future work is to investigate the applicability of proposed architecture as well as scalability issues related to large implementation scale.

The proposed architecture will be a base for further investigation related to pricing in heterogeneous and dynamic QoS environment.

Acknowledgments

This work is supported by the Croatian Ministry of Education, Science and Sports through the projects 165-0362027-1479 and 165-0361630-1636.

References

1. Fulp, E.W., Reeves, D.S.: Optimal Provisioning and Pricing of Internet Differentiated Services in Hierarchical Markets. In: Proceedings of the IEEE International Conference on Networking (2001)
2. Gupta, A., Stahl, D.O., Whinston, A.B.: The Economics of network management. Communications of the ACM 42(9) (September 1999)
3. Dutta-Roy, A.: The cost of quality in Internet-style networks. IEEE spectrum, 57–62 (September 2000)
4. Pras, A., Beijnum, B.J., Sprenkels, R., Parhonyi, R.: Internet Accounting. IEEE Communications Magazine, 108–113 (May 2001)
5. Dube, P., Liu, Z., Wyner, L., Xia, C.: Competitive equilibrium in e-commerce: Pricing and outsourcing. Computers & Operations Research (2006)
6. Hayel, Y., Tuffin, B.: A mathematical analysis of the cumulus pricing scheme. Computer Networks (2004)
7. Jin, N., Jordan, S.: The effect of bandwidth and buffer pricing on resource allocation and QoS. Computer Networks 46 (2004)
8. Ros, D., Tuffin, B.: A mathematical model of the Paris Metro Pricing scheme for charging packet networks. Computer Networks 46 (2004)
9. Li, T., Iraqi, Y., Boutaba, R.: Pricing and admission control for QoS enabled Internet. Computer Networks 46 (2004)
10. Blefari-Melazzi, N., Di Sorte, D., Reali, G.: Accounting and pricing: a forecast of the scenario of the next generation Internet. Computer Communications 26, 2037–2051 (2003)
11. Wang, X., Schulzrinne, H.: Comparative study of two congestion pricing schemes: auction and tatonement. Computer Networks 46, 111–131 (2004)
12. Di Sorte, D., Reali, G.: Pricing and brokering services over interconnected networks. Journal of Network and Computer Applications 28, 249–283 (2005)
13. Žagar, D., Vilendečić, D., Mlinarić, K.: Network Resource Management for the Services with Variable QoS Requirements. In: Conference on Telecommunications, ConTel 2003, Zagreb (2003)
14. Turk, T., Blažič, B.J.: User's responsivness in the price-controlled best-effort QoS model. Computer Comunication 24, 1637–1647 (2001)
15. Wang, M., Liu, J., Wang, H., Cheung, W.K., Xie, X.: On-demand e-supply chain integration: A multi-agent constraint-based approach. Expert Systems with Applications 34, 2683–2692 (2008)
16. Wang, M., Wang, H., Vogel, D., Kumar, K., Chiu, D.K.W.: Agent-based negotiation and decision making for dynamic supply chain formation. Engineering Applications of Artificial Intelligence (2008)
17. Comuzzi, M., Francalanci, C., Giacomazzi, P.: Pricing the quality of differentiated services for media-oriented real-time applications: A multi-attribute negotiation approach. Computer Networks 52, 3373–3391 (2008)
18. Ferguson, P., Huston, G.: Quality of Service on the Internet: Fact, Fiction, or Compromise? In: Proceedings of the INET 1998, Geneva (1998)
19. Skorin Kapov, L., Mosmondor, M., Dobrijevic, O., Matijašević, M.: Application-level QoS negotiation and Signalling for Advanced Multimedia Services in the IMS. IEEE Communications magazine 45(7), 108–116
20. Skorin Kapov, L., Matijašević, M.: A QoS Negotiation and Adaptation Framework for Maltimedia Services in NGN. In: Proceedings: Conference on Telecommunications, ConTel 2009, Zagreb (2009)

21. Malinowski, K.: Optimisation network flow Control and price coordination with feedback: proposal of a new distributed algorithm. Computer Communications 25, 1028–1036 (2002)
22. Wooldridge, M.: An introduction to multiagent systems. J. Wiley, England (2002)
23. Fulp, E.W., Reeves, D.S.: Bandwidth Provisioning and Pricing for Networks with Multiple Classes of Service. Computer Networks 46, 41–52 (2004)
24. Yuksel, M., Kalyanaranaman, S.: Effect of pricing intervals on the congestion sensitivity of network service prices. Proceedings of the IEEE INFOCOM (2001)
25. Yang, H., Zhang, C.: Application of MAS in Implementing Rational IP Routers on the Priced Internet. In: Dickson, L., Zhang, C. (eds.) DAI 1996. LNCS, vol. 1286, pp. 166–180. Springer, Heidelberg (1997) ISBN:3-540-63412-6
26. Odell, J.J., Van Dyke Parunak, H., Bauer, B.: Representing Agent Interaction Protocols in UML. In: Ciancarini, P., Wooldridge, M.J. (eds.) AOSE 2000. LNCS, vol. 1957, pp. 121–140. Springer, Heidelberg (2001)
27. Lima, E.F., Machado, P.D., Figueiredo, J.C., Sampaio, F.R.: Implementing Mobile Agent Design Patterns in the JADE framework. Special Issue on Jade of the TILAB Journal EXP (2003)
28. http://jade.cselt.it/

JABAT Middleware as a Tool for Solving Optimization Problems

Dariusz Barbucha, Ireneusz Czarnowski, Piotr Jędrzejowicz,
Ewa Ratajczak-Ropel, and Izabela Wierzbowska

Department of Information Systems,
Gdynia Maritime University
Morska 83, 81-225, Gdynia, Poland
{barbucha,irek,pj,ewra,iza}@am.gdynia.pl

Abstract. JABAT supports designing and implementing A-Team architectures for solving difficult optimization problems. This paper presents several applications of JABAT as a tool for solving such problems. List of implementations and extensions of JABAT shows how useful and flexible the system can be. The paper summarises experiences of authors gained while developing various A-Teams. Some conclusions concerning such details of the A-Team model like the composition of the team of agents, the choice of rules determining how the agents interact with the population of solutions, or how synchronisation or cooperation of agents influence the quality of results are offered.

Keywords: JADE-Based A-Team, A-Team, optimization, compution-ally hard problems, multi-agents systems.

1 Introduction

Last years a number of significant advances have been made in both the design and implementation of autonomous agents. A number of applications of the agent technology is growing systematically. One of the successful approaches to agent-based optimization is the concept of an asynchronous team (A-Team), originally introduced by Talukdar [33].

A-Team is a multi agent architecture, which has been proposed in [33] and [32], where, it has been shown that the A-Team framework enables users to easily combine disparate problem solving strategies, each in the form of an autonomous agent, and enables these agents to cooperate to evolve diverse and high quality solutions. Asynchronous team was defined as collection of software agents that solve a problem by dynamically evolving a population of solutions. Each agent works to create, modify or remove solutions from the population. The quality of the solutions gradually evolves over time as improved solutions are added and poor solutions are removed. Cooperation between agents emerges as one agent works on solutions produced by another. Each agent encapsulates a particular problem-solving method along with methods to decide when to work, what to work on and how often to work.

N.T. Nguyen and R. Kowalczyk (Eds.): Transactions on CCI II, LNCS 6450, pp. 181–195, 2010.

The reported implementations of the A-Team concept include two broad classes of systems: dedicated A-Teams and platforms, environments or shells used as tools for constructing specialized A-Team solutions. Dedicated (or specialized) A-Teams are usually not flexible and can be used for solving only particular types of problems. Among example A-Teams of such type one can mention the OPTIMA system for the general component insertion optimization problem [25] or A-Team with a collaboration protocol based on a conditional measure of agent effectiveness designed for Flow optimization of railroad traffic [7].

Among platforms and environments used to implement A-Team concept some well known include IBM A-Team written in C++ with own configuration language [26] and Bang 3 - a platform for the development of Multi-Agent Systems (MAS) [23]. Some implementations of A-Team were based on universal tools like Matlab [32]. Some other were written using algorithmic languages like, for example the parallel A-Team of [9] written in C and run under PVM operating system.

The above discussed platforms and environments belong to the first generation of A-Team tools. They are either not portable or have limited portability, they also have none or limited scalability. Agents are not in conformity with the FIPA (The Foundation of Intelligent Psychical Agents) standards and there are no interoperability nor Internet accessibility. Migration of agents is either impossible or limited to a single software platform.

Next generation A-Teams started to appear roughly after the year 2004. Major diferences in comparison with the first generation solutions can be found with respect to accessibility, scalability and portability of the next generation solutions. However, there exists still two major classes of solutions. The first includes specialized A-teams designed to solve instances of particular problems. Their architecture is problem-specific and not flexible. The second class covers middleware platforms allowing for an easy implementation of the A-Teams ready to solve instances of arbitrary problems.

Good example of the problem specific A-Team is the implementation proposed by Meneses et al. [22] dedicated to solving probe selection problems. Kernel of the system is a multithreaded preprocessing program written in C++. A dialog-based framework was used to allow for rapid development of the program. Classes from the Microsoft Foundation Class (MFC) library were utilized for storage of probes, clones and solutions. Individual probes were stored as CStrings. CStringArrays were used to store input clones, probes and probe solutions, and a CObArray was used for Memory M1. A random-number generator was used to randomly select the agent to be called at each iteration.

The middleware platforms, supporting implementation of A-Teams, are represented by the JADE-Based A-Team environment (JABAT), first proposed in [21] and intended to become the first step towards next generation A-Teams which are portable, scalable and in conformity with the FIPA standards.

JABAT supports designing and implementing A-Team architectures for solving difficult optimization problems. This paper presents several applications of JABAT as a tool for solving such problems. List of implementations and extensions of JABAT shows how useful and flexible the system can be. The paper summarises experiences of authors gained while developing various A-Teams. Although it might be slightly premature to expect at this stage fully validated generalizations some conclusions concerning such details of the A-Team model like the composition of the team of agents, the choice of rules determining how the agents interact with the population of solutions, or how synchronisation or cooperation of agents influence the quality of results are offered.

2   JABAT

The main features of JABAT include the following:

- The system can solve instances of several different problems in parallel.
- The user, having a list of all optimization agents working in the system (e.g. optimization algorithms implemented for the given problem) may choose how many and which of them should be used.
- The optimization process can be carried out on many computers. The user can easily add or delete a computer from the system. In both cases JABAT will adapt to the changes, commanding the optimizing agents working within the system to migrate. JABAT may also clone some already working agents and migrate the clones, thus increasing the number of concurrently operating agents.
- The system is fed in the batch mode - consecutive problems may be stored and solved later, when the system assesses that there is enough resources to undertake new searches for solutions.

JABAT produces solutions to combinatorial optimization problems using a set of optimizing agents, each representing an improvement algorithm. The process of solving of the single task (i.e. the problem instance) consists of several steps. At first the initial population of solutions is generated. Individuals forming the initial population are, at the following computation stages, improved by independently acting agents, thus increasing chances for reaching the global optimum. Finally, when the stopping criterion is met, the best solution in the population is taken as the result. How the above steps are carried out is determined by the "working strategy". There might be different strategies defined in the system, each of them specifying:

- How the initial population of solutions is created.
- How to choose solutions which are forwarded to the optimizing agents for improvement.
- How to merge the improved solutions returned by the optimizing agents with the whole population (for example they may be added, or may replace random or worse solutions).
- When to stop searching for better solutions (for example after a given time, or after no better solution has been found within a given time).

For each user's task the system creates report files that include:

- The best solution obtained so far (that of the maximum or minimum value of fitness).
- Average value of fitness among solutions from the current population.
- Actual time of running and list of changes of the best solution (for each change of the best solution in the process of solving the time and the new value of fitness is given).

The report on the process of searching for the best solution may be later analyzed by the user. It can be easily read into a spreadsheet and converted into a summary report with the use of the pivot table.

The JABAT middleware is built with the use of JADE (Java Agent Development Framework, [6]), a software framework proposed by TILAB [34] for the development and run-time execution of peer-to-peer applications. JADE is based on the agents paradigm in compliance with the FIPA specifications and provides a comprehensive set of system services and agents necessary for distributed peer-to peer applications in the fixed or mobile environment. It includes both the libraries required to develop application agents and the run-time environment that provides the basic services and must be running on the device before agents can be activated.

2.1   Extensions

eJabat. In [3] JABAT was extended to become a fully Internet-accessible solution, with the ability not only to access the system in order to solve own combinatorial problems, but also to add own computer to the system with a view to increase the amount of computational resources used for solving the problem at hand.

Registered users obtained a web interface in which tasks could be uploaded for solving. The uploaded tasks were sequenced and solved in the order of uploading. They could be solved in parallel (even the tasks of different problems). After a task was solved the user could download the results saved in a text file in the users space.

The interface made it easy to choose which agents from those available for the given problem were to be used for solving the task. The user gave the minimum and the maximum number of running copies of each agent. The system initially used the minimal specified number and could increase it when there were enough computational resources available.

cJABAT. In the standard JABAT optimizing agents work asynchronously (each at its own speed) and in parallel. Each agent receives the required number of solutions (one or more) to be improved, immediately after it requests for them. There are a few advantages of this approach, for example agents do not have to waste their time waiting.

On the other hand, taking into account that such agents represent improvement algorithms of various complexity (simple local search heuristic vs. tabu search for example), it is possible that agents representing rather simple, fast and less effective heuristics are much more often invoked than agents representing more complex algorithms, requiring much more time to improve a solution. The consequence of calling too often less effective optimization agents is the increased requirement of consumption of the computational resources by the system without adequate increase of the effectiveness of the proposed approach. It has been also shown that at the initial stages of searching for a solution all optimization agents contribute to improvement. However after a while, only some optimization agents are able to improve the solution, while the remaining ones are employed without a positive effect, decreasing efficiency of the approach.

Taking into consideration the above, cJABAT (cooperative JADE-based A-Team) was designed [2], in which implementation of a reinforcement learning mechanism was introduced. The main goal of the proposed changes was to promote those optimization agents that have positive impact on solution improvement and often improve the best known solution in the process of searching.

In cJABAT, to increase computational efficiency, reinforcement learning technique is used. A reward is assigned to optimization agents each time they find a solution better than its previous best found solution. Such reward inreases the weights of agents. It is also possible to decrease the weight after the agent fails to improve a solution (negative change of agent's weight).

The solutions from the population are not send immediately after request has been made, but only after all agents have made such requests. Then the required number of solutions read from the common memory is sent to only one optimization agent, chosen by a function that takes into account the agents' weight. The rest of the optimization agents remains waiting until the next choice is being made in the next cycle.

2.2 Implementations

JABAT-based A-Teams have been designed and implemented to solve a range of difficult optimalization problems, among them the following:

- RCPSP (Resource Constrained Project Scheduling Problem) and MRCPSP (Multi-Mode Resource Constrained Project Scheduling Problem) [19,17], with agents representing the following optimization algorithms:
  - local search algorithm,
  - crossing algorithm,
  - precedence tree algorithm,
  - tabu search algorithm,
  - MCS-based algorithm,
- RCPSP/max (Resource Constrained Project Scheduling Problem with minimal and maximal time lags, e.g. time windows) [20,18,28], with the following optimization algorithms:
  - local search algorithm,
  - path relinking algorithm,
  - gene expression programing algorithm,
  - tabu search algorithm,

- Euclidean planar TSP (Travelling Salesman Problem) with:
  - LinKernighan heuristics,
  - 2-opt and 3-opt heuristics,
  - crossover algorithm,
  - mutation algorithm,
- Clustering Problem and Distributed Clustering with:
  - random local search,
  - hill-climbing local search,
  - tabu search
- VRP (Vehicle Routing Problem) with:
  - 2-opt and 3-opt heuristics,
  - local search algorithm,
  - λ-interchange local optimization method,
  - crossover algorithms,
- Data Reduction Problem and Distributed Data Reduction Problem with
  - simulated annealing for instance selection,
  - simulated annealing for feature selection.
  - local search algorithm,
  - local search algorithm with tabu list.

2.3   Some Results

Some of the above listed JABAT-based implementations produce a very good or even competetive results as compared with state-of-art approaches reported in the literature. The following subsection report on such implementations.

In some of the implementations listed in Subsection 2.2 the results obtained in JABAT environment were significantly better than other results described in contemporary papers. Below some examples of such good results are listed.

RCPSP/max. Table 1 shows some results from [28] for RCPSP/max and benchmark instances from PSPLIB [24]. Three test sets were considered: j10, j20 and j30, each consisting of 270 instances of the problem. The experiment involved computation with the fixed number of optimization agents representing LSA, TSA, PRA and GEPA algorithms, one of each type. Population of solutions in the common memory consisting of 25 or 50 individuals was used. The computation was interrupted if better solution had not been found after 30 or 60 seconds.

The computation results were evaluated in terms of the mean relative error (Mean RE) calculated as the deviation from the lower bound. Each instance was solved five times and the results presented in Table 1 are averaged over these solutions. The results can be compared with the results reported in the literature. Such a comparison with ISES (Iterative Sampling Earliest Solutions, [8]) is presented in Table 2, and it is clear that the results obtained in the JABAT environment are better than ISES results.

Table 1. Experiment results obtained by JABAT for RCPSP/max

#Activities	Population size	Time [s]	Mean RE
10	25	30	0.32%
20	25	30	4.25%
30	25	30	9.13%
10	50	30	0.32%
20	50	30	4.16%
30	50	30	9.28%
10	25	60	0.32%
20	25	60	4.25%
30	25	60	9.13%
10	50	60	0.32%
20	50	60	4.16%
30	50	60	9.28%

Table 2. Results obtained by ISES, [8]

#Activities	Mean RE
10	0.99%
20	4.99%
30	10.37%

Clustering Problem. Another example of good quality results obtained in the JABAT environment come from [11] and apply to solving non-distributed and distributed clustering based on employing three kinds of optimization agents - random local search, hill-climbing local search and tabu search agents. The results can be seen in Table 3. For comparison in the same paper results from [15] were presented, here shown in Table 4. In both tables results for benchmark instances (Ruspini, Iris and other published in [30] and [1]) of the problem being solved are given. The clustering accuracy is calculated through comparison with known solutions. In both tables the results shown are chosen as the best results from 10 runs of algorithms being compared.

Data Reduction. In [13] a method of data reduction through simultaneous instance and feature selection was proposed, as a combination of the simulated annealing algorithm with agent-based population models. Details on the definitions of agents (algorithms) working within the system may be found in [13], but this is worth noting that two of the approaches proposed in the paper, e.g. ABSA #2 and ABSA #3 gave better results for data from [1] than traditional simulated annealing algorithm and also better than other approached described in other, contemporary papers. The results are presented in 5.

Table 3. The clustering results as produced by the JABAT A-Team

	Ruspini	Iris	Heart	Credit	ImgSeg
	Non-distributed				
Clustering accuracy	100%	100%	100%	99%	90%
Number of clusters produced	4	3	2	2	7
Square error	12881.1	74.4	338.2	528.6	773.9
	Distributed				
Clustering accuracy	91%	83%	74%	82%	78%
Number of clusters produced	4	3	3	2	7
Square error	29401.3	77.9	373.0	586.3	906.2

Table 4. The clustering results as produced by the k-means algorithm

	Ruspini	Iris	Heart	Credit	ImgSeg
	Non-distributed				
Clustering accuracy	100%	89%	93%	94%	82%
Number of clusters produced	4	3	2	2	7
Square error	12881.1	78.9	343.0	548.8	859.9
	Distributed				
Clustering accuracy	90%	71%	73%	78%	71%
Number of clusters produced	4	3	3	2	7
Square error	36164.56	142.65	461.187	802.62	1131.4

Two-Level Architecture. An interesting implementation of JABAT was described in [10]. The paper deals with distributed learning based on data reduction carried out at separated sites. The proposed approach to the distributed learning uses a set of agents which process the local data and communicate results to other agents controlling and managing the knowledge discovery process. The approach involves two stages, both supported by agent collaboration:

- local, in which the selection of prototypes from the distributed data takes place (at first clusters of data are induced, next, the prototypes are selected from thus obtained clusters by applying the agent-based population learning algorithm),
- global, consisting of pooling of the selected data (that is the selected feature vectors) and producing the global model.

The selection of prototypes for each part of the distributed data corresponds with how JABAT in its basic form finds solutions to tasks of a given problem: there is a population of random solutions and a set of optimizing agents, then the agents try to improve solutions from the population until a stopping criterion

Table 5. Comparison of different classifiers and data reduction approaches (I - instance selection only; F - feature selection only; IF - instance and feature selection; N - no data reduction)

Classifier	Reduction Type	Heart	Cancer	Credit	Sonar
ABSA #2	IF	87.49	**96.53**	**88.38**	83.06
ABSA #3	IF	**87.69**	96.47	88.22	**83.35**
SA	IF	82.00	93.05	83.22	75.68
k-NN [35]	N	81.19	96.28	84.78	58.80
k-NN+RELIEF [27]	F	77.85	72.12	79.57	-
CNN [35]	I	73.95	95.71	77.68	74.12
SNN [35]	I	76.25	93.85	81.31	79.81
IB3+RELIEF [27]	IF	79.94	73.25	71.75	-
RMHC [31]	IF	82.30	70.90	-	-
GA-KJ [29]	IF	74.70	95.50	-	55.30

is met. The computations in the local stages are being carrried out in parallel. In implementation described in [10] a new agent was added with the view to initialize and manage local stages. In more details the so called global level managing agent does the following:

- for the given task initializes local stages in required number,
- collects results from local stages and
- creates the global solution by integrating local solutions and finally producing meta-classifier.

The above solution to the problem of distributed learning based on data reduction is strongly dependent on the actual alghorithms used for optimizing agents at the local stages and also on how the meta-classifier is designed. However, in the case of the experiment described in details in [10] the whole model proved to produce meta-classifiers of good quality, comparable or better than the standard approach to distributed learning when the data are pooled together in centralized data repository.

2.4   Enviroments

JABAT itself has been designed in such a way, that it can be easily instantiated in new environments where Java and JADE are available. To do so, JABAT with at least one set of objects (e.g. task, solutions, optimizing agent) intended to solve instances of the given problem have to be set up on a computer, and in the minimal configuration it is enough to solve an instance of the problem. Such a minimal configuration may be extended by adding more optimizing agents, more working strategies, new agents for solving more problems, more resources, e.g. attaching a computer (or computers) to which the optimizing agents could migrate to work on.

So far JABAT worked in the following environments:

- consisting of several MS Windows PC computers connected within the local area network (Fast Ethernet),
- MS Windows Server accessed through the Internet, e.g. eJABAT described in Subsection 2.1,
- cluster Holk: a cluster of computers with Linux at the Academic Computer Centre TASK [14].

It is worth noting that the cluster implementation required only changing the configuration file and recompiling. Thus, it has been confirmed that JABAT can be easily set up in various environments and indeed it is flexible, adaptive and stable.

3   Experiences from the Current Implementations

3.1   Synergetic Effects

The ground principal of asynchronous teams rests on combining algorithms into effective problem solving organizations, possibly creating a synergetic effect, in which the combined effect of cooperation between agents is greater than the sum of their separate efforts. To evaluate the existence and strength of the synergetic effect produced by joint effort of optimization agents, some experiments have been carried out.

In the first series of experiments [5] an implementation of JABAT for solving VRP problem was used. Investigated factors included the number of optimizing agents and composition of the team. Two criteria were evaluated: mean relative error and computation time.

It could be observed that in many cases adding a new agent to the team of running agents brings improvement to the final soultion: for many instances tested in the experiment the average value of mean relative error decreases when the number of optimizing agents used in the process of solving the problem increases. However, applying more agents may require more computation time, especially when the agents added are more complex in terms of computational complexity. What is more, scale-effectiveness (performance improvement with scale) could be observed only up to a point: adding yet another agent to the team consisting of a certain number of agents did not improve the solution.

The experiment also showed that there existed synergetic effect from cooperation of different types of agents, e.g. agents representing different optimizing algorithms. The strength of synergetic effect strongly dependeds on the structure of the agents team and often diversifying composition of the team resulted in producing solutions of a better quality.

Another experiment was described in [16]. In this case an implementation of JABAT for solving TSP was used, with 5 types of relatively low quality optimizing agents. The experiment involved solving TSP tasks with the use of different sizes of the common population of solutions. The number of individuals in the population ranged from 2 to 15.

A synergetic effect appeared, on average, for all sizes of the common memory. For larger problem instances such an effect to appear required some computation-time lag. However, small size instances could be effectively solved using a number of homogenous local-search optimizing agents working together for a certain time, which would be shorter than the time required by a heterogeneous A-Team to achieve a comparable quality. All these findings refer to the working strategy used in the experiment where escaping from the local optima was based on inserting to the common memory some random solutions from time to time during the computation process.

Unfortunately the experiment results do not allow to draw any general rules for construction of an A-Team from heterogeneous optimizing agents with a view to achieving a synergetic effect, even for the specific problem type.

The existence of the synergetic effect was also shown by the experiment described in [12]. There, tasks from data reduction problem were solved with the use of different two agent teams. There were two homogenous teams consisting of agents implementing simulated annealing and tabu search algorithms respectively, and eight teams consisting of both types of agents (simulated annealing and tabu search algorithms), varying by some parameters of the algorithms. It was shown that the results obtained from heterogenous teams were more accurate. In fact each heterogenous team gave better results than both homogenous teams.

3.2   Common Memory Maintenance Strategy

JABAT platform offers considerable freedom with respect to defining and implementing a working strategy understood as a procedure or a set of rules responsible for the process of maintaining the common memory and selecting individuals, which at the given computation stage should be forwarded to optimizing agents for improvement. Designing effective and useful working strategy could be supported by use of the knowledge on how a different working strategies may influence the A-Team performance. In [4] ten different working strategies were examinated on four different problems (EPTSP, VRP, CP and RCPSP) to answer that question. The research confirmed the importance of choosing an effective working strategy when employing A-Teams searching for solutions of computationally difficult combinatorial problems.

According to [4], the strategy that appeared to produce solutions of the above average quality was build on selection with blocking (RB) and replacement of the worse with exchange (RE). Selection RB is the selection of a random solution (solutions) from the population to be improved by an optimizing agent. The selection RB is connected with the so called blocking, which means that once selected individual (or subset of individuals) cannot be selected again until all other individuals or their subsets have been tried.

Replacement of the worse with exchange (RE) defines what happens with solutions returned from optimizing agents. In case of RE the returning individual replaces the first found worse individual. If a worse individual can not be found within a certain number of reviews (review is understood as a search for the worse individual after an improved solution is returned) then the worst individual in the common memory is replaced by the randomly generated one representing a feasible solution.

Good performance of the working strategy based on selection with blocking (RB) and replacement of the worse with exchange (RE) can be attributed to the fact that such selection assures that all individuals from the common memory have a chance to contribute to finding an improved solution. On the other hand replacement with exchange (RE) provides a useful mechanism of escaping from the local optimum.

[4] identified the following pieces of knowledge as useful in the process of designing an implementation of the A-Team dedicated to solving a particular optimization problem:

- The quality of solutions produced by the A-Team will not be independent from the working strategy used.
- Not all working strategies are equally effective, moreover the choice of strategy might be problem dependent.

3.3   Learning Mechanism

Described in Subsection 2.1 extension of JABAT with synchronous search for solutions was used to evaluate the effectiveness of the reinforcement learning mechanism implemented in it. [2] describes a computational experiment evaluating how the implemented reinforcement learning mechanism influences computation results, measured as mean relative error (MRE). Results are compared with the results obtained without any reinforcement, where all optimization agents have the same probability of being chosen to try to improve a solution (solutions) from the population.

The experiment from [2] involved solving some task from the vehicle routing problem. It was shown that combination of cooperative searching for the best solution with learning mechanism, where agents adapted their behavior to the new conditions of environment during the process of solving the problem, might bring potential benefits and results in producing solutions of a better quality. As it was observed, the positive impact of such learning on the quality of solution depended on the form of reward assigned to software agents during the process of solving the problem.

Rewards in this experiment were designed as positive (or sometimes negative) changes in the weights assigned to agents. Among the various cases of combinations of positive and negative reinforcement the best results were observed for all combinations in which slow positive increase of agent's weight (by adding 1 each time the agents improved a solution) was included. It can be concluded that such gradually raise of weight during the process of solving the problem allows to choose all optimization agents with almost the same probability at early stages of computation, simultaneously promoting the best ones in following stages.

On the other hand, in all cases in which no negative changes were considered, the results were worse than in those with some negative changes. Deeper analysis of the behavior of agents running in the system brings the observation that in case in which only positive changes of agents' weights are considered, only one optimization agent producing relatively good solutions at early stages of process of searching is promoted and called in next stages. As consequence, the local optimum is reached very fast and there is no chance for diversification of searching.

4 Conclusions

JABAT middleware has proven to be useful and effective tool supporting the design and implementation of the A-Team architectures for solving difficult optimization problems. Main advantages of the tool include agent conformity with the FIPA standards, inherent parallelization of the computation process, reusability of agents, ability to run on numerous computation platforms, and scalability. Experiments with various A-Teams have shown that it is possible to achieve a synergetic effect from cooperation of the different types of the optimization agents.

There are also some disadvantages of the approach. Among them one should mention high communication overhead and a necessity to fine-tune the A-Team composed of heterogeneous optimizing agents. Deciding on the number of individuals in the common memory, selecting a strategy for maintaining the population of solutions in this memory and deciding on the number and mixture of the optimizing agents has been, so far, based on a trials and errors procedure. Experiments carried out with a different combinatorial optimization problems and different compositions of the optimizing agents have not resulted in finding and validating some general rules or fine-tuning procedures applicable to a wider class of optimization problems. Some response to the fine-tuning problem was proposed through introduction of the cJABAT which incorporates some reinforced learning principles. The approach requires, however, further studies, which are intended as the future research.

There are also several other intended directions of future research. The existing set of agent classes will be extended by expert agent whose role would be to analyze the problem at hand and suggest a mix of optimization agents to be used out of the pool of the available ones. Another possible extension is to introduce agents allowing for interactions between the A-Team and the user during the process of search for a solution with a view to better use an expert knowledge of the user.

Acknowledgments. This research has been supported by KBN grant N N519 576438. Calculations have been performed in the Academic Computer Centre TASK in Gdask.

References

1. Asuncion, A., Newman, D.J.: UCI Machine Learning Repository. University of California School of Information and Computer Science. Irvine (2007), http://www.ics.uci.edu/~mlearn/MLRepository.html
2. Barbucha, D.: Cooperative Solution to the Vehicle Routing. In: Jędrzejowicz, P., et al. (eds.) KES-AMSTA 2010. LNCS (LNAI), vol. 6071, pp. 180–189. Springer, Heidelberg (2010)
3. Barbucha, D., Czarnowski, I., Jędrzejowicz, P., Ratajczak-Ropel, E., Wierzbowska, I.: e-Jabat An Implementation of the Web-Based A-Team. In: Nguyen, N.T., Jain, L.C. (eds.) Inteligent Agents in the Evolution of Web and Applications, vol. 5786, Springer, Heidelberg (2009)
4. Barbucha, D., Czarnowski, I., Jędrzejowicz, P., Ratajczak-Ropel, E., Wierzbowska, I.: Influence of the Working Strategy on A-Team Performance. In: Szczerbicki, E., et al. (eds.) Smart Information and Knowledge Management, pp. 83–102. Springer, Heidelberg (2010)
5. Barbucha, D., Jędrzejowicz, P.: An experimental investigation of the synergetic effect of multiple agents working together in the A-Team. System Science 34(2), 55–62 (2008)
6. Bellifemine, F., Caire, G., Poggi, A., Rimassa, G.: JADE. A White Paper, Exp. 3(3), 6–20 (2003)
7. Blum, J., Eskandarian, A.: Enhancing intelligent agent collaboration for flow optimization of railroad traffic. Transportation Research Part A 36, 919–930 (2002)
8. Cesta, A., Oddi, A., Smith, S.F.: A Constraint-Based Method for Project Scheduling with Time Windows. Journal of Heuristics 8, 108–136 (2002)
9. Correa, R., Gomes, F.C., Oliveira, C., Pardalos, P.M.: A parallel implementation of an asynchronous team to the point-to-point connection problem. Parallel Computing 29, 447–466 (2003)
10. Czarnowski, I.: Prototype selection algorithms for distributed learning. Pattern recognition 43(6), 2292–2300 (2010)
11. Czarnowski, I., Jędrzejowicz, P.: Agent-Based Non-distributed and Distributed Clustering. In: Perner, P. (ed.) Machine Learning and Data Mining in Pattern Recognition. LNCS, vol. 5632, pp. 347–360. Springer, Heidelberg (2009)
12. Czarnowski, I., Jędrzejowicz, P.: Agent-based Simulated Annealing and Tabu Search Procedures Applied to Solving the Data Reduction Problem (to appear, 2010)
13. Czarnowski, I., Jędrzejowicz, P.: An Agent-Based Simulated Annealing Algorithm for Data Reduction. In: Jędrzejowicz, P., Nguyen, N.T., Howlet, R.J., Jain, L.C. (eds.) KES-AMSTA 2010. LNCS (LNAI), vol. 6071, pp. 130–139. Springer, Heidelberg (2010)
14. Czarnowski, I., Jędrzejowicz, P., Wierzbowska, I.: A-Team Middleware on a Cluster. In: Hakansson, A., et al. (eds.) KES-AMSTA 2009. Lecture Notes in Computer Science, LNAI, vol. 5559, pp. 764–772. Springer, Heidelberg (2009)
15. Januzaj, E., Kriegel, H.P., Pfeifle, M.: Towards Effective and Efficient Distributed Clustering. In: Proceedings of International Workshop on Clustering Large Data Sets, 3rd International Conference on Data Mining (ICDM), pp. 49–58 (2003)
16. Jędrzejowicz, P., Wierzbowska, I.: Experimental Investigation of the Synergetic Effect Produced by Agents Solving Together Instances of the Euclidean Planar Travelling Salesman Problem. In: Jędrzejowicz, P., et al. (eds.) KES-AMSTA 2010. LNCS (LNAI), vol. 6071, pp. 160–169. Springer, Heidelberg (2010)

17. Jędrzejowicz, P., Ratajczak, E.: Agent-Based Approach to Solving the Resource Constrained Project Scheduling Problem. In: Beliczynski, B., Dzielinski, A., Iwanowski, M., Ribeiro, B. (eds.) ICANNGA 2007. LNCS, vol. 4431, pp. 480–487. Springer, Heidelberg (2007)
18. Jędrzejowicz, P., Ratajczak-Ropel, E.: Agent Based Gene Expression Programming for Solving the RCPSP/max Problem. In: Kolehmainen, M., et al. (eds.) Adaptive and Natural Computing Algorithms. LNCS, vol. 5495, pp. 203–212. Springer, Heidelberg (2009)
19. Jędrzejowicz, P., Ratajczak, E.: Agent-Based, Self-tuning, Population Learning Algorithm for the Resource Constrained Project Scheduling. Foundations of Computing and Decision Sciences 32(3), 213–225 (2007)
20. Jędrzejowicz, P., Ratajczak-Ropel, E.: Solving the RCPSP/max Problem by the Team of Agents. In: Hakansson, A., et al. (eds.) KES-AMSTA 2009. Lecture Notes in Computer Science, LNAI, vol. 5559, pp. 734–743. Springer, Heidelberg (2009)
21. Jędrzejowicz, P., Wierzbowska, I.: JADE-Based A-Team Environment. In: Alexandrov, V.N., van Albada, G.D., Sloot, P.M.A., Dongarra, J. (eds.) ICCS 2006. LNCS, vol. 3993, pp. 719–726. Springer, Heidelberg (2006)
22. Meneses, C.N., Pardalos, P.M., Ragle, M.: Asynchronous Teams for probe selection problems. Discrete Optimization 5, 74–87 (2008)
23. Neruda, R., Krusina, P., Kudova, P., Rydvan, P., Beuster, G.: Bang 3: A Computational Multi Agent System. In: Proceedings of the IEEE/WIC/ACM International Conference on Intelligent Agent Technology, IAT (2004)
24. PSPLIB, http://129.187.106.231/psplib
25. Rabak, C.S., Sichman, J.S.: Using A-Teams to optimize automatic insertion of electronic components. Advanced Engineering Informatics 17, 95–106 (2003)
26. Rachlin, J., Goodwin, R., Murthy, S., Akkiraju, R., Wu, F., Kumaran, S., Das, R.: A-Teams: An Agent Architecture for Optimization and Decision-Support. In: Muller, J.P., et al. (eds.) ATAL 1998. LNCS (LNAI), vol. 1555, pp. 261–276. Springer, Heidelberg (1999)
27. Raman, B.: Enhancing learning using feature and example selection. Texas A&M University, College Station, TX, USA (2003)
28. Ratajczak-Ropel, E.: Experimental Evaluation of the A-Team Solving Instances of the RCPSP/max Problem. In: Jędrzejowicz, P., et al. (eds.) KES-AMSTA 2010. LNCS (LNAI), vol. 6071, pp. 210–219. Springer, Heidelberg (2010)
29. Rozsypal, A., Kubat, M.: Selecting Representative Examples and Attributes by a Genetic Algorithm. Intelligent Data Analysis 7(4), 291–304 (2003)
30. Ruspini, E.H.: Numerical method for fuzzy clustering. Inform. Sci. 2(3), 19–150 (1970)
31. Skalak, D.B.: Prototype and Feature Selection by Sampling and Random Mutation Hill Climbing Algorithm. In: Proceedings of the International Conference on Machine Learning, pp. 293–301 (1994)
32. Talukdar, S., Baerentzen, L., Gove, A., de Souza, P.: Asynchronous teams: cooperation schemes for autonomous agents. Journal of Heuristics 4, 295–321 (1998)
33. Talukdar, S.N., de Souza, P., Murthy, S.: Organizations for Computer-Based Agents. Engineering Intelligent Systems 1(2) (1993)
34. TILAB, http://jade.tilab.com/
35. Wilson, D.R., Martinez, T.R.: Reduction Techniques for Instance-based Learning Algorithm. Machine Learning 33(3), 257–286 (2000)

Author Index

Printing: Mercedes-Druck, Berlin
Binding: Stein + Lehmann, Berlin